the best spas
in Britain

By the Good Spa Spies

the
good
spa
guide

The Best Spas in Britain

Published by The Good Spa Guide

Second edition

© The Good Spa Guide 2010

The Good Spa Guide Ltd
Unit 6 Hove Business Centre
Hove Park Villas
Hove BN3 6HA

www.goodspaguide.co.uk

www.goodspaguide.com

Photographs copyright their copyright holder;
see listing of photo credits on pages 303–306

Cover photograph © Veer/Kate Kunz

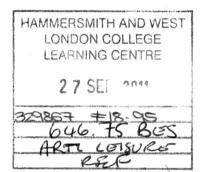

ISBN: 978-0-9558908-1-9

British Library Cataloguing in Publication data: A CIP catalogue record
for this book is available from The British Library.

Text	Anna McGrail, Daphne Metland, Jane Knight and the rest of the Spies
Design	Paul Williams
Layout	Julie Stanford
Printing	Ashford Press, Southampton

Contents

Loch Lomond Golf Club, see page 141

Hello, gorgeous!

Another busy year for The Spies. Even in the post-credit crunch world, new spas have been opening, new product lines launched, and new treatments invented. We thought there might be a drop in spa-going, as people tightened their belts. After all, if it's a choice between paying your mortgage and lying on a treatment table being slathered in mud, then the mud's going to go, right?

Wrong. There has been a huge change over the past couple of years in the way people approach their spa-going. Once, a trip to a spa was seen as something pampering, self-indulgent, a bit of a treat. It can be that, and there's nothing wrong with a treat. But more and more people are taking the approach that time at a spa is an essential part of maintaining their own wellness. They might choose an afternoon on a lounger by a pool, a day alone or with friends, or an invigorating week of walks, swims and gym: whatever people need to keep their lives in balance, their bodies fit, and their minds soothed. For many people, a spa day or stay is now an essential, not a treat. That's why we're having spa treatments at the airport, to give us strength to cope with the security queues. That's why teenagers take time out with an aromatherapeutic massage. That's why you're also seeing more and more men in spas. It's the me-time that gives people the energy and focus to cope with their work-and-family-life time.

But these are difficult times, too, so you want to spend your spa pound wisely. That's where The Good Spa Guide comes in. Our mission is to provide you with the information you need so that you can choose **a spa that's right for you**, with the **right treatments**, in the **right place**, for the **right price**. Sometimes you want to surround yourself in luxury; sometimes you want a good-value massage without too many frills.

In this book (our fifth!), we've brought together what we think are the best spas in Britain. We rate spas according to the bubble system: 1 means you probably won't get us through the door again, 5 bubbles means the spa owner probably had trouble getting us to leave. (See more about our ratings on page 13.) This book contains only the spas we've recently given our highest awards of 4 or 5 bubbles. A 4-bubble spa is very good and we recommend a visit. A 5-bubble spa is *exceptional* and worth travelling that bit further to enjoy.

Just because a spa is a 'best' spa, that doesn't necessarily mean it is an expensive spa. Some of the spas featured in this book offer great value treatments and affordable spa days. We judge spas on what they offer: what they do and how well they do it. We don't mark a spa down because it doesn't have peacock feathers on the wall, treatments that contain diamond dust, or caviar for breakfast. Some spas may have just one or two treatment rooms, and specialise in a small range of therapies, but do those really, really well. So that's a best spa.

If you want to choose from a wider range, and perhaps find out more about spas that are local to you, you can find details of *all* the spas in the UK in an A–Z listing on our website: www.goodspaguide.co.uk

There you'll also find details of new spas, notifications of which ones have closed (there have been casualties) and which are undergoing refurbishment. You'll also find answers to those spa questions you don't know who to ask, especially if you've never been to a spa before: Will I have to take all my clothes off? Does my therapist expect a tip? If so, how much?

To help you make the most of your spa visit, we've once again included our **A–Z of treatments** (see page 243) as so many people told us they found it helpful. It is designed to help you decide whether a particular treatment is worth spending your money on, and to encourage the adventurous.

Do you need your treatment in a spa near you? Find out where they are with our series of spa maps, starting on page 289.

The Spies have also put together their new **Spa Spy Favourites**, which you can find sprinkled throughout the book. Thanks to them, and also to all the spas and product houses, who provided us with information and sent us their alluring photos.

You can let us know of any spa finds or secrets you want to share, too, by emailing us at reviews@goodspaguide.co.uk

Enjoy!

Anna
x

Anna McGrail
Managing Editor
The Good Spa Guide
www.goodspaguide.co.uk

Finding *your* best spa

A spa trip doesn't mean a dreary weight-loss programme with three runs around the back field before breakfast and only a celery stick for lunch. It means fluffy towels, heavenly massage, uplifting aromas, cool pools and serious me-time. It means you can leave radiant from your facial, silky from your exfoliation, and gorgeously glam from your fingers to your toes.

Unless you've been to the wrong spa. In which case, you might be leaving even more stressed than when you went in. Maybe it was because the therapist turned out to have fairy fingers and didn't touch the knots in your muscles. Not good when you're lying there thinking you've paid a pound a minute for a bit of dabbing about.

Maybe you thought you'd go for a swim and it turned out there wasn't a pool. Or perhaps your serious solitude was rendered less than solitary by the hen party in the steam room next door. And when did they start calling an exercise bike in the back room a gym? Or maybe you *wanted* a weight-loss programme and a celery stick for lunch, only to find that they're coming

The Spies discuss the bubble ratings

at you with organic chocolate cake and, heaven forfend, chocolate facials as well.

Or maybe where you went wasn't even a spa. All kinds of places are suddenly calling themselves spas, because they know there's such demand for the spa experience. So 'spa' is now used to describe all kinds of things, from a traditional health farm to a hair salon.

There are more than 500 spas and treatment rooms in the UK. Wherever you are, you're probably not very far from a good one. But how do you know what a good one is? It's easy to get carried away when you see the spa's dreamy images and read their tempting invitations. But what are they really like? Wouldn't you rather hear about it first hand, from someone who's actually been there?

Independent and unbiased

The Good Spa Guide was set up by Daphne Metland and Anna McGrail in 2004. Both health journalists, they realised such a guide was needed after they booked into a spa to complete a particularly stressful manuscript they were working on together... and had a terrible time.

Snotty therapists who hung round at the end of a treatment expecting a tip, food that was mainly alfalfa, and a bedroom that felt like someone had died in it. And journalists are intelligent people; they'd looked at the website, called the spa up, and everything. That's when they realised that what you see in Spa Land is not necessarily what you get. And set out to put that right.

Our website is updated daily. We're constantly visiting spas – selflessly being scrubbed, massaged and covered in seaweed, just so that we can bring you an honest review, and some first-hand advice about what to have, where to have it and when. We'll tell you which spas are pagodas of pleasure, and which ones, say, will appeal to amateur microbiologists keen to examine the scum in the sauna. You may even recognise us if you see us at a spa because of our insistence on visiting every shower, using every pool, sniffing the moisturiser and mentally noting marks out of ten midway through our algae wrap.

We try all sorts of spa experiences – sometimes, so you don't have to. And we visit spas all over the country, large and small, new and old, those that charge a high price and those that don't.

The key to spa success

You won't be able to work out whether *you* will like a spa unless you know what you want out of your spa visit.

This is crucial: **to find the spa that's right for you, you need to know what you're looking for**. Spas these days all offer a different experience, different treatments, facilities and packages, and different brands, all of which suit different people at different times.

So the first step on the spa journey is to work out what a spa actually is, anyway...

What is a spa, anyway?

Spa-ing is far from a new thing. It's been around for millennia, literally, in various forms. The Romans were great spa fans, and Roman baths form the model for many spas today, with most having a hot pool (caldarium), lukewarm area (tepidarium) and cold pool (frigidarium). Romans would also be familiar with the steam rooms and saunas we see in spas today.

The Romans built baths all over their empire, often around naturally occurring hot springs, such as the ones in Bath, now gloriously reopened. In the UK, you can often recognise the spa towns by their name; some of them use the word spa, such as Leamington Spa, and others wells, like Tunbridge Wells or, well, just Wells.

A spa has always traditionally been based around water. Some people believe that the word 'spa' comes from the Latin, meaning 'sanitas per aqua', or 'health through water'. (Some people think it's just named after a particularly spa-ey Belgian town.) People used water to cleanse, invigorate and heal. Spas were about wellness, inner rather than outer beauty.

For many years, spas were associated with the idea of a 'health farm', too. The health aspect is still there, but now you're more likely to find an emphasis on the stress-relieving benefits of various treatments, and the importance of calm. Many spas have brought in ayurvedic or Eastern treatments, from cultures that have long recognised the need to keep your body and mind balanced. You're more likely to hear the word 'chakra' than 'celery stick' in a spa these days.

So what types of spa can you find now?

Spa categories

There are places you can pop into for a specific treatment, spas where you can spend the day and spas where you can stay as long as you like. Some spas are based round their water facilities; others are themed around a certain country or treatment. You'll find spas that specialise in steam, mud, algae, chocolate, truffles, yoga or Thai massage. Happily, as we've all got different tastes and timetables, there is a variety of different approaches, too – from health farm to holistics to healing. There are so many spas to choose from, and so many different ways to experience them that you're not going to be bored while you find something to suit you.

These are the main categories of spa that you have to choose from.

Day spas

What are they? A spa where you go just for the day, which has no residential option. Most day spas are based around natural mineral springs and water-based treatments, offering a variety of pools and baths, all designed to help you refresh, relax and restore. A few don't have a pool, but still allow you space to chill for the whole day. Most offer a range of spa treatments, by various product houses, including massages and facials, as well as manicures and other beauty treatments.

To get the most out of your visit Get there as early as you can and leave as late as you can without hitting the rush for the hairdryers in the changing rooms. You're only there for the day, so make it a real treat. If you're there in the summer, check whether they have any outdoor facilities to make the most of the sunshine. Some day spas have gardens you can sit in, or outdoor pools with loungers. If you want a treatment, try to book it towards the end of your day. You don't want to have a concoction of startlingly-priced unguents slathered over your skin at 10 in the morning, only to find them soaking nicely out again at 3pm, when you're on your third mineralised hydrotherapy bath of the day. Also check what's included in your package and what's not – some packages include treatments as well as use of the facilities, and these can add up to very good value.

Treatment rooms

What are they? These are the little sisters of day spas in that they are day spas without pools. They often do not have water of any kind except the sort you can drink in the changing rooms. There may be no sauna or steam room, either. The focus in treatment rooms is usually more utilitarian and time-limited, with many people booking single treatments and going in and out. However, they offer more of a spa experience than beauty salons do; you get to change into a fluffy towelling robe, drink some herbal tea, and sojourn in a relaxation room as well as enjoy your treatment. Some offer 'rituals', which means you get to spend a half or a whole day in a dedicated spa environment. Chill out without the splashing about. You'll usually find treatment rooms in town centres or shopping centres, or even some large department stores.

To get the most out of your visit Make sure you know what's on offer. If your definition of a spa means a swim is essential, you're not going

St David's
Hotel and Spa
see page 221

to be happy with just a rose rub, however relaxing. If you want to look good, consider going to a day spa with a focus on beauty treatments and makeovers. If you want to retreat and relax, look for treatment rooms that offer that little bit more. You'll still be able to get your hair and make-up done, as well as your eyebrows shaped and your feet pedicured. Switch off the outside world, and relax.

Hotel spas

What are they? Spas attached to a hotel. More and more hotels are adding spas and barely a new hotel opens without some kind of spa offering. You will find hotel spas in the heart of the urban environment and in country house hotels. Some hotel spas are free to use for hotel residents, others make a small charge.

The thing that distinguishes a spa in any hotel from other spas is that you could stay in the hotel without visiting the spa, or visit the spa without staying in the hotel. See, we're only on our third entry and the classification is beginning to get murky. If you're staying in the hotel, you may want to breeze down for a swim, a sauna, a steam, and perhaps one or two treatments. Then you could retreat to your room and prepare for your conference, adjust your PowerPoints and watch *Strictly*. If you're not staying, you might come to the hotel to use the facilities and have a favourite treatment.

This is all great, and pleases most of the people most of the time. If you're travelling, hotels with spas offer that me-time that is so hard to catch on a business trip. If you're local, the luxurious facilities and treatments have undoubted appeal. Both sets of spa-goers can have a fab time. The thing to remember is that you are mixing two sorts of spa-goers. If you're looking for relaxation, you need to be prepared for a flotilla of business people heading straight for your pet Jacuzzi as soon as their conference is over. Families with children could be splashing about in the pool. There may be no towelling robe, no spa slippers, and no relaxation area – because the majority of the clientele can relax in their rooms – but some certainly have one (we say, with fond memories of Chancery Court). If there is a towelling robe in your wardrobe and you don it to wander down to the spa, you may

The Best Spas in Britain • www.goodspaguide.co.uk

share the lift with a party of golfers. Unless you're in St David's Hotel in Cardiff, of course, where they have their very own spa lift!

To get the most out of your visit Call ahead for information before you book your treatments, and find out the most cost-efficient ways of spending as long as possible at the spa and getting your money's worth.

Destination spas

What are they? It's quite simple. You go here for the spa. The spa is the destination. You're not going anywhere else. You're going to stay here for as long as your need or budget prescribes and you're going to relax. Or have fun with a friend. This is not a hotel with a pool you can dip into after a few rounds of golf. This is not a base for touring the Cotswolds or the Borders. This is a place you go to just to spa. A destination spa can offer everything from beautiful surroundings to the most comfortable beds, delicious food, friendly service and the highest quality of facilities and treatments, which themselves can range from manicures to yoga to Tui Na (Chinese medical massage).

A destination spa aims to hit every 'restore' button you have, whoever you are. It is a place where you can spend anything from a few days to a few months. People tend to visit because they want to relax and unwind, and the

emphasis is often just as much on pampering and indulgence as on health. If you want a wrap and to eat cake – or even to wrap yourself in cake – a destination spa is the place for you.

Some destination spas are set in stunning countryside or mountain areas, without telephones, TVs or other things that can distract you from your focus on well-being.

Of course, it gets complicated because destination spas usually let people in just for the day, too. But the difference between a hotel spa and a destination spa is that, at lunchtime, people will be in towelling robes. They will be for breakfast, as well. These are people seriously chilling, not fitting in a gym spree or sauna after their management consultancy day job. They are here to stay and put their own needs first.

There are several varieties of destination spa.

There's the just all-out gorgeous. Here the setting is not Spartan or forbidding. The focus in on you, looking after you, and doing what's best for you. These destination spas are often like well-appointed country-house hotels, with the difference that everyone is there to spa. Anyone not in a towelling robe looks odd – not the other way around. When the day guests go, those staying congratulate themselves on their wise choice of putting off a return to the real world for at least another night.

There are the health farms, beloved of so many. These take a 'let's improve' approach to your health and well-being. Providing personal consultations, health farms offer health assessments, body and facial treatments, complementary therapies, and diet and exercise advice, all tailored to your individual needs. You may well also have an opportunity to learn about an aspect of health and beauty in a class or talk. Quite often, people choose to visit a health farm because they want to lose weight or make permanent changes to their lifestyle. A stay on a health farm can give a diet or exercise programme a morale-boosting kickstart.

A holistic spa is one that seeks to nurture you in a more thorough way than simply pampering. They offer an opportunity to look at your whole lifestyle, and to work on a range of different aspects of your self. Generally speaking, the range of treatments available is narrower, but more focused, or themed, and a lot of energy goes into finding out about you, and your specific issues and needs. You're more likely to go for a series of visits or a residential stay so that you can have some consistent input into your overall health and well-being. Some holistic spas run meditation, yoga and other workshops and short courses that you can take when you're there, and take with you when you leave. Some holistic spas may even offer you 'treatments' such as counselling, numerology and even hypnotherapy.

To get the most out of your visit Choose a destination spa carefully, as they are not cheap, and plan what you want to get out of your trip. Pampering? Weight loss? Yoga before breakfast? All is on offer. You can be as focused or as open as you want and you'll often find that while you're there, there are opportunities for you to try out and learn about new things. You might also want to be open-minded about complementary therapies. Be honest about your lifestyle, and your priorities for your visit. The more you tell your therapists, the more appropriate their advice will be.

When you're there, do what you feel you want to. If that's to walk through the natural surroundings of the estate for four hours every day before lunch, do it. If you want to eat alone, do that. Use your stay as a relaxation holiday and explore all the ways you can release your tension and stress.

Resort spas

What are they? Dedicated spas that happen to be – hello – in the grounds of a family holiday resort. Which genius thought of that? Family holidays *and* a chance for pampering.

Resorts offer a large range of activities and family experiences in extensive grounds. You'll find something for everyone in the family to enjoy, and get plenty of fresh air while you're doing it. Spa-ing is just one of the available options for pleasure. Which you can book in advance. For you. On your own. By yourself. Every happy family has a happy mummy at its heart. And happiness begins with a massage and a manicure, obviously.

To get the most out of your visit Plan and book ahead. There's more to a family holiday than a spa timetable. If you get there and find activities or treatments you want are already booked up, you'll be disappointed.

Vineyard Spa
see page 237

Beyond our brief

Health clubs

What are they? Some health or fitness clubs offer spa facilities, such as steam rooms, massages and beauty treatments. The facilities may be available for members only or on a day-member basis, where you can pay a small supplement to use them. Alternatively, use of the facilities may come free if you book a treatment. You'd usually expect a health club to have personal trainers available to help you plan and pursue an exercise programme.

To get the most out of your visit Find out whether you can use the club facilities for all or part of the day. That way you can stretch out the relaxation and exercise and spend happy hours swimming, steaming, lounging, taking part in a class, or pumping it up at the gym.

Beauty salons

Some high-street hair and beauty salons offer 'spa' treatments but they're not really a spa as such. Some treatments are no doubt very good, but hair and beauty is their primary trade. As with anything, it depends what you're looking for. If you find a good beauty salon that does offer great treatments, this can be cost-effective and convenient, but you shouldn't expect the full spa experience.

Dental spas

What are they? Dental spas are less common here than in the US but they are a new trend. A dental spa combines regular dental treatment with other spa-type treatments, perhaps to make it less daunting. They can be anything from a fancy dentist with aromatherapy candles to a spa that offers teeth whitening, via a place that offers you an Indian head massage and a cup of green tea after you've had your porcelain polished and your 'smile design consultation'.

To get the most out of your visit Have a good collagen facial that will plump up your skin and lips and even out your skin tone to provide the perfect setting for those beautiful biters.

Medi-spas

What are they? The idea of a medi-spa is to combine cosmetic surgery with the experience of a day spa. So you could have a massage and collagen injections all on the same day. Or have your colon irrigated and a bit of liposuction. Would madam care for a herbal tea after her tummy tuck? This kind of spa is not much in evidence – yet – in the UK, although there are a few.

To get the most out of your visit Make sure you know what to do in advance, and how to care for yourself when you get back home.

How we rate spas

We rate our spas with bubbles – anywhere between 1 and 5.

Generally speaking, our bubble rating will give you a good idea of our overall impression – how we felt about being there, and whether the spa lived up to expectations.

5 bubbles	=	fantastic (*'Shut the doors, I'm not leaving'*)
4 bubbles	=	great (*'Mmm, take me back'*)
3 bubbles	=	okay (*'Nice, might go there again, especially if I was nearby'*)
2 bubbles	=	poor (*'Not doing that again'*)
1 bubble	=	shocking (*'Let me out!'*)

In this book, we feature the 4- and 5-bubble spas we've visited recently. A 4-bubble spa is worth a drive; a 5-bubble spa is worth a journey.

A 5-bubble spa is not necessarily an expensive spa; some very good value spas and treatment rooms earn 5 bubbles because what they set

Clean?
Quiet?
Chlorine?

out to do, they do well. It's all about setting expectations and meeting their promises.

Our criteria for judging spas – large and small – are thorough. We take a lot of different things into account. Overleaf we list the things we look out for when we visit and rate a spa.

Ambience

○ Does the spa have a relaxed and positive atmosphere?

○ Are staff polite, friendly and attentive? Are they professional at all times, and focused on you and your spa experience?

ONE Spa
see page 159

Booking

○ Is booking efficient and confirmed before your arrival?

○ When you arrive at the spa, do you get what you ordered without last-minute changes on their part?

Cleanliness

Whichever and wherever your spa, and however much your visit costs, you should expect a very high standard of cleanliness. If this means you see the odd mop and bucket whilst you're gliding from pool to treatment, so be it. Better that than fungus.

○ Is the spa spotless throughout, from the reception to the pools to the toilets?

Facilities

We're not demanding that every spa offers full tennis courts, a croquet lawn and a rooftop pool. But how good is what the spa actually has? You should expect the spa facilities to be finished, working, clean and appropriate for their intended use. You should also expect the standard of the facilities to live up to what the spa has promised you in advance.

○ Are the pools or changing rooms too small or too few for the number of people using them?

- Are there enough toilets?
- Are there enough towels?
- Did you have to queue for the aroma room?
- Are there tiles missing or is paint peeling off the walls?
- Is the hydrotherapy pool that looked so huge on the website actually more like a small garden water feature?
- Does the Turkish hammam feel more like a cupboard?

Friendliness and courtesy

It is the job of a spa to make you feel relaxed. Friendliness and courtesy is where this starts. You should never feel intimidated, nor struggle to get the attention of the spa staff.

Of course you don't want overfriendliness, either. You're (probably!) not going a spa to make friends and influence people. Staff at a spa should be sensitive to your mood and pick up on whether and how much you want to talk. In some spas, staff ask you whether you'd like to talk or not. A therapist should ask you if you're happy and comfortable during your treatment. A therapist shouldn't ask you about work or your Christmas shopping.

- Were staff polite and the right amount of friendly at all times?

Information

It's amazing the difference good communication makes at a spa, in terms of treatments, facilities and your whole visit. Good information is a vitally important part of your spa experience. You should be able to start enjoying it before you even get there, to get full value for money. But standards vary enormously.

You should expect information about the spa and the treatments available to be forthcoming, meaningful and accurate. The spa should confirm your booking in writing, and also include information on terms and conditions, any cancellation fees and timings. They should also give you details of how to get there, how long ahead of your treatment you should arrive, and other facilities available or included in your treatment or package. The spa should also make clear exactly what your package includes – there's nothing more disruptive to a spa day than people coming up to you with another bill to sign because you innocently ordered sparkling instead of still water and 'sparkling water isn't included in your package'.

Some good spas also include 'All you need to know'-style information, telling you what you do and don't need to bring and what to expect.

A good spa should keep you informed of anything that is going on while you're there.

This includes, for example, telling you when the pool might be closed for cleaning, what time you can use the steam room until, and whether the sauna is broken. They should let you know these things before you find them out yourself.

- Does the spa provide all the information you need to know before you arrive?
- While you are there?
- Are you informed about any difficulties (such as out-of-action saunas) before you find them out yourself?

Quality of the treatment

No matter whether you're paying a fortune or have found a bargain, you should expect your therapist to know what she is doing and to do it well and professionally. Therapists should be sensitive to your feelings and check that you are okay during the treatment. And they should tell you when it has finished, too. You shouldn't have to gather it's finished because they're leaving the room, or the plinky-plonky music has stopped.

- Does your therapist actually tell you about what's going to happen during your treatment and why?
- Does she check whether or not you are allergic to anything?
- Does she appear to have looked at the consultation form you filled in?

- Does she tell you what oils she's going to use, and is there any choice?
- Does she ask you if you're okay, and what you're happy with during the treatment?

A good spa should not subject you to any kind of 'sell'. You're not at a convention, and you're not necessarily going to a spa on the lookout for Christmas presents, either. Your therapist should tell you what products she has used during your treatment. If you loved that cream she used, you'll probably be happy to buy it. A good spa will have plenty of free samples for you to try. But they shouldn't ask you to attend a presentation on them or do a hard sell while you're still in post-massage semi-consciousness.

Tipping

It is normal to tip at a spa if you felt your therapist did a good job. Most people tip between 10 and 15 per cent. But you should not be expected or pressured to tip. Your therapist shouldn't loiter meaningfully as you're coming round from your Indian head massage. Why should you be pestered for money when you're wearing nothing but a pair of paper knickers?

We suggest that spas are upfront about tipping. Why not have a sign on your front desk saying: 'If you would like to tip any of our therapists, please feel free to do so when you pay your bill'?

- Did the spa make it easy to tip or not to tip?

Value for money

Price is not necessarily a guide to how good a spa is. In some expensive spas, however, you'd be justified in expecting thoughtful orchids on your towels or perhaps a welcome basket of fruit or free products in your room.

○ Was the spa a good experience for the price?

Water

Water is essential in a spa. For example, if you've been in a sauna for half an hour and don't have enough fluid, you could pass out.

Almost every body or heat treatment you have in a spa will get your lymphatic system going in some way and this will accelerate how quickly your body loses fluid. You are likely to find yourself needing to go to toilet a lot more than usual; and as toxins come out in water, you'll need to replace that water. We're not talking about fancying a little light refreshment, either. Have a good massage, or spend any time in a sauna, steam room or gym, and you will need to drink plenty. Availability of water and advice to drink plenty of it are indicators of a good spa.

○ Is water available throughout the spa?

○ Are you offered drinks throughout your visit, as well as actively advised to drink plenty?

Barnsley House, see page 36

Choosing the right spa

So, now you know. There are many different ways you can indulge in spa fun, tailored to suit different purses, pet peeves and personalities. The trouble is, the perfect spa experience for one person may be someone else's idea of boredom. So to make sure you choose the right spa and treatments for you, ask yourself a few questions before you sign up:

What are you looking for?

○ A handy urban spa where you can pop in for a bit of fangotherapy at lunchtime?

○ A whole day of gliding from pool to sauna before some reflexology?

○ A weekend of complementary spa treatments, all delivered to you in a teepee?

○ A great local venue to catch up with friends in the steam room?

○ Somewhere far away with tranquil grounds for some solitude?

○ Somewhere to unwrinkle, unwind and leave looking better in a basque? (A little bit of collagen, a relaxing massage and a spray tan?)

○ Somewhere you can stay for a week?

Once you know what you're looking for, then you can start to narrow down your choices.

○ Do you want seclusion or somewhere you can go with all your friends?

○ How much are you looking to spend?

○ Do you want a completely all-in package where you don't think about your wallet from the moment you arrive to the minute you leave, or would you prefer to pay as you go?

○ Do you want long solitary walks in stunning countryside, or do you like to temper your spa experience with a bit of shopping?

○ Do you want to go with your family, or get away from them?

○ Do you want to go with your partner, and enjoy a spa that provides a range of treatments specifically for couples?

○ Do you want to make health and lifestyle changes, or just to unwind?

○ Do you want healthy eating or chocolate cake? Or the option of both?

○ Do you want a range of outdoor as well as indoor activities?

○ Do you want to exercise while you're there?

○ Do you want to try a new treatment? Or something you've tried already?

○ Do you want a range of water facilities? Or a thermal suite?

○ Do you want to wear a robe 24/7?

Whatever you're looking for, you can probably find it somewhere. The key is knowing what you want and what to expect.

Let us know how you get on.

The spas

Agua at Sanderson

Bloomsbury, London

The Sanderson is uber-stylish with a sense of fun; the spa, Agua, a celestial retreat from the hustle and bustle of nearby Oxford Street. Here you will find professionally delivered indulgent treatments in an immaculate designer-white environment.

Spa type
Hotel spa

Where?
Agua at Sanderson
50 Berners Street
Bloomsbury
London W1T 3NG
020 7300 1414

Signature treatment
Agua Milk and Honey:
gentle ayurvedic massage

Brands
Aromatherapy Associates
Eve Lom
Natura Bissé

Expect to pay
Treatments:
£75 for 50 minutes
Stay: Prices start from
£255 per night for a
standard room

Bubble rating
4 out of 5 bubbles

What's on offer

Fourteen treatment rooms with stylised white décor, surrounded by white curtains. There's also a gym and a steam room but no pools.

Treatments include the famous cleansing Eve Lom facial; aromatherapy, deep-tissue or custom massage; Aromatherapy Associates body treatments, including a jet-lag massage. Pep yourself up with a Bed of Roses Body Booster.

We loved

The original, if over-the-top, white surroundings; white makes a refreshing change to the fashionable neutral stone and wood décor of many spas.

The 'private relaxation suites' – more of a tall curtained cubicle than a suite – where you can enjoy the most artistically presented (and expensive) fresh fruit you'll probably ever consume in your life.

We didn't love

The treatment rooms don't have walls, only Agua's trademark white curtains, which unfortunately don't share the soundproofing qualities of an actual wall.

Food file

Fruit, water. Anything from the hotel's room service menu.

Who would like it

Blancophiles; interior designers; people who enjoy eavesdropping while spa-ing.

Don't miss

The impressive intergalactic holographic lift from the hotel to the first-floor spa.

Alexandra House

Huddersfield, Yorkshire

This grand Victorian house has been converted into a spacious and welcoming holistic health and well-being set of treatment rooms within easy access of the M62 and just five minutes from Huddersfield city centre.

What's on offer

Facial and body treatments, plus holistic therapies such as reflexology, chakra balancing, reiki, Indian head massage, yoga and Hopi ear candles. Relaxation and meditation, foot and hand rituals, hypnosis, homeopathy and even physic readings. There are Angel cards everywhere.

There are four treatment rooms, two relaxation rooms and gardens. A tasteful dual treatment room and also a very cosy double relaxation lounger. No pools, heat experiences or wet areas. Robes and slippers are provided.

We loved

The hospitality and friendliness of the staff. The calm atmosphere. Our excellent treatments performed by skilled and experienced therapists. Our lymphatic drainage body massage and body mud mask that uses a combination of Karin Herzog products. We really did notice a reduction in the dimples on our thighs.

We didn't love

There is only one changing room; we're not sure the place could cope with a group who arrived at the same time.

Food file

Fresh homemade cakes to have with your tea. Smoothies with fresh fruit, and a selection of hot drinks. You can pre-order sandwiches if you would like.

Who would like it

Anyone looking for a retreat: on your own, as a couple, or in a group.

Don't miss

The inflatable footbath.

Spa type
Treatment rooms

Where?
Alexandra House
2 Murray Road
Edgerton
Huddersfield
West Yorkshire HD2 2AD
01484 303786

Signature treatment
Karin Herzog chocolate body wrap

Brands
Karin Herzog
Eve Taylor

Expect to pay
Treatments:
£40 for 60 minutes

Bubble rating
4 out of 5 bubbles

Amala Spa

Hyatt Regency Hotel, Birmingham

The Hyatt Regency is a large, high-rise hotel, close to Birmingham's International Convention Centre and Symphony Hall. Amala Spa is located in the basement but is cleverly lit and spacious, with high ceilings. The spa has a pleasantly relaxing ambience and a wide range of treatments to leave you glowing inside and out.

Spa type
Hotel spa

Where?
Hyatt Regency Hotel
2 Bridge Street
Birmingham B1 2JZ
0121 643 1234

Signature treatment
Hammam Signature Ritual

Brands
Karin Herzog

Expect to pay
Treatments:
£60 for 60 minutes
Stay: from £99 per night
in a King room

Bubble rating
4 out of 5 bubbles

What's on offer

Amala's décor is neutral tones of natural dark wood and beige, with minimal Asian-inspired furnishings. Although the spa is on a lower ground floor, the hotel is on a slight incline, so the bright, airy pool room has large windows running along its length. There's also a grey marble Turkish hammam, a Jacuzzi, sauna, steam room and plunge pool. For the active, there's a gym; for the less active, some very inviting loungers by the pool.

You can choose from a good range of Karin Herzog treatments, a brand famous for its oxygen products, and facials and body envelopments that use products infused with chocolate. Amala also offers massages and alternative therapies.

We loved

The Karin Herzog Orange and Cinnamon facial left our Spy's dry skin soft, smooth and glowing, as she drifted around in wafts of orange-scented moisturiser.

We didn't love

There's no proper relaxation room, only a sofa and a couple of chairs at either end of the reception area. It's a shame that the spa hasn't used this space to create a proper chill-out zone.

Food file

Modern European cuisine in the Aria restaurant; the Regency Club lounge.

Who would like it

Amala is just right for a chic take on a girls' weekend in the city.

Don't miss

The TV inside the sauna: a good way to sit back and relax – for the recommended 10 minutes at least!

Amida Day Spa

Beckenham, Kent

High-tech and totally vast, Amida Day Spa is jam-packed with excellent facilities. If you want to follow up your workout in a top-notch 200-station gym with a long lounge in a hydrotherapy pool, Amida is the place for you.

What's on offer

A 25-metre swimming pool, perfect for lap lovers; a large hydrotherapy pool, plunge pool and relaxation pool; a steam room, sauna and sanarium; also, an excellent gym.

Teenage treatments; Ionithermie detox; anti-ageing treatments; facials; body treatments including scrubs and wraps; treatments for men and mums-to-be; a range of Elemis day-spa packages. Bridal packages include optional wedding dance lessons alongside the more standard make-up and manicures.

We loved

The huge, top-of-the-range gym – just above the pool, and sensibly divided into spacious sections for treadmills, stretching, weights, and so on.

Friendly receptionists and, luckily, more than one of them; this is a health club with some 7,000 members.

We didn't love

No seats to use beside the pool; as Amida is purpose-built, and packed with facilities, we felt it should really have a quiet relaxation room.

Food file

The café and bar next to the pool serve light bites and filling meals.

Who would like it

Sporty types. Amida is handy for families, too, as there's a crèche and activities for kids on offer.

Don't miss

The excellent hydrotherapy area. We wish we'd had more time to spend there.

Spa type
Day spa

Where?
Amida Day Spa
Stanhope Grove
Beckenham
Kent BR3 3HL
020 8662 6161

Signature treatment
Elemis Amida Stone
Back Massage

Brands
Elemis
Mama Mio
Murad

Expect to pay
Treatments:
£55 for 55 minutes

Bubble rating
4 out of 5 bubbles

Aquarias Spa

Whatley Manor, Malmesbury, Wiltshire

A beautiful Cotswold manor house in a picturesque setting, Whatley Manor offers traditional luxury with an emphasis on your comfort and convenience. Aquarias is a relaxing spa offering a wide range of indulgent treatments, with beautifully designed hydrotherapy and thermal areas.

What's on offer

The hotel is relatively small with 23 rooms and suites, and this helps to give Whatley Manor its exclusive, private feel. Great attention has been paid to design throughout the hotel and spa with extravagant but classy touches.

The main hydrotherapy pool, designed more for lolling than swimming, has underwater loungers, swan pipes and a central powerful Jacuzzi area; it extends outside, too, and has beautiful views of the valley below. There is also a thermal suite which includes a tepidarium, laconium, caldarium, sauna, experience showers, and two salt scrub showers, all immaculate and finished to a beautifully tiled standard.

When it comes to treatments, you can choose from a good range of La Prairie treatments, including the popular Deluxe Caviar Facial, as well as massages, some complementary therapies, and beauty finishing touches.

We loved

Reclining on the heated loungers in the thermal suite and gliding from one heated treat to the next.

We didn't love

Not living closer so we could lounge around the pool more often.

Food file

Delicious smoothies and snacks in the spa café, a light space overlooking the pool and gardens (try a Tropical Sunset smoothie). There are two restaurants in the hotel: a brasserie, Le Mazot, and the impressive and more formal Dining Room.

Who would like it

Anyone who appreciates, and can afford, a little serious luxury in their life. The evening spa experience is affordable, however, and we noticed people taking advantage of the time to chill, warm up and catch up.

Don't miss

Scheduling a stroll in the hotel's serene and surprising gardens into your spa day or stay; the Wave Dream Sensory room to soothe your soul with sound and colour.

Spa type
Hotel spa

Where?
Whatley Manor
Easton Gray, Malmesbury
Wiltshire SN16 0RB
01666 827070

Signature treatment
La Prairie Signature Experience: developed exclusively for Whatley Manor, this facial uses La Prairie caviar extracts and hot stones

Brands
La Prairie

Expect to pay
Treatments:
£84 for 60 minutes
Stay: from £295 for one night in a standard room

Bubble rating
5 out of 5 bubbles

Aquila Health Spa
Spread Eagle Hotel, Midhurst, West Sussex

An historic hotel in the middle of a picturesque Sussex market town, surrounded by glorious countryside. The Aquila Spa, adjacent to the hotel, is modern, brick and wood-framed, and has plenty of natural light. A perfect balance between retreat spa and urban spa.

What's on offer

A 14-metre blue mosaic pool with a golden spread eagle on the bottom. Next to the pool is a Turkish steam room, a Scandinavian sauna, and a wooden hot tub. There is also a small gym.

Three treatment rooms – quite small, but very clean and warm, with soft music and fragrant oil burners. A full range of Elemis therapies. Reflexology and Indian head massage are also available.

We loved

The great market town location; the heritage of the hotel.

The Elemis back, neck and shoulder massage; the therapist said you should feel less knotted after just one massage, and this proved to be true for us a week later.

Swimming a few laps in the perfect-temperature pool water.

We didn't love

How expensive the taxi from the nearest station was. The changing-room lockers are slightly awkward to access if there are more than a few spa-goers.

There are around 400 day spa members, as well as hotel guests using the spa, so it can get quite busy.

Food file

Many of the packages at the spa include a one-course lunch in the hotel restaurant. The choice is excellent, and many spa visitors are attracted by the great modern-traditional food here. The honey-glazed bacon with mustard mash and spinach was delicious.

Who would like it

The Spread Eagle is perfect for a family break. Children can use the pool at allotted times, and mum and dad could alternate treatment slots.

Don't miss

Swimming and relaxing in natural light, in the gorgeously bubbly hot tub.

Spa type
Hotel spa

Where?
Spread Eagle Hotel
South Street
Midhurst
West Sussex GU29 9NH
01730 819829

Signature treatment
Elemis Exotic Lime & Ginger Salt Glow body exfoliation ritual

Brands
Elemis

Expect to pay
Treatments:
£53 for 55 minutes

Bubble rating
5 out of 5 bubbles

Armathwaite Hall Hotel

Keswick, Cumbria

This seventeenth-century stately-home hotel in the Lake District happily houses a state-of-the-art modern spa. In both, you'll find luxury and love.

What's on offer

Armathwaite Hall is set in 400 acres of private estate in the beautiful Lake District, with a fabulous view along Bassenthwaite Lake. In the spa, you'll be spoiled with immaculate changing rooms, a big, airy, well equipped gym, a dance studio, and a 16-metre infinity pool that seems to disappear through the window and out into the glorious landscape. There is a cascading waterfall, an outside hot tub (big enough not to have to play footsie with strangers) and a sauna with views to the lake. A large thermal suite including hydrotherapy pool with neck shower, aroma room, steam room, experience tropical shower and rain-dance shower. There are ten spacious treatment rooms, including a double treatment room with private whirlpool bath, and a relaxing spa lounge with a feature fireplace.

Our treatments were excellent, with professional and attentive therapists. Our massages and facials began with a vanilla, lemon, and parma rose Tranquillity Welcome and ended in mmmm noises as we dozed off. Afterwards, we retreated to the Hush Room to chill out. Our skin stayed gloriously smooth for ages.

We loved

Everything, but especially the sauna with its woodland view. And our soft, plump honeycomb towelling robes…

We didn't love

The evening meal could have made more of the wealth of fine produce on offer in Cumbria. (There's not a lot of squid in Bassenthwaite!)

Food file

Lunch in the spa was a choice of light, salady options. We made our way through a giant plate of antipasti, and tian of crab. In the evening, we had a six-course formal *table d'hôte* meal in the hotel.

Who would like it

Anyone who needs some me-time, or a bit of a massage at the end of an energetic day in the Lakes. The décor is gender neutral, so Armathwaite Hall would appeal to men as much as women.

Don't miss

Relaxing in the outside tub, enjoying the glorious view of the woodland and lake.

Spa type
Hotel spa

Where?
Armathwaite Hall Hotel
Bassenthwaite
Keswick
Cumbria CA12 4RE
017687 88900

Signature treatment
Bassenthwaite ritual

Brands
[comfort zone]
Terraké

Expect to pay
Treatments:
£60 for 60 minutes
Stay: from £125 per night
in a double room

Bubble rating
5 out of 5 bubbles

Do you need to book a spa break for a **special occasion?**

The Good Spa Guide booking service is here to help!

A romantic retreat in a luxury hotel? A detox day in a yurt? Whether you're looking for an essential escape or a girly getaway, we can organise the perfect tailor-made spa package for you and your friends. What's more, because we know so many spas so well, we have access to secret spa offers that are unavailable anywhere else...

We can offer you spa days and stays that you simply can't book by booking direct with a spa

We will handle everything, in person, from your initial call through to your dinner reservations. Our team of spa experts will research, book everything for you, and provide you with a personal spa itinerary, so all goes smoothly. We'll also send you our 'How to spa' booklet to ensure that you get the most out of your spa visit. Do you need us to organise your travel and some luscious extras, too? No problem!

Dive in and enjoy our special booking service bringing you exclusive tailor-made spa packages.

Perfect for birthdays, anniversaries or just spending some relaxing time away

Photo courtesy of Formby Hall Golf Resort and Spa

Make the most of our personal and friendly service by contacting our spa bookings hotline, **Monday to Friday between 9am and 5pm, on 0845 6 809 909**.

Calls are charged at local rates. See? We're making life easier for you already.

the
good
spa
guide

Aura Day Spa

Belfast, Northern Ireland

This day spa on the prestigious Lisburn Road might be small but it packs a powerful pampering punch. Its boutique treatment rooms are stylishly decorated, the staff are professional and friendly, and our experience was blissfully relaxing.

What's on offer

No pools or saunas, just a wide range of luxurious treatments and some unusual rituals (many featuring the spa's Japanese Slipper Bath), an infra-red sauna and dry-floatation therapy. There are treatments specifically for men and mums-to-be. The lounge area is stylishly decorated with comfortable seating, and there's a clean, tidy refreshment station.

We loved

Our Aromatherapy Associates Enrich Body treatment, a wonderfully decadent way to moisturise parched skin. Our professional, friendly therapist used an

invigorating sea-salt, frankincense and coffee full-body exfoliation, a moisturising serum scented with patchouli, tuberose and vanilla and Enrich Oil, all topped off with a generous layer of Body Butter. In the quiet, dimly-lit Chill Out Room, we felt dozy, and deliciously soft and fragrant.

We didn't love

It's a pity that you have to enjoy your lunch in the waiting area, which doesn't have tables. Also, although clean and well stocked with soap and shampoo, the showers looked a little dated.

Food file

Complimentary refreshments available at all times. Many treatments include a light lunch. You can also order afternoon tea, including home-baked scones.

Who would like it

Shoppers looking to relax after hitting the Lisburn Road retail emporia.

Don't miss

The Aromatherapy Associates Enrich Body treatment. Worth every penny.

Spa type
Treatment rooms

Where?
Aura Day Spa
615 Lisburn Road
Belfast
Northern Ireland BT9 7GT
028 90 666 277

Signature treatment
Hydradermie facial

Brands
Aromatherapy Associates
Guinot

Expect to pay
Treatments:
£50 for 55 minutes

Bubble rating
4 out of 5 bubbles

Aveda Institute

Covent Garden, London

This huge, glass-fronted beauty factory is Aveda's flagship salon. Combining a busy, trendy hair salon with a relaxing and peaceful spa, the Aveda Institute is perfect for those who want some spa indulgence but not to leave with messy hair!

Spa type
Treatment rooms

Where?
Aveda Institute
174 High Holborn
Covent Garden
London WC1V 7AA
020 7759 7355

Signature treatments
Elemental Nature facial
Customised facial

Brands
Aveda

Expect to pay
Treatments:
£75 for 60 minutes

Bubble rating
4 out of 5 bubbles

What's on offer

The popular Aveda hair salon, manicure stations and café on the ground floor. The spa treatment rooms are downstairs.

All the hair services you would expect from a top-end salon; the full range of Aveda spa treatments.

We loved

We absolutely loved the Caribbean Body Scrub. We definitely recommend it for a pre-holiday treat.

Friendly therapists.

The therapist finishes your spa treatment with a blow-dry, so you leave looking rather fab. A blow-dry is a great way to finish a day at the spa!

We didn't love

The shower is out in the corridor. You have to shuffle out of the treatment room in your robe to wash your scrub off. We think the shower may be a little small for some.

Food file

A café on the ground floor, serving healthy, light meals.

Who would like it

Young urbanites. However, customers on our visit covered quite an age range, so: anyone out on a day's shopping trip who needs a treat; anyone getting ready for a night out in London.

Don't miss

Showing off your glowing skin and swishy hair in the Covent Garden shops post-treatment.

Ayush Wellness Spa

Hotel de France, St Helier, Jersey

The first completely ayurvedic hotel spa in the UK, and the largest hotel in the Channel Islands. The only spa treatments on offer are ayurvedic treatments, with traditional spa therapies adapted to ayurvedic principles. If wellness is what you're after, you'll find it here.

What's on offer

A large infinity pool where you can have a proper swim, with a water curtain at one end where you can rest between lengths. A deep massage pool with a hydrotherapy bench and three swan pipes. A caldarium, a frigidarium and a large, hot sauna which could fit at least eight people without everyone sweating on each other. The mosaic-tiled steam room contains real steam – nicely hot with a thick fog and twinkly lights. The excellent gym is divided into two wooden-floored rooms.

Treatments include Vata, Pitta and Kapha facials, a wide variety of massages, including Shirodhara, where a stream of herbal-infused oil is poured onto your forehead, and Pizzichill, where two therapists massage you in gallons of warm oil. There's a hair and beauty salon elsewhere in the hotel, so you don't need to be without your manicure or make-up.

We loved

The proper ayurvedic consultation before the Abhyanga massage.

We also loved our authentic treatment with two therapists, as well as the breathtaking amount of space in the spa.

We didn't love

Because the hotel is so large, it can feel a little impersonal.

Food file

Café Aroma has an outside terrace overlooking the lawn. There's a range of snacks and grander dinner menu options.

Who would like it

Everyone who values their own well-being.

Don't miss

The extremely good four-handed Abhyanga massage.

Spa type
Hotel spa

Where?
Hotel de France
St Saviour's Road
St Helier
Jersey JE1 7XP
01534 614171

Signature treatment
Abhyanga four-hand oil massage with Bashpa Sweda herbalised steam detox

Brands
Ayush
Maharishi Ayurveda

Expect to pay
Treatments:
£65 for 55 minutes
Stay: from £75 per person in a standard double room

Bubble rating
5 out of 5 bubbles

Bailiffscourt Hotel

Arundel, West Sussex

A classic English manor house, all medieval mellow stone and mullioned windows.
Bailiffscourt sits in 30 acres of gardens where peacocks stroll casually by. The Temple
Spa aromatherapy products are unusual and irresistible; the spa offers well-priced
and excellent treatments in a very pleasant environment.

Spa type
Hotel spa

Where?
Bailiffscourt Hotel
Climping
Arundel
West Sussex
BN17 5RW
01903 723576

Signature treatment
Mediterranean Sea Massage:
a water-bed massage using
Drift Away oil

Brands
Temple Spa

Expect to pay
Treatments:
£72 for 55 minutes
Stay: £225 per room for bed
and breakfast in a small
standard double room

Bubble rating
4 out of 5 bubbles

What's on offer

Temple Spa individual therapies and
day-retreat packages; a large indoor
pool; a sauna, steam room and Jacuzzi;
an outdoor pool and hot tub overlooking
the gardens; a medium-size gym, wood-
floored, overlooking the outdoor pool
so it's nice and bright.

We loved

Reading and swimming and steaming in
the pool area. You can recover from your
swimming exertions in the Jacuzzi and
lounge around to your heart's content.

You can see the gardens through the
window, which adds to the 'get-away-
from-real-life-for-a-bit' atmosphere.

The gorgeously aromatic Temple Spa
products used in the treatments.

We didn't love

The small changing rooms. Bailiffscourt
is also a health club for members lucky
enough to live nearby, so there are times
when the changing area is busier than is
comfortable for dedicated spa goers.

Food file

There's a sunny room in the spa that
doubles as a relaxation area and café.
Sandwiches are brought over from the
main hotel kitchen.

Who would like it

Anyone looking for R&R; anyone looking
to escape real life for a day, or for a few
days, and rediscover their energy.

Don't miss

If you want to sit in a hot tub and watch
peacocks stroll by, this is the place to go.

Balmoral Spa

Balmoral Hotel, Edinburgh

A very grand hotel on Princes Street, with a basement spa. Usually a recipe for darkness but the Balmoral Spa is kept brighter by the glass roof in the pool area. It creates a very effective light-well in the centre of this popular spa.

What's on offer

A reasonable sized pool – 15-metres. It was temptingly empty early in the morning. There's a sauna and a large steam room, and it's all very handy in the centre of the city.

There are five treatment rooms, and a good range of treatments to choose from; we loved the organic Ytsara facials. Be aware that this is a popular spa: you have to book 4-6 weeks ahead for a spa day at the weekend.

We loved

You dip your feet in a bamboo bowl filled with warm water and rose petals to start your Thai-inspired Kamala treatment.

Having the relaxation room to ourselves; there were five wooden loungers with cushions and blankets so you could snuggle down, and classy magazines.

We didn't love

The layout of the spa is quite awkward and it's hard to find your way around. The changing rooms are a long way from the treatment rooms and you have to cross the pool area to get to them.

The spa is a bit mean with their towels. When we asked why they didn't have extra towels around, we were told that the health club members would use them.

Food file

Hadrian's, the hotel brasserie; you can have an excellent healthy lunch.

Who would like it

A great spa to meet a friend at on a midweek morning, have lunch and then hit the shopping hot spots of Edinburgh.

Don't miss

The brilliant afternoon tea in the Palm Court – a very grand room with a harp.

Spa type
Hotel spa

Where?
Balmoral Hotel
1 Princes Street
Edinburgh EH2 2EQ
0131 622 8880

Signature treatment
Kamala – Ytsara hot herbal treatment for face and body

Brands
ESPA
Ytsara

Expect to pay
Treatments:
£70 for 55 minutes
Stay: from £360 per night in a Classic double room

Bubble rating
4 out of 5 bubbles

Barnsley House

Cirencester, Gloucestershire

Enjoy holistic spa treatments in a cool country retreat. This lovely Cotswold stone manor house is in the centre of a quintessentially English village. The spa is a new addition and has been sympathetically designed using local stone.

Spa type
Hotel spa

Where?
Barnsley House
Barnsley
Cirencester
Gloucestershire GL7 5EE
01285 740000

Signature treatment
The Barnsley House:
exfoliation, hot stone
therapy, massage and facial

Brands
Barnsley House
REN

Expect to pay
Stay: from £275 per night
in a twin room

Bubble rating
4 out of 5 bubbles

What's on offer

There's no swimming pool but the outside hydrotherapy pool, heated to a cosy 36–38 degrees, offers a steamy refuge from which to admire the rural view. There's also a steam room and a sauna.

Six treatment rooms offer spa treatments with a holistic focus, and there's a good range of massages. The Aromatherapy Massage and Deep Tissue Massage use Barnsley House's signature blends of essential oils. There are only four facials to choose from, though.

We loved

Reclining on black leather loungers in the glass-walled relaxation room.

The decadent warmth of underfloor heating in the small but perfectly formed changing room.

We didn't love

The spa team were friendly and helpful but lacked information on the products.

The treatments felt rather disjointed. They weren't as slick as they could have been.

Food file

It's a short journey over the road to the sweet and rustic Village Pub, also owned by Barnsley House. The food was nothing special. This is the less formal alternative to the in-house restaurant.

Who would like it

People seeking an intimate, romantic refuge; City types looking for a cool and relaxing country retreat.

Don't miss

Visiting in summer when Rosemary Verey's celebrated garden is in bloom.

www.goodspaguide.co.uk • The Best Spas in Britain

Bath Spa Hotel

Bath, Somerset

Imagine an elegant Georgian building in mellow Bath stone, with attractive formal gardens, just a 15-minute walk from the centre of Bath. Add an informal spa with Roman-style murals. Then add your own butler, attending to your every whim. That's the Bath Spa Hotel.

What's on offer

A smallish indoor pool; an outside hydrotherapy pool; and a real thermal suite including an ice cave, steam room, properly hot sauna, salt infusion room and infra-red cabin.

There are also seven treatment rooms, one of which is a double room; a large room for manicures and pedicures, including a massage chair. There's a nice range of beauty and well-being treatments.

We loved

Our facial: the process was all very gentle and relaxing.

Lazing in bubbling bath-hot water in the outdoor hydrotherapy pool, and the dimly lit relaxation room, with comfortable black leather loungers.

Our own butler, who showed us to our room. Later, he arrived with champagne and canapés. Just what a girl needs while changing for dinner.

We didn't love

When we visited, the spa was suffering from pesky plumbing problems.

Food file

Hotel restaurants, plus a spa terrace menu in the summer.

Who would like it

Your American cousins; they will love the grandeur of the house and the spa.

Don't miss

Taking advantage of the high service levels throught the hotel.

Spa type

Hotel spa

Where?

Bath Spa Hotel
Sydney Road
Bath
Somerset BA2 6JF
01225 476862

Signature treatment

Decléor Aroma ultimate body massage

Brands

Decléor

Expect to pay

Treatments:
£70 for 60 minutes

Bubble rating

4 out of 5 bubbles

The Bath Priory

The Garden Spa, Bath, Somerset

This country house hotel has a new spa that makes the most of the beautiful gardens. Hence the name: The Garden Spa. With an award-winning restaurant, too, The Bath Priory provides a perfect indulgent day or stay.

What's on offer

A mellow Bath stone building in a row of Georgian houses on the edge of Bath city centre. Traditionally styled bedrooms with impressive modern bathrooms, complete with Molton Brown products.

A 10-metre pool more suited to relaxing swims than serious laps; underwater lighting gives the pool an aquamarine glow; it's surrounded by half-a-dozen loungers and a comfy couple's chaise. Modern graphite walls and flooring contrast with the more traditional hotel.

An 'elliptical steam pod', which is a nicely hot steam room within a large circular column at the far end of the pool, tiled in aubergine mosaic. A warming sauna. A changing area with, oddly, no doors.

The treatment rooms are in an adjacent building; not ideal, but the spa rooms do have their own changing area.

We loved

The Garden Spa signature treatment: The Awakening. This Li'Tya treatment incorporates a body cleanse and exfoliation, full body massage, facial, and head massage. Comprehensively blissful.

We didn't love

There's no relaxation room, and the pool area might struggle to cope under a determined influx of spa-goers.

Food file

After your treatment: a shot glass of fruit smoothie and some fresh fruit. The Bath Priory's restaurant serves delights such as seared scallops and pancetta, and roast fillet of beef with celeriac purée, in the traditional but unstuffy dining room.

Who would like it

The Bath Priory is perfect for anyone who enjoys the finer things in life. The spa is suited to couples or small groups relaxing for an hour or two and soaking up the ambience, rather than spending the whole day; the spa is quite compact and there's no communal chill-out area.

Don't miss

The Aboriginal-inspired treatments, such as the mala mayi mud wrap, though you can have Decléor treatments, too.

Spa type
Hotel Spa

Where?
The Bath Priory
Garden Spa
Weston Road
Bath, Somerset BA1 2XT
01225 478395

Signature treatment
The Awakening: foot soak, body exfoliation, Kodo massage, hair mask and facial.

Brands
Decléor, Li'Tya

Expect to pay
Treatments:
£70 for 60 minutes
Stay: from £185 per night for a classic double room

Bubble rating
5 out of 5 bubbles

Bedruthan Steps

Mawgan Porth, Cornwall

Bedruthan Steps is not the most economical of family holiday destinations, but the level of thought that has gone into Bedruthan's family facilities, come rain or shine, will make it hard to stay away for long. That's without even mentioning the indulgent Ocean Spa treatments...

Spa type
Hotel spa

Where?
Bedruthan Steps
Mawgan Porth
Cornwall TR8 4BU
01637 861219

Signature treatment
The Maharlika massage

Brands
Mama Mio
REN
Voya

Expect to pay
Treatments:
£50 for 55 minutes
Stay: from £87 per person
for one night in a sea-view
room

Bubble rating
4 out of 5 bubbles

What's on offer

A good choice of watery options: an indoor pool, a heated outdoor pool with a separate toddler area, and a larger outdoor pool with a hot tub on the side. There's also a hammam.

You can have REN and Voya facials, massages, scrubs and wraps. You can also have Thai massage, a delicious REN Guerande salt scrub and massage using rose oil; manicures and pedicures using Zoya nail polish (free from 'key chemical nasties'); personal fitness training; surfing lessons.

We loved

The stunning sea-view location and the beautiful stone hammam (although any hammam treatments have to be booked in advance).

The brilliant facilities for families: there are Ofsted-registered kids clubs offering fun for five age groups.

We didn't love

There is no separate relaxation room in the spa. There are a few loungers by the sea-view infinity spa pool, and a square formation of corner sofas, but nowhere dedicated to reclined relaxation.

Food file

Modern British with an emphasis on seasonal, local food.

Who would like it

Busy parents looking to re-introduce some me-time into their lives.

Don't miss

The Maharlika massage, with elements of shiatsu and Thai massage.

Berkeley Spa

The Berkeley Hotel, Knightsbridge, London

In so many hotels, the spa is sulking in the basement. Not at The Berkeley. Take the lift up to the seventh floor for top-notch spa treats and treatments. With the views over Hyde Park and the delicious poolside lunch, you won't want to come down.

What's on offer

The star of the show is the rooftop swimming pool with views over Hyde Park. There's a gym next to the pool and single-sex saunas and steam rooms within the changing rooms.

The spa uses [comfort zone] products for its signature spa treatments. Tailor-made jetlag recovery is available in 25-, 55- and 85-minute sessions, depending on your degree of disgruntlement. You can also try VOYA organic treatments, an ancient form of body treatment based on kelp from Northern Ireland.

We loved

The view; the fact that you can sit at your poolside table and feel so removed from real life is a real bonus.

The steam room is wonderfully hot and a good size for a hotel heat room.

We didn't love

No showers in the treatment rooms. You'll have to return to the changing rooms to shower off your exfoliant mid-treatment.

Shouty children in the swimming pool. The lack of a relaxation room.

Food file

Our poolside club sandwich could have won a competition for getting the most ingredients into a sandwich.

Who would like it

People staying at the hotel; local health-club members; anyone who fancies being really, really kind to themselves.

Don't miss

Splashing in the rooftop pool: a welcome antidote to London.

Spa type

Hotel spa

Where?

The Berkeley Hotel
Wilton Place
Knightsbridge
London SW1X 7RL
020 7201 1699

Signature treatment

Sacred Space: The ultimate massage ritual

Brands

[comfort zone]
Mama Mio
VOYA

Expect to pay

Treatments:
£90 for 55 minutes
Stay: from £289 per night in a Superior King room

Bubble rating

4 out of 5 bubbles

Bishopstrow House

Country Hotel and Halcyon Spa, Warminster, Wiltshire

Bishopstrow is a quintessential English country house and the Halcyon Spa is a quintessential contemporary luxury spa. Indoor and outdoor pools, over 40 treatments to choose from, and its own river to stroll along.

Spa type
Hotel spa

Where?
Bishopstrow House Country
Hotel and Spa
The Wylye Valley
Warminster
Wiltshire BA12 9HH
01985 212512

Signature treatment
Halcyon Spa luxurious face,
back and scalp treatment

Brands
Elemis

Expect to pay
Treatments:
£60 for 60 minutes
Stay: from £169 per night
for a double room

Bubble rating
4 out of 5 bubbles

What's on offer

An ivy covered Georgian country mansion in beautiful countryside with stylish and spacious rooms.

Two swimming pools, a sizeable Jacuzzi, a steam room and sauna, and experience showers. Tennis courts, a fully equipped gym and, of course, croquet.

The Halcyon Spa has four treatment rooms and a mud therapy room. Elemis facials, massages, wraps and scrubs. reiki and reflexology, treatments for mums to be, and for men. All the finishing beauty touches, and a hair studio.

We loved

The friendly, helpful and professional staff. The Elemis facial, which left us glowing with radiance. Swimming in the outdoor pool; a balmy 30 degrees in perfectly manicured gardens. Champagne and delicious pre-dinner canapés.

We didn't love

The changing rooms are small. An area next-door has hair driers and mirrors, but it is a passageway rather than a room. More signs might help, too.

Food file

The 2AA Rosette Mulberry Restaurant overlooking the gardens has a modern English menu and sensational food.

Who would like it

Bishopstrow makes a perfect romantic getaway. Families would also enjoy the pools; time your swim carefully if you fancy child-free serious swimming.

Don't miss

Swimming indoors and out. Afternoon tea on the lawn.

Bliss London

Chelsea, London

Terrific subterranean treatment rooms where you can luxuriate in an all-round superior environment with pricy but top-notch treatments. Fantastic for visible results.

What's on offer

Seven simple but stylish treatment rooms; a clinical feel but the warmed couches and fleecy blankets all say 'spa'.

A huge range of facials and skin-care treatments, from the Hangover Herbie for post-party people to a Quadruple Thighpass anti-cellulite treatment. Pedis, manis, treatments for eyes and necks, massages, peels, scrubs and rubs. They'll even wax your ears. For men, there's an Homme Improvement oxygen facial.

Our Tri-oxygen Treatment was a roller-coaster of a facial: if you can stand the pain of the fruit-acid wash and extractions, your skin will feel supple and moist. We came out looking as if we'd had Botox. It takes a few days for your skin to settle down, so this is not a treatment to book the day before your wedding. Bliss is busy, so book well in advance.

We loved

The quality robe and havaianas – a really nice touch – and you'd be hard pushed to find a more comfortable massage couch. Our facial was one of the best (if painful and expensive) we've ever had.

We didn't love

While the waiting and relaxation area is stylish, it is small with no loungers.

Food file

The chocolate brownie is a slice of heaven, washed down with lashings of refreshing home-made lemonade. A cheese-plate is also available.

Who would like it

Image-conscious *Vogue* and *Grazia* readers; self-appointed beautiful people.

Don't miss

One of the best facials on earth. If you're brave enough.

Spa type
Treatment rooms

Where?
Bliss London
60 Sloane Avenue
Chelsea
London SW3 3DD
020 7584 3888

Signature treatment
Blissage 75: a 75-minute head-to-toe massage

Brands
Bliss

Expect to pay
Treatments:
£100 for 75 minutes

Bubble rating
5 out of 5 bubbles

Boath House

Nairn, Inverness-shire

Boath House offers gourmet food, distinctively individual accommodation, and personal and friendly service. It's not really a spa, having just two treatment rooms and no pools or other spa features. However, you can have an indulgent and relaxing stay at this hotel, with the Aveda treatments an enhancing well-being add-on.

Spa type
Hotel spa

Where?
Boath House
Auldearn
Nairn
Inverness-shire IV12 5TE
01667 454896

Signature treatment
Aveda Elemental facial

Brands
Aveda

Expect to pay
Stay: from £220 for
bed and breakfast

Bubble rating
4 out of 5 bubbles

What's on offer

A former cellar with a low, arched ceiling has been converted with a partition screen into two treatment rooms. These are dimly lit, just with candles.

You can try a good variety of Aveda facials, including a glycolic peel, Thai or hot stone massage, and an Essential Back Treatment to make your spine feel fine. You can choose from a small range of beauty treatments, reflexology, and a menu of three half-day spa packages.

We loved

The warm Highland welcome. First impressions count, and ours was a very good one.

Our lovingly furnished two-bedroomed cottage a stone's throw from the main Georgian hotel. With the bathroom's deep, free-standing bath peppered with Molton Brown products, Boath House gave us a sense of pampering before we'd even set foot in the main building.

The spa and restaurant are open to non-residents, so you don't have to stay at the hotel to sample some of the Boath House indulgence.

We didn't love

Boath House is not a spa, although it doesn't pretend to be one. There's no pool, no sauna or steam room, no gym.

Food file

Divine. The lemon-balm ice cream with chocolate-and-cocoa-nib cake still evokes happy memories.

Who would like it

Gourmet spa-goers.

Don't miss

The Aveda treatments; Boath House is the only location in the north of Scotland that offers them.

Body Experience

Richmond, Surrey

Australian-themed treatment rooms. There aren't many spas where you can take a pleasant stroll along the River Thames and end your afternoon with a massage inspired by Aboriginal healing techniques. Body Experience is one such place.

What's on offer

Lots of aboriginal-inspired treatments using the entirely organic Australian skincare brand Li'Tya; there's a Mud, Aroma Steam and Kiradjee Indulgence, for example, or try a luxurious Deep Ocean Renewal Facial. Body Experience's 'Lifestyle Clinic' offers medispa treatments and IPL hair removal.

There's no sauna, steam room, pool or classes – just a great spa menu of unusual treatments.

We loved

The very relaxing relaxation room, decked out with loungers and decorated with floaty white fabric on the walls.

The aboriginal-inspired Li'tya Mikiri deep cleansing facial. Relaxing and effective.

We didn't love

The scarcity of information about the treatments on the website. It's hard for a newbie to tell your kiradjee from your kodo melody.

Therapists can be a bit 'selly' on pushing the products at the end of the treatments.

Food file

Spa lunches, afternoon tea, champagne, smoothies. You can enjoy a generous fruit salad after your treatment.

Who would like it

People who like to relax, and who like spa-ing without leaving town.

Don't miss

The 'tranquil garden' patio area; this is perfect for a post-treatment chill-out in the fresh air.

Spa type
Treatment rooms

Where?
Body Experience
50 Hill Rise
Richmond
Surrey TW10 6UB
020 8334 9999

Signature treatment
Kodo Melody body massage

Brands
Elemis
Li'Tya
Thalgo

Expect to pay
Treatments:
£65 for 60 minutes

Bubble rating
4 out of 5 bubbles

Bodysgallen Hall and Spa

Conwy, North Wales

A small and exclusive grey-stone manor house hotel with just 18 bedrooms and a scattering of cottages hidden in the grounds. Bodysgallen's intimate spa is in the grounds, in a rebuilt stone and slate farm building. It feels more like a small, private country house.

Spa type
Hotel spa

Where?
Bodysgallen Hall and Spa
Near Llanrhos
Llandudno
Conwy
North Wales LL30 1RS
01492 562500

Signature treatment
Anne Sémonin 100% Active
Decrease facial

Brands
Anne Sémonin
CACI
Decléor

Expect to pay
Treatments:
£48 for 55 minutes
Stay: £175 per night in a
standard queen-size room

Bubble rating
4 out of 5 bubbles

What's on offer

A 50-foot pool, a sauna, a steam room and a Jacuzzi; roof lights keep this area bright. The gym is small but well equipped. Treatments include customised Anne Sémonin cosmeceutical face and body treatments, CACI electronic 'non-surgical facelifts', microdermabrasion and oxygen infusion treatments.

We loved

A log fire and the offer of afternoon tea were perfect after a long drive on a cold March day.

The spa is more like your own private space than a spa; you are treated as if you are the only person there.

We didn't love

The spa is a walk through the woods from the hotel. Pack your trainers.

The pool, steam and Jacuzzi area is in need of a lick of paint and the white plastic chairs by the pool are rather downmarket for a luxurious destination.

Food file

The Club Room serves healthy meals and drinks. In the summer, guests can also use the sun terrace.

Who would like it

The hotel and setting are very romantic, so Bodysgallen is great for couples. It also feels exclusive; the morning we were there, David Cameron helicoptered in for breakfast.

Don't miss

The Anne Sémonin express radiance cubes. Not actually Botox ice cubes, but something they call 'neurocosmetics'.

Bowood Hotel, Spa and Resort

Calne, Wiltshire

There is a real sense of grandeur at this stylish hotel and spa in the grounds of a stately home. Bowood has something for everyone: an enthusiastic, friendly welcome, a championship golf course, Elemis treatments and a traditional adventure playground. Not to mention a fab pool and gym with great views.

What's on offer

A 15-metre pool, poolside Jacuzzi, sauna, crystal steam room and shiny new gym with a view over the Wiltshire countryside.

There are no dedicated treatment rooms, so treatments are given in one of the deluxe bedrooms, fitted with massage couches, draped in Indian fabric and filled with tea-lights and ambient music. The spa focuses on just four Elemis body treatments and four Elemis facials.

We loved

The stately grounds, the treatments and the pool with a view. Our relaxing Elemis deep-tissue massage – just the thing for a tender lower back.

We didn't love

The trip to the first-floor treatment room/bedroom, which breaks up the flow of the spa journey. There is no dedicated treatment relaxation area either.

Food file

The spa has its own bar/cafe area offering healthy snacks and light refreshments. There are two dining options in the hotel:

The Shelbourne, which serves traditional, seasonal cuisine and uses estate-grown and local produce, and the less formal Brasserie at the golf clubhouse. Choose from Caesar salad or spaghetti carbonara or the favourite 'steak stone steak', cooked at your table.

Who would like it

Anyone looking to combine a rural break in a luxury hotel with a tempting pool and a relaxing treatment; families; couples looking for a golf and spa retreat.

Don't miss

The beautiful blue mosaic pool with floor-to-ceiling picture windows on three sides, overlooking the 18-hole championship golf course and Wiltshire countryside.

Spa type
Hotel spa

Where?
Bowood Hotel,
Spa and Golf Resort
Bowood, Derry Hill
Calne
Wiltshire SN11 9PQ
01249 823883

Signature treatment
Face and body sensation

Brands
Elemis

Expect to pay
Treatments:
£50 for 60 minutes
Stay: from £150 per night
in a double room

Bubble rating
4 out of 5 bubbles

Brandshatch Place

Fawkham, Kent

This elegant, red-brick Georgian mansion, built by the Duke of Norfolk in 12 acres of lush countryside in the Garden of England in 1806, had a multi-million pound refurbishment. Result? A perfect spa destination. And the best cauliflower soup we've ever tasted.

Spa type
Hotel spa

Where?
Brandshatch Place
Brandshatch Road
Fawkham
Kent DA3 8NQ
01474 875040

Signature treatment
The Neom Complete
Organic Bliss

Brands
ESPA
MD Formulations
NEOM

Expect to pay
Treatments:
£55 for 55 minutes
Stay: from £95 per night
in a classic room

Bubble rating
4 out of 5 bubbles

What's on offer

Fully air-conditioned gym, indoor swimming pool, hydrotherapy pool, sauna, Jacuzzi and crystal steam room. The bright, modern Amber Lounge. A wide range of effective and professional treatments: wraps, facials, massages, aromatherapy treatments, holistic therapies, hot-stone therapies, complementary therapies, manicures and pedicures, treatments for men, and treatments for pregnant women.

You can also have driving tuition at the Brands Hatch race-track nearby.

We loved

The spa's signature treatment, the Neom Complete Organic Bliss. Beginning with a foot ritual, this uses a combination of reflexology, Thai and Swedish massage, aromatherapy, crystal therapy and relaxation techniques (the aroma is heavenly).

We didn't love

The very small pool and the dearth of loungers. The space would definitely feel noisy with more than a few people in it.

Food file

After a long gin and tonic, gazing out on the peaceful countryside, we ate in the award-winning 2 AA-Rosette Hatchwood Restaurant. It offers excellent traditional English dishes. For lunch, a tempting menu is available in the Amber Lounge.

Who would like it

Mothers and daughters; groups of friends; couples.

Don't miss

The Neom Complete Organic Bliss treatment. Very special.

Brooklands Retreat

Garstang, Lancashire

Brooklands is a true retreat with a small and exclusive spa. No business travellers in a hurry or small children rushing round on bicycles. Why watch the clock for your appointment times, when you can just lounge by the pool till someone calls your name?

What's on offer

Here you'll find a swimming pool, hydrotherapy pool, sanarium, steam room, gym, and aerobics studio. A varied programme of exercise, too – including an aqua-fit session.

A wide range of body and facial treatments and many different stay packages. Brooklands' tagline is 'as individual as you' so they really can mix you up your own preferred combination.

We loved

The very warm welcome – you'll feel very cared for throughout your visit; the earthiness of the Spa Find products; the warm and comfortable Spa Find mud wrap; rose petals in the foot baths; no rush between treatments.

We didn't love

The sanarium and the steam room are fairly basic. Air fresheners in the corridors are not very 'spa'.

Food file

Beautifully prepared and presented, the right balance between virtuous and

ever-so-slightly naughty. We loved the surprisingly alcoholic grapes and ice cream with a fruit coulis.

Who would like it

Mums and daughters, mums and mums, groups of girlfriends. It's very girly.

Don't miss

The 24-hour residential package: arrive at 4pm for tea, leave at 4pm the next day. The room and the meals are a fabulous complement to your treatments.

Spa type
Spa retreat

Where?
Brooklands
Calder House Lane
Garstang
Lancashire PR3 1QB
01995 605162

Signature treatment
Sculptured Silhouette face and body experience

Brands
Clarins, Decléor, Spa Find

Expect to pay
Treatments:
£42 for 40 minutes
Stay: from £212 in a standard room including meals and some treatments

Bubble rating
4 out of 5 bubbles

Good Spa Spy Favourites

Student Spy

Age 18 **Skin type** Combination **Spa likes** Good food; friendly therapists; decent music to listen to during a treatment; therapists who understand that exams make you really stressed **Spa dislikes** Robes that are too big for people who are only five foot tall; swimming pools with no room to swim; too much healthy food

Best spa experiences this year

I loved the hammam at the **Le Kalon Spa** at the Bentley Hotel. I got very hot, but you could pour cold water over yourself to cool yourself down, and that was a lot of fun. The massage afterwards was very relaxing. I also like the **Aquitaine Spa** at the Runnymede Hotel. I have been to this spa before, and like it very much. Although an Espa massage is still my favourite treatment.

Worst spa experiences this year

A spa menu that contained all the foods that I don't like. There's a lot of those.

Favourite products

Superdrug Tea Tree & Peppermint Moisturiser

It gets rid of dry skin quickly! It doesn't cause my skin to feel clogged up, or bring it out in spots. The moisturiser also makes my skin feel very soft. Easily absorbed, it also feels refreshing. Plus, it's a very good price!

Imperial Leather Japanese Spa Foam Burst

This 'ultimate shower experience' contains green tea, rice milk and jasmine. It is fun to use because a tiny amount of the transparent gel turns into a lot of rich and creamy lather. It washes off very easily, leaving my skin soft and clean. There are others in the range but I think this one has the nicest smell.

Thalgo Foaming Marine Cleanser

This is the wash I use in the morning and evening. It's a very soft foam that I keep coming back to because I think it makes my skin the cleanest and clearest. When you first put it on your skin, it feels different to soap because it isn't as hard, and it rinses off very easily. I use it as part of Thalgo's PURITY Range for combination skin, which is the best set of products I've ever found for teenage skin. Must be all those marine extracts. Each one in the range is very good value as this product lasts a long time.

Pantene Hold and Gloss hair spray

I like this spray because it has an 'ultra-strong hold'. This means it is actually very good at keeping your hair in the style you want, even when you go out. You just need to remember to wash it out the next day otherwise you then have hard and crackly hair.

Brown's Hotel

Mayfair, London

Brown's is the epitome of hotel elegance in central London. The spa's interior is minimalist and modern with pristine white walls and clean lines. Well suited to those who want a professional treatment in a smart, discreet location.

What's on offer

A gym; three treatment rooms; a good range of massage and a few Carita facials; Natura Bissé wraps; an Aromatherapy Associates body polish, Mama Mio pregnancy treatments.

We loved

The Natura Bissé Diamond facial; it certainly left our Spy's skin sparkling.

The minimal design and clean, uncluttered treatment rooms; ask for the large double room – you'll have plenty of space.

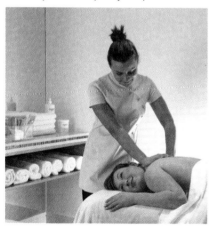

If you're staying, the Egyptian cotton bedsheets will make you want to spend the next 24 hours in bed.

We didn't love

There is no relaxation area and the waiting area consisted only of a padded bench; there wasn't even a table to put a teacup on. A few spa touches in the reception area also wouldn't go amiss.

Food file

At the spa, traditional loose tea served on a tray with some fresh, juicy grapes. In the hotel, modern British at the Albermarle, or afternoon tea at the English Tea Room.

Who would like it

Hotel guests at Brown's; it's so easy to pop in the lift and visit the spa. There's no pool, so if getting your laps in is a crucial part of your spa day, Brown's isn't for you.

Don't miss

The use of a tuning fork to make sound vibrations, which are meant to energise your muscles and tighten your skin, in the Natura Bissé Diamond facial.

Spa type
Hotel spa

Where?
Brown's Hotel
Albemarle Street
Mayfair
London W1S 4BP
020 7518 4009

Signature treatment
Natura Bissé Diamond facial

Brands
Aromatherapy Associates, Carita, Dr Sebagh, Mama Mio, Natura Bissé

Expect to pay
Treatments:
£80 for 60 minutes
Stay: from £475 per night in a Queen room

Bubble rating
4 out of 5 bubbles

Calcot Spa

Calcot Manor, Tetbury, Gloucestershire

A luxury Cotswold country house retreat that manages to hit the spot for families and child-free chill seekers alike. The hotel offers practical luxury and a lot of thought has gone into combining guest comfort with style. There's a well-heeled but not overly flashy clientele.

What's on offer

A relaxed garden area with a large, square hot tub, open fire and café tables. A dry floatation room and hammam; we liked relaxing in the sauna that has a window overlooking the pool. The large indoor pool has an area roped off for serious swimmers. There's an immaculate all-weather tennis court and a jogging/trim trail. Hire a bike – there's even a trailer for those with young children.

A comprehensive array of aromatherapy body treatments and facials, some using the organic Spiezia range from Cornwall, as well as a maternity massage based on Aromatherapy Associates Rose products.

We loved

The luxury Zenspa pedicure in a £2,000 leather Balzac chair, and the Borders-scale magazine selection in the relaxation room.

The facilities for children at Calcot: our spacious suite was complete with a cosy children's bedroom in the eaves, books, toys and a stairgate. The Ofsted accredited crèche is also impressive. Children are welcome to use the indoor pool at clearly designated times, ensuring no resentment between families and tranquillity seekers.

We didn't love

Being taken on a one-to-one run by the circuits instructor when no-one else turned up for the scheduled circuits class!

Food file

Choose from the smart but thankfully unstuffy Conservatory, or the Gumstool Inn, which feels like an upmarket Harvester.

The Conservatory is light and airy and serves imaginative, if not hugely portioned modern food. The Gumstool offers a livelier option, and bigger portions of gastro-pub cuisine. It's also where the children's 'high tea' is served between 5.30–6pm.

Who would like it

Anyone looking for a luxurious but bling-free indulgent escape; people escaping with – or from – the children.

Don't miss

The hot tub with a log-fire backdrop. Pretty special, if rather surreal on a hot summer's day. It's the first time you'll ever be sunburned sitting in front of a fire.

Spa type

Hotel spa

Where?

Calcot Manor
Tetbury
Gloucestershire GL8 8YJ
01666 891232

Signature treatment

Luxury Bliss: body brush, body massage, facial and scalp massage

Brands

Aromatherapy Associates, CACI, Guinot, Thalgo

Expect to pay

Treatments:
£60 for 55 minutes
Stay: from £245 per night in a standard double bedroom

Bubble rating

5 out of 5 bubbles

Cameron House

Spa at the Carrick, Loch Lomond, Scotland

Don't walk, don't run – take the complimentary 4x4 to Cameron House hotel's spa. It's a spacious spa, with curved walls and candlelight being key themes throughout. There aren't many places where you can enjoy views of surrounding Scottish mountains from a tepidarium but this is one of them.

Spa type
Hotel spa

Where?
Cameron House
Alexandria
Loch Lomond
Dunbartonshire G83 8QZ
01389 713659

Signature treatment
Caviar facial using
Kerstin Florian products

Brands
Carita
Kerstin Florian

Expect to pay
Stay: from £179 for bed and breakfast in a classic garden view room

Bubble rating
4 out of 5 bubbles

What's on offer

A spectacular rooftop infinity pool; we loved watching the local birds fly by. Thermal experiences include an infra-red sauna, caldarium, aroma steam bath, and hydro-pool. The tepidarium is light and airy, with large windows so you can revel in the views of the surrounding mountains and hills.

A Golfer's Spa menu includes soothing facials, foot treatments, and back, neck, and shoulder massages.

We loved

The Lavender Dream Ultimate Kur: it combines a series of treatments traditionally offered in European spas, using mud, thermal mineral water and other natural products. The Kur includes a full body exfoliation, scalp massage and hot-stone pressure-point massage.

The relaxation room: ten single beds offer private space with plenty of room. You can relax under a duvet in a darkened room with colour-therapy lighting.

We didn't love

The spa at Cameron House is two-and-a-half miles from the hotel. That's why there is a complimentary 4x4 taxi service.

Food file

Formal dining or lighter meals, with a view over the loch.

Who would like it

Cameron House is a great venue for a weekend or midweek treat.

Don't miss

Taking the complimentary taxi back to the hotel; post-treatment, our Spy thought it would be good to meander back to the hotel through peaceful greenery. She was wrong. You need to cross some very busy roads.

Center Parcs Elveden

(Aqua Sana Spa), Brandon, Suffolk

A warm haven of a spa in a popular holiday village offering stunningly good value for money, an enormous choice of spa experiences and spot-on customer care. A wide range of heat experience rooms include a Roman laconium, Balinese multi-steam bath, and Indian Blossom steam room.

What's on offer

Aqua Sana spa is in the tradition of Roman baths where people go to socialise and gossip. Spa hostesses welcome you and answer questions – great for spa virgins. At the centre of the spa area is a small, 7-metre, open-air hydrotherapy pool, circled by massage jets.

A good range of Carita, Decléor and Elemis facials and body treatments. Dual treatments for friends, couples, and mothers and daughters, and treatments for mums-to-be, teens and men. We had the Elemis Absolute Spa Ritual, a great combination treatment with deep-tissue

massage and relaxing facial. Everything is clean and well maintained.

We loved

The range of experiences and the friendly staff. The heat experience rooms, tiled and decorated in different styles.

We didn't love

The small changing rooms; they get very crowded at the end of an afternoon. The wooden staircase to the treatment rooms can be rather noisy.

Food file

The Zilli Café offers Italian cuisine. There are daily pasta specials and seasonal salads to wash down with a glass of San Pellegrino (or Prosecco!).

Who would like it

Anyone who likes a bargain; groups of friends; anyone who wants to take a day out to recharge batteries.

Don't miss

Sitting in the warm hydrotherapy pool having your back massaged and looking up at the sky.

Spa type
Day spa

Where?
Center Parcs
Elveden Forest
Brandon
Suffolk IP27 0YZ
08448 266200

Signature treatments
Bliss Dual Treatment,
Harmony Dual Treatment,
Indulgence Dual Treatment

Brands
Carita, Decléor, Elemis

Expect to pay
Treatments:
£65 for 55 minutes
Stay: from £229 for a four-night midweek break in a two-bedroom comfort villa

Bubble rating
4 out of 5 bubbles

Center Parcs Longleat

(Aqua Sana Spa), Warminster, Wiltshire

Aqua Sana provides the perfect escape from the activity frenzy that is a typical Center Parcs holiday. The facilities at the impressive Roman-style Aqua Sana are high quality and extensive, although it can be a busy World of Spa...

Spa type
Day spa

Where?
Center Parcs
Longleat Forest
Warminster
Wiltshire BA12 7PU
08448 266200

Signature treatment
Bliss Dual Treatment,
Harmony Dual Treatment,
Indulgence Dual Treatment

Brands
Carita, Decléor, Elemis

Expect to pay
Treatments:
£65 for 55 minutes
Stay: from £229 for a four-night midweek break in a two-bedroom comfort villa

Bubble rating
4 out of 5 bubbles

What's on offer

World of Spa, Aqua Sana's boldly entitled spa area, contains spa treats from around the world: Greek herbal baths; a large Indian Blossom steam room; a Japanese salt room; an intensely steamy Turkish hammam; a Tyrolean and a Finnish sauna.

Dry floatation treatments include volcanic mud and zesty citrus wraps. You can try a serail mud treatment, too. If you work during the day, you can visit during a Twilight Spa session and enjoy the heated outdoor pool by moonlight.

We loved

Aqua Sana's attempt to recreate an authentic feel in the spa. The steam rooms are all beautifully tiled and each has its own individual characteristics.

The seriously firm deep-tissue massage in the Elemis Absolute Spa Ritual.

We didn't love

Aqua Sana could do with more changing space when the spa is busy. It got quite cosy when we were there with a dozen or so other spa goers.

Food file

The Zilli Café serves morning coffee and breakfast, healthy lunches, fresh juices and afternoon tea.

Who would like it

Aqua Sana is well suited to groups of friends as the facilities are extensive. Aqua Sana is also a good way to combine some spa me-time with a family holiday.

Don't miss

The cream-leather aqua meditation room has mesmerising bubbling water cylinders.

Center Parcs Sherwood

(Aqua Sana Spa), Rufford, Newark, Nottinghamshire

Everywhere is spotlessly clean and in good condition at this attractive, very sociable spa in the holiday village. It's great value, offers great treatments and has a great range of facilities. In fact, it's just great!

What's on offer

A calm, cool reception, spotless changing rooms and a spa hostess to greet you. The spa is built around an open-air pool, with 20 different heat and experience rooms. Waterbeds, reclining chairs, a Zen garden and an outdoor terrace where you can sit wrapped in 'furs'.

A wide range of treatments including reiki, reflexology, massages, facials, pampering for mums to be, treatments for men, and teen treatments. We tried the Elemis Rediscover Romance treatment, a gorgeous massage for two with both therapists working to deliver a soft, soothing Hawaiian-style 'wave' massage.

We loved

The scents: ylang-ylang in the Indian Blossom steam room, jasmine and mint in the Japanese salt steam bath. The outdoor pool; it's small, but we had fun swimming outside on a cold, grey day, the steam rising gently around us.

We didn't love

Towards the café and treatment area, the floor gets very wet and slippery. The café could be more luxurious and comfortable,

too, and they charge a few pounds for a piece of carrot cake!

Food file

The Conservatory Café has options from sandwiches to crayfish with crème fraiche and herbs.

Who would like it

Us and all our friends! Couples; mums and groups escaping for a couple of hours.

Don't miss

The key to the pleasure here is the way the spa stimulates all your senses. Soft water, stone floors, 'fur' blankets, wonderful aromas. So sample them all.

Spa type
Day spa

Where?
Center Parcs, Sherwood
Rufford
Newark NG22 9DN
08448 266200

Signature treatments
Bliss Dual Treatment,
Harmony Dual Treatment,
Indulgence Dual Treatment

Brands
Carita, Decléor, Elemis

Expect to pay
Treatments:
£65 for 55 minutes
Stay: from £229 for a four-night midweek break in a two-bedroom comfort villa

Bubble rating
4 out of 5 bubbles

Center Parcs, Whinfell Forest

(Aqua Sana Spa), Penrith, Cumbria

Blending perfectly with its forest surroundings in the holiday village, this good value, imaginative spa is small from the outside, huge on the inside. Seven different heat rooms, four flavours of massage, two excellent treatments and one impressive World of Spa!

Spa type
Day spa

Where?
Center Parcs
Whinfell Forest
Penrith, Cumbria CA10 2DW
08448 266200

Signature treatments
Bliss Dual Treatment,
Harmony Dual Treatment,
Indulgence Dual Treatment

Brands
Carita, Decléor, Elemis

Expect to pay
Treatments:
£65 for 55 minutes
Stay: from £229 for a four-night midweek break in a two-bedroom comfort villa

Bubble rating
4 out of 5 bubbles

What's on offer

Not solitude and luxury but friendly, fun spa time. Inspired heat rooms, a 12-metre outdoor heated pool big enough for a tiny swim, a large outdoor hydrotherapy pool with strong massage jets.

Professional therapists and good quality treatments with a huge range of various massages, wraps, aroma treatments and facials. You can have a dry floatation with an organic honey and milk wrap, or a serial mud treatment. There are teen treatments, and a nail and hair studio, too.

We loved

The imaginative approach to the heat experiences. You can spend a happy couple of hours trying everything. Twice.

We didn't love

Having our make-up applied among the products in the reception area. We felt a little jostled as people rummaging for bath oil peered at our blusher. The spa can get very busy in the afternoon, too.

Food file

The Conservatory Café has options from sandwiches to coriander chicken and lime. We found it a little disappointing, with high prices and a limited range of healthy options.

Who would like it

Spa beginners, couples and groups. Aqua Sana isn't a 'girlie' spa and men will feel at home here.

Don't miss

All the heat rooms, reviving yourself with bracing ice flakes or a minty mist in the multi-sensory shower.

Champneys Brighton

(A Town and City Spa), Brighton, East Sussex

Good customer service and a cool vibe in a great location, with a wide range of reasonably priced treatments – Champneys facials, massages and a St Tropez tanning station. No robes or splashing about, this Champneys is more quick-fix treatment room than spa sanctuary.

What's on offer

A shabby chic/kitsch retro décor (gorgeous black and gold wallpaper), and good customer service from the amiable, young, perfectly groomed staff. Excellent disabled access. A small reception/waiting area and large shop. Seven treatment rooms spread over four floors. A massive front window so you can watch the world go by as you have your manis and pedis. Everywhere tidy and spotless.

We had the Ultimate Hip and Thigh Detoxifier, which uses a (noisy!) machine, exclusive to Champneys, to relax the muscles, then a seaweed mask followed by a dreamy massage. It felt great, and truly revived and refreshed our legs.

We loved

The warm, toasty treatment bed. The location in Brighton's cool South Lanes.

We didn't love

The busy waiting area – not the most relaxing of places – and the absence of a relaxation room, wet facilities, or lockers to store your bags.

Food file

We were offered water or fruit tea in a good selection of flavours.

Who would like it

This is quite a girly place – there are only two treatments on the menu for men. Great for best buddies; mums and daughters; anyone out shopping who feels the need for some pampering.

Don't miss

The CACI eye treatment, which uses a technique for training muscles into shape. A course of six is recommended but we felt an instant difference after one session.

Spa type
Treatment rooms

Where?
Champneys Town and City Spa – Brighton
24 East Street
Brighton BN1 1HL
01273 777155

Signature treatment
Spa Heaven Cocoon

Brands
CACI, Champneys, Elemis, MD Formulations

Expect to pay
Treatments:
£50 for 55 minutes

Bubble rating
4 out of 5 bubbles

Champneys Chichester

(A Town and City Spa), Chichester, West Sussex

These white, bright treatment rooms situated in one of the main shopping streets in Chichester are a perfect place to recover from over-zealous retail exertions. As long as you don't dip too deep into the spa's shelf after shelf of appealingly presented Champneys products...

Spa type
Treatment rooms

Where?
Champneys Town
and City Spa
60 East Street
Chichester
West Sussex PO19 1HL
01243 819010

Signature treatments
Collagen Enriched
Anti-Ageing Facial
Spa Heaven Cocoon

Brands
CACI, Champneys,
Dr Sebagh, Elemis

Expect to pay
Treatments:
£50 for 55 minutes

Bubble rating
4 out of 5 bubbles

What's on offer

A short and simple menu of Champneys, CACI, Dr Sebagh and Elemis facials in these eight treatment rooms. Body treatments include a chocolate wrap, aromatherapy body massage and pregnancy massage. There's also St Tropez spray tanning, a small selection of treatments for men, and all the usual beauty treatments you would expect: waxing, eyebrow shaping and manicures, including the Minx nail design service.

Because of the heavy retail focus, it does feel a little like a shop that just happens

to have some treatment rooms attached to it, rather than a spa in its own right.

We loved

The helpful attitude of the staff. The way they explain everything that will happen. Our Relaxing Facial: it lived up to its name. Our back, neck and shoulder massage that left us almost asleep.

We didn't love

The lack of a relaxation area. Sitting in the waiting area is not special.

Our treatment room was a little chilly and some parts of the spa need some TLC.

Food file

Water and herbal teas.

Who would like it

Nervous first-time spa-goers and shoppers looking for a quick fix.

Don't miss

The brilliant retro black and white photos of Champneys from the 1960s.

Champneys Henlow

Henlow, Bedfordshire

A health-farm-style spa in a converted country house. With an emphasis on well-being, and a wide range of activities, Champneys Henlow is an affordable spa to get away to with friends, rather than the ultimate in exclusive pampering.

What's on offer

A country manor house surrounded by fields. Spacious changing rooms and 35 treatment rooms. A 25-metre pool with whirlpool, in a light and airy atmosphere. Steam room and laconium. A bookable thalassotherapy pool.

Everything from facials and manicures to fortune telling and colonic irrigation. Wraps, scrubs, massages, hypnotherapy, a wax bath, tui na and dry floats. A range of 'finishing touches' is also on offer, plus a hair salon.

You can work out in the light and well-equipped gym, or go to one of the dawn 'til dusk classes in the two studios.

We loved

The pool: perfect for getting those lengths in. The personalised Champneys facial with a gorgeous head massage while your mask works its magic.

We didn't love

Some of the communal areas could do with a lick of paint. The spa can also get very busy; book off-peak if you can.

Food file

Mostly good. Plenty of choice with a lunch-time buffet and evening waitress service. Menus are well marked, showing low fat options, for example. There's a table for single diners to share.

Who would like it

Anyone looking for an affordable spa break, or a packed spa programme.

Don't miss

The lovely grounds: a change of scene if you're staying for a few nights.

Spa type
Spa retreat

Where?
Champneys Henlow
The Grange, Henlow
Bedfordshire SG16 6DB
08703 300 300

Signature treatment
The Wax Bath

Brands
Babor
Champneys
Elemis

Expect to pay
Treatments:
£70 for 55 minutes
Stay: from £278 per night
in a standard double

Bubble rating
4 out of 5 bubbles

Champneys Tring

Tring, Hertfordshire

The UK's first health farm remains true to its roots. Champneys Tring is still very much a traditional health spa. The emphasis here is on weight loss and lifestyle change, coupled with indulgent Champneys spa therapies. Following their multi-million pound refurb, the facilities are great.

What's on offer

The new thalassotherapy area is large and impressive. There's also a well-equipped gym and a glass-roofed 25-metre indoor swimming pool. Daily activities run from dawn until dusk at Tring. Choose from an early-morning walk, aqua classes, tai chi, aerobics, boot camp circuit…

As well as all the standard spa treatments you would expect, there are more health-based offerings such as cellulite/colon therapy, chiropody, postural analysis and nutritional testing. Try holistic Aura Soma Colour Therapy, or a session with the Tring clairvoyant.

Residential packages range from a Luxury Day to a seven-night residential package.

We loved

The grounds are impressive and there's a good feeling of space which, with 170 acres, we suppose there should be.

The helipad. (We always forget to bring something…)

The communal table for guests who are dining on their own.

We didn't love

The relaxation area; it's a rather under-whelming room consisting of six loungers, a carved wooden screen and some calming music.

Everywhere you look, there seems to be a Champneys logo. We defy anyone to visit and emerge oblivious to the fact that they have their own product range.

Food file

A self-service buffet lunch; you eat lunch in your robes, which gives the feeling of being in a traditional health farm. There are many healthy options, and 'Light Diet' dishes, although you can splurge on desserts and champagne at dinner, should you wish.

Who would like it

Fans of more traditional health farms; people who are serious about adopting a healthier lifestyle or losing weight; C-list celebrity spotters.

Don't miss

The smart new thalassotherapy area.

Spa type
Spa retreat

Where?
Champneys Tring
Tring
Berkhamsted
Hertfordshire HP23 6HY
08703 300 300

Signature treatment
East Meets West: full body treatment combining shiatsu and Swedish massage

Brands
Carita, Champneys, Crystal Clear, Elemis

Expect to pay
Stay: £318 per night in a standard double room

Bubble rating
5 out of 5 bubbles

Chancery Court Spa

Holborn, London

This is a peaceful city-centre spa that aims to soothe your soul as well as pamper you from here to who-knows-where. Chancery Court does what it sets out to do very well, and that is to provide a soothing haven in the midst of busy working lives.

What's on offer

Chancery Court offers a wide range of treatments influenced by Oriental culture. You can try a Thai Herbal Heat Massage, or a Replenishing Intensive Facial, which promises 'connective energy bonding between therapist and client'. You can have ayurvedic rituals tailored to your individual dosha, too.

You can also book the couples' suite ('London's most exclusive'), or book the entire spa for your exclusive use for four hours, for up to 15 people.

You'll be disappointed if you're looking to combine your spa treatments with several laps, as there's no pool, although there is a light and bright gym upstairs.

We loved

The limestone walls, soft floor lighting and wooden bridges over rippling water and pebbles; hard to believe you're in the middle of Holborn. We also liked the heated changing room floor; take your plastic slippers off and do a barefoot shuffle just because you can.

Chilling out in the relaxation room: this circular room in the centre of the spa is a joy. It's filled with candles and gold-plated pillars reflecting the light.

We didn't love

The cost of the Ashtaang eight-hand massage; for £540, we expected to turn around and find ourselves being massaged by Brad Pitt. The most expensive massage in London? Perhaps it's worth it just to say you've had it.

Food file

Fruit to eat in the relaxation room, and water, but no tea. After our dual massage, the therapists wheeled a little trolley over and left it in between our massage tables. There was a beautiful display of anti-oxidising berries – blueberries, strawberries, blackberries, raspberries – and water. Sadly, still no tea.

Who would like it

Anyone with a City bonus and someone to impress.

Don't miss

Soaking up the peace in the circular relaxation room.

Spa type

Hotel spa

Where?

Chancery Court Hotel
252 High Holborn
Holborn
London WC1V 7EN
020 7829 7058

Signature treatment

Ashtaang eight-hand massage for two in the Harmony Suite

Brands

Cosmeceuticals, ESPA, PRIORI

Expect to pay

Treatments:
£80 for 55 minutes
Stay: from £240 per night in a standard room

Bubble rating

5 out of 5 bubbles

Good Spa Spy Favourites

Sweet Spy

Age 24 **Skin type** Quite dry and a little bit sensitive **Spa likes** Empty swimming pools; proper food; well stocked changing rooms; good value for money **Spa dislikes** Congested changing areas; being kept waiting around before a treatment; cold treatment rooms

Best spa experiences this year

Stepping off a snowy London Street to be scrubbed, wrapped, and polished at **Sanook**.

Worst spa experiences this year

Being massaged in a chilly treatment room; it's very hard to unwind and relax when you're shivering away on the treatment bed.

Favourite products

Neal's Yard Orange Flower Facial Oil

My skin always needs a little bit more moisture, whether it's July (when the sun dries it out) or January (when the central heating dries it out). So, Neal's Yard Orange Flower Facial Oil is perfect for me all year round. Pomegranate, orange-flower and mandarin oils are combined with vitamin-rich evening primrose and seabuckthorn oils to produce a moisture-balancing treat that leaves my skin looking healthy and radiant. A little bit goes a long way, so it's quite economical, too!

Burt's Bees Coconut Foot Crème

I've said it before and I'll say it again: This is by far my favourite foot product. I don't have time to faff around with pumice stones or foot files, but the Burt's Bees Coconut Foot Crème fixes dry, cracked heels without needing to reach for anything else. I just apply liberally, pop some socks on, go to bed, and awake to smooth coconutty feet. Lovely.

ila Body Scrub for a Blissful Experience

My other products are quite thrifty, really. So, I feel like I can afford to splash out on this last one. The ila Body Scrub for a Blissful Experience is, without doubt, a special occasion product. And I don't mean 'weekend' special – I mean 'wedding day and birthday party and Christmas-do all on the same day' special. But, assuming you have the excuse to *really* splash out and pamper yourself, this is the product I'd go for. The Himalayan salt crystals (oooh) get to work straight away, seriously exfoliating any dead skin. Then the essential oils do their bit (aaah) replenishing any lost moisture. The result? Soft, sweet-smelling, hydrated skin. And a 'strengthened bio-energy field' to boot. What's not to *love*?

Charlton House Hotel & Spa
Shepton Mallet, Somerset

This tiny jewel of a spa is part of a traditional country house hotel but you can also visit for treatments, or for a luxurious day being pampered. The keynote throughout is richness; in the colours – red, purple and blue – and in their own hand-made and natural essential-oil products.

What's on offer

There is a small and gently lit pool with several hydrotherapy stations, and a heat-experience area with a black slate sauna, laconium, and steam room with a huge crystal embedded in the wall. Upstairs, you'll find a small gym and a tiny weights and exercise area.

On the treatment menu is a choice of ten spelt and walnut-oil facials and massages, plus other facials, envelopments and massages, all using the spa's own natural products. You can enjoy a good range of complementary therapies including counselling and acupuncture, too.

We loved

The waiting area, with soft and squishy sofas in velvety reds, oranges, rich browns and midnight blues. You can sit in a soft purple robe, clutch a purple towel, drink mint tea and feel that you are inside a jewellery box.

We didn't love

A main corridor through the hotel bisects the spa area, so people come and go all the time.

Food file

Fascinating and delicious food in the restaurant, using local, organic, and seasonal ingredients.

Who would like it

Romantics. This is the place to whisk your best-beloved away to for a couple of days.

Don't miss

The nourishing spelt treatments, using spelt oil produced at the nearby Sharpham Park farm.

Spa type
Hotel spa

Where?
Charlton House
Shepton Mallet
Bath, Somerset BA4 4PR
01749 342008

Signature treatment
Ultimate Body Therapy: body brushing, scrub, massage, moisturising treatment, scalp massage and hair mask

Brands
Monty's

Expect to pay
Treatments:
£60 for 60 minutes
Stay: from £155 per night for a small double room

Bubble rating
4 out of 5 bubbles

Chelsea Club Escape Spa

Stamford Bridge, London

Part of the Chelsea Football Club stadium complex, this smart, classy spa is perfect for men and women alike. No blue and white, just immaculate, well-designed space and a sense of exclusivity.

What's on offer

Enormous changing rooms, good-sized sauna, plunge pool and Jacuzzi. A Pilates room, golf simulator and a 25-metre beauty of a pool, flooded with natural daylight. Wow.

A huge gym with stylish Japanese paper windows letting in soft daylight, a cardio-vascular room, resistance room, kinesis room, state-of-the-art TechnoGym equipment. Wow again.

In the dark-wood-and-turquoise spa, the atmosphere becomes dimly-lit and hushed. There's a bijou seating area and four treatment rooms with direct access to the relaxation room.

Therapies include ONLY YOURx facials and peels, including a mighty 35% glycolic acid Ultra Cellular Sweep, Elemis facials, wraps and massage, Endermologie anti-cellulite treatment, manis, pedis and beauty treatments.

We loved

The large pool and gym, the thoughtful design, the sense of space. The elevated 200-metre track where you can jog along the roof, taking in views of a cemetery, railway, and major football ground.

We didn't love

No-one gave us a consultation form; if you're pregnant or allergic to anything, do pipe up before your treatment. The music that came on halfway through the treatment, jolting us out of our pineapple-scented reverie. Our spa bubble deflating as we left through a crowd of football fans.

Food file

The spacious dining area is no health-club snackerie, more of a cross between formal restaurant and relaxed bar. You can dine at a table or lounge on a comfy chair, with your paninis and smoothies.

Who would like it

Anyone looking for gentle me-time, sociable spa day or top-notch spa experience in central London; football widows; well-heeled Chelsea-ites. Men will feel right at home, too. The gym and pool are for members only, but you can buy a gym day pass. To make a day of it, you'll need that pass.

Don't miss

The ONLY YOURx facial. Our Papaya Purifying Peel was wonderful.

Spa type
Day spa

Where?
Chelsea Club Escape Spa
Stamford Bridge
Fulham Road
Chelsea, London SW6 1HS
020 7915 2215

Signature treatments
ONLY YOURx facials:
the Papaya Purifying
Peel in particular
Elemis absolute spa ritual

Brands
Elemis
ONLY YOURx

Expect to pay
Treatments:
£60 for 60 minutes

Bubble rating
5 out of 5 bubbles

Chewton Glen

New Milton, Hampshire

Chewton Glen is a real country-house hotel with all the class, comfort and quality you could wish for. A place for lavishing and pampering; don't book in for a few days and expect to come away thinner. The food is simply too good. But breathe in the country air and you'll already feel healthier.

What's on offer

A 17-metre ozone-treated swimming pool and a large separate hydrotherapy pool. A small but bright gym. Yoga and pilates classes. Outside, you can try the outdoor hot tub, nine-hole golf course, tennis courts, and an outdoor pool. Borrow some wellies and a map and go for a hike in the New Forest, or just stroll round the grounds and play croquet on the lawn.

Treatments include a range of sensory experiences using ila products, many designed specially by ila, using raw materials such as herbs from Chewton's own gardens, as well as exclusive Linda Meredith facials. There's a grooming lounge, where you can have mini-treatments such as manicures.

We loved

Chewton Glen limits the number of day-spa guests so that the spa never has an overcrowded feel. No queuing for the showers here.

The hotel bulletin, delivered each evening with the turndown service, contains details of available treatment times in the spa the following day, which is a nice touch. Class times are also listed.

We didn't love

Despite the double doors to cut down on noise, if you're in the treatment rooms which open off the waiting area, you may hear some intrusive chat from outside.

Food file

The Pool Bar offers freshly-made salads and indulgent puddings. You can eat at tables overlooking the pool or drink tea on sofas overlooking the parkland.

In the main restaurant, the excellent food tends to the foie gras, scallops and crème brulée sort of menu. It is gourmet-cooking of Michelin-star-winning quality.

Who would like it

People looking for a country-house stay with spa treatments. As a stay destination, it's not for the faint of pocket. However, with their trained army of every-whim-catering staff, Chewton Glen really looks after you when you're there.

Don't miss

The spa is quiet in the evenings and this is a good time to enjoy it. De-stress before your gourmet dinner.

Spa type
Hotel Spa

Where?
Chewton Glen
New Milton
Hampshire BH25 6QS
01425 282251

Signature treatment
ila Larch and Beech
Anti-Aging facial

Brands
ila
Linda Meredith

Expect to pay
Stay: from £313 based on a Bronze room with shower

Bubble rating
5 out of 5 bubbles

The CityPoint Club

Barbican, London

The CityPoint tower is the third tallest skyscraper in the City of London, so it's pretty hard to miss. The CityPoint Club is just as much a spa with health-club facilities, as it is a health club with spa facilities, so it offers the best of both worlds. Modern, more functional than feminine, but perfectly suited to pampering as well as active well-being.

What's on offer

As CityPoint is a health club and spa, there is plenty to do. There are two squash courts, and a well-equipped gym with all the latest machinery. A 20-metre ozone-treated pool is set up with lanes for serious swimmers and poolside loungers for lazy folk. There are separate male and female heat areas. In each, there's a sauna, steam room and plunge pool.

CityPoint offers acupuncture, osteopathy, physiotherapy, nutrition and sports massage, plus shiatsu and Thai massage as alternatives to the standard spa treatments on offer. Classes include Boxercise, core stability and pole dancing.

The CityPoint Club feels surprisingly spacious for a lower-ground-floor spa. High ceilings and day-bright lighting make you forget that there aren't any windows.

We loved

The equal split between pampering space and fitness space. We felt perfectly at home wandering around the whole club in our robes, as many guests were doing.

The spacious, modern changing rooms have everything you need: plenty of locker space, changing space, lots of spare clean towels and robes. There's shower gel, shampoo and conditioner (often an oversight in health clubs).

You get a personal treatment schedule, complete with timings, so you won't forget when to get out of the steam room!

We didn't love

Having a pedicure in a vibrating massage chair. Pity any poor therapist trying to paint the nails on a busily bouncing spa-goer.

Food file

A smart café with a contemporary bistro feel; refreshments on arrival are included for day package guests. Your low-GI food needs are catered for.

Who would like it

Anyone who works in the City; we can't think of how a club could please this market better.

Don't miss

The dimly lit relaxation room with hypnotic fish tank and duvets This space is perfect for a post-treatment rest.

Spa type
Day spa

Where?
The CityPoint Club
1 Ropemaker Street
Barbican
London EC2Y 9AW
020 7920 6200

Signature treatments
Tibet pebbles, Dead Sea salt and oil scrub and massage

Brands
Crystal Clear
Elemis
Gerard's

Expect to pay:
Treatments:
£60 for 55 minutes

Bubble rating
5 out of 5 bubbles

The Club Hotel and Spa

St Helier, Jersey

This smart town-house hotel in the centre of St Helier has a top-notch bijou spa. The hotel is very handy for the shops just round the corner, and the beach, while the spa offers pleasing pick-me-up and beauty treatments. It's not a cheap place to stay, but it's good value if 'luxury', 'upmarket' and 'sophisticated' tick your boxes.

Spa type
Hotel spa

Where?
The Club Hotel and Spa
Green Street
St Helier
Jersey JE2 4UH
01534 876500

Signature treatment
The Club Minerale
Envelopment

Brands
Algotherm, Aromatherapy Associates, Carita, Darphin, Payot, Thalgo, Yon Ka

Expect to pay
Stay: from £215 per night in a Deluxe double room, bed and breakfast

Bubble rating
4 out of 5 bubbles

What's on offer

A subterranean salt-water pool with subdued lighting, which gives an atmosphere of calm; a relaxation lounge; a sauna; a small outdoor pool; a steam room and something called a salt cabin which mysteriously didn't contain any salt. The Club Hotel specialises in marine-based spa therapies, and you can have rasul mud treatments, too.

We loved

The fact that the spa is very much a separate area of the hotel; hotel guests can only use the small pool between certain hours. This keeps the pool crowd-free and means that your drifting away is not interrupted by small children.

The Frette bedlinen; you have to go to bed with nothing on just to get a full appreciation of the thread count.

We didn't love

The changing rooms are compact. There are eight lockers – though you wouldn't want eight people in there at once – and just one shower.

Food file

The Michelin-starred Bohemia restaurant offers gourmet dining. Our room service order of home-made pea soup with garlic bread and a Caesar salad was divine.

Who would like it

If large chain hotels don't appeal and you like a personal service, you'll love The Club.

Don't miss

The outdoor pool in summer; the mineral envelopment body treatment that is unique to the spa.

Clumber Park Hotel and Spa

(New Leaf Spa), Sherwood Forest, Nottinghamshire

The hot tub is great fun and the treatments enjoyable at this smart, good-value day spa in a recently extended hotel. There's a small pool but a large Jacuzzi.

What's on offer

A sparkling spa and health club with pool, gym and treatment rooms, in an old coaching inn close to a main road. A small, 12-metre pool, large Jacuzzi, steam room and reasonable-sized sauna, an outside hot tub, very well equipped gym, and seven treatment rooms.

A good range of therapies, facials for anti-ageing, skin solutions and skin specifics, body therapies including body sculpting cellulite, colon therapy, packages for mothers to be and men, complimentary therapies, and beauty treatments.

We loved

The spa's signature treatment, a relaxing Elemis Cooling Hot Stone Body Facial, including a good firm back massage. Drifting off to sleep in the warm, dimly lit relaxation room.

We didn't love

The small pool; four people doing laps and it's full. We were woken by traffic noise in the morning – we'll book a room at the back of the hotel next time. Oh… and this is a spa with no paper knickers!

Food file

The spa bar area is pleasant and the spacious café area has big, squashy sofas and views beyond the pool area to the forest. The hotel brasserie offers a good selection from sandwiches to pie and peas. The restaurant is much quieter than the brasserie and the classic modern food quite good.

Who would like it

Anyone who wants some time out for a swim and a massage. The spa takes a maximum of ten day-spa guests each day.

Don't miss

The outdoor hot tub: room for four people and a chatty, sociable atmosphere.

Spa type

Hotel spa

Where?

Clumber Park Hotel and Spa (New Leaf Spa) Clumber Park Sherwood Forest Nottinghamshire S80 3PA 01623 835333

Signature treatment

Elemis Cooling Hot Stone Body Facial

Brands

Elemis

Expect to pay

Treatments: £65 for 55 minutes

Stay: from £70 per night for a superior double room

Bubble rating

4 out of 5 bubbles

COMO Shambhala Urban Escape

Metropolitan Hotel, Mayfair, London

Shambhala means 'a sacred place of bliss'. This small but perfectly formed urban retreat with holistic therapies, intuitive counselling, and skin care treatments is indeed bliss in the heart of London.

Spa type
Hotel spa

Where?
COMO Shambhala
Urban Escape
The Metropolitan Hotel
Old Park Lane
London W1K 1LB
020 7447 1000

Signature treatment
COMO Shambhala
massage

Brands
COMO Shambhala
Dr Perricone
Environ

Expect to pay
Treatments:
£75 for 60 minutes
Stay: from £375 per night
in a City room

Bubble rating
5 out of 5 bubbles

What's on offer

A warm, relaxing retreat. Small but elegant, with beautifully lit and immaculate treatment rooms. Once the door closes, you forget you're in the centre of a busy capital.

Choose from massage therapies including deep-tissue massage, Thai massage, reflexology, reiki and acupuncture, and well-being, rejuvenating and holistic facials. Personal trainers and yoga instructors, single-sex steam rooms and a well equipped gym.

We loved

The enormous showers with shower-heads the size of small plates. The staff's loose fitting uniforms, the kind worn in Thailand, which say 'therapist' rather than 'beautician'.

We didn't love

The lack of a relaxation room.

Food file

Delicious ginger and manuka honey tea in the spa. Have lunch in the sophisticated, contemporary lobby of the hotel. Our wild rice salad with seared tuna and roast pumpkin was fantastic.

Who would like it

Anyone looking to escape for a few hours or in need of recovery after a hard day's shopping in the West End.

Don't miss

The holistic 75-minute luxury COMO Shambhala Purify facial, a mood-elevating, deep cleansing and nourishing facial using natural botanical ingredients.

C.Side

Cowley Manor, Cheltenham, Gloucestershire

Cowley Manor is an impressive, discreet, very rural hotel. Once through the entrance, you get a glimpse of beautiful grounds. The glass-fronted C.Side spa is an inspired piece of modern design, sunk into the hill to one side of the hotel.

What's on offer

In the hotel, the traditional country-house exterior hides a contemporary interior. In the spa, there are good-sized modern indoor and outdoor pools, plus a unisex steam room and sauna. There are four glass-walled treatment rooms and a gym. For treatments, try Thai yoga massage, or reiki, Ashtanga yoga, reflexology or Breema – a form of 'physical and mental energy workout'.

C.Side is open to day guests so you don't have to invest in a hotel stay to enjoy a day at the spa.

We loved

The beautifully designed indoor and outdoor pools, and the cup of 'love' herbal tea and strawberry dipped into chocolate after our treatment.

You can borrow (clean!) swimwear from the spa; could save you an emergency visit to a leisure centre en route.

We didn't love

The spa's previously pristine looking décor now looks a little tired. Peeling paint is never a good accessory for

a spa day or stay. There's no dedicated relaxation area, just the reception area overlooking the pool.

Food file

Modern English with some local and organic ingredients.

Who would like it

City types with a penchant for the country; country types with a penchant for the city.

Don't miss

C.Side's own range of products, developed by an aromatherapist.

Spa type
Hotel spa

Where?
Cowley Manor
near Cheltenham
Gloucestershire GL53 9NL
01242 870902

Signature treatment
Green & Spring Indulgence

Brands
Green & Spring (C.Side spa's own products)

Expect to pay
Treatments:
£75 for 60 minutes
Stay: from £250 per night in a Good room
Day packages from £125 including lunch

Bubble rating
4 out of 5 bubbles

Culloden

Holywood, Belfast, Northern Ireland

Culloden Estate, high on the Holywood Hills, is just five miles from Belfast city centre. It's a spa fairytale you can book, where you can let luxurious Culloden weave its magic from dawn to dusk.

What's on offer

A storybook building with a turret. Antiques, silks and velvets in the bedrooms. Idyllic views from every window.

The leisure pool is at the centre of the health-club complex; there's a Jacuzzi, a marble steam room with twinkling chromatherapy lights. A modern, spacious fitness studio with high-tech equipment.

In the spa, curved, softly lit corridors and eight treatment rooms. Small, private dressing areas beautifully scented by ESPA candles.

Mesmerising massages. Culloden's signature treatments include Thai massage, reflexology, reiki, deep sports, Swedish and Indian head massage. ESPA treatments include facials and massages, hot-stone therapy and wraps. There's a range of treatments on offer for male spa-goers, too. You can also enjoy manicures, pedicures, fake tans, and beauty treatments.

We loved

The two relaxation areas. 'Dawn' is where you wait for your therapist to collect you.

'Dusk' is the post-treatment relaxation area, dimly lit and very quiet – designed for optimum relaxation.

Our ESPA aromatherapy massage: produced a complete state of bliss.

We didn't love

Not being able to live there.

Food file

Excellent local food and wine. We had a light lunch of salmon salad in the Mezzanine restaurant in the health club. Dinner in the AA-rosette Mitre Restaurant in the hotel was outstanding; the food is often sourced locally.

Who would like it

Anyone. Everyone. The spa facilities at Culloden are top class, and the atmosphere in the spa and hotel is professional but friendly and not intimidating.

Don't miss

Swimming in the round, glass roofed pool against the counter-current.

Spa type

Hotel spa

Where?

Culloden Estate and Spa
Bangor Road
Holywood
Belfast
Northern Ireland BT18 0EX
02890 421135

Signature treatments

Reflexology; Reiki; Chakra Balancing with Hot Stones

Brands

ESPA

Expect to pay

Treatments:
£70 for 55 minutes
Stay: from £240 per night in a superior double

Bubble rating

5 out of 5 bubbles

Cupcake Spa

Wandsworth, London

Cupcake is a private members' club and spa for mums and mums-to-be, which is very handy for the many yummy-mummies who live in south London. Once you've made it past the fleet of Bugaboos in reception, you'll find pregnancy treats galore. And cupcakes, of course.

Spa type
Treatment rooms

Where?
Cupcake
10 Point Pleasant
London SW18 1GG
020 8875 1065

Signature treatment
Cupcake in the Oven
pregnancy massage

Brands
Belli
Mama Mio
Thalgo

Expect to pay
Treatments:
£65 for 60 minutes

Bubble rating
4 out of 5 bubbles

What's on offer

All sorts of treats for mums, and mums-to-be; the 'What's Up, Doc?' package aims to leave you 'confident, relaxed and prepared for [your] pregnancy checkups'.

If you sign up for membership, you can make use of Cupcake's ante- and post-natal classes, seminars and 'wellness classes'. You may also be interested in baby massage or baby yoga, or a seminar on 'Conquering the Workforce as a Mum'.

If that wasn't enough, there's an on-site crèche, sleep pod, and child-friendly café.

We loved

Being asked whether or not we would like to be chatted to by our therapist during the treatment, and being shown where the toilets are beforehand. We also loved the luxurious Belli products, all especially designed for pregnant women, and the egg-shaped sleep pod: perfect for a nap.

We didn't love

The water-filled layer on top of the massage couch. Every time the therapist puts her hands under your back, the plastic layer makes a squeaking noise.

Food file

We were impressed by the balance between healthy salads and lunches, and not-so-healthy treats in the café. We enjoyed a particularly delicious blueberry muffin. And, of course, a cupcake.

Who would like it

Mothers and mothers-to-be who need some pampering.

Don't miss

A session of 'mummy-lates'. Prams are left downstairs whilst mums do their Pilates upstairs. Babies can enjoy Cupcake's on-site crèche.

Danesfield House

Marlow, Buckinghamshire

Danesfield House is a glorious country house in a magical setting. It's built of white stone and has courtyards, twisty brick chimneys, leaded windows, and a wide terrace at the back overlooking the Thames. There's a spacious spa and excellent food, which makes this place perfect for romantics, and foodies.

What's on offer

Perennial ESPA face and body favourites when it comes to treatments; a 20-metre ozone pool with deep blue tiles which make it look cool and refreshing. Beside the pool, you'll find a Jacuzzi, steam room, sauna and showers. There's plenty of room for wooden recliners next to it and there's a terrace outside for warm days.

There's also a gym, fitness studio and exercise classes; you can try Hatha yoga, Pilates, Fitball or Cardio-tone.

We loved

The glorious views; the hotel is built on a rise, so you can gaze down at the fields, the water, and passing boats and swans.

The changing rooms; they are spacious, light and airy with large lockers and seating areas all finished in pale wood and light-blue glass.

We didn't love

Danesfield has quite a large health-club membership, so has busy times of the day, especially morning and evening. The area for food is more 'bar' than 'spa'.

Food file

The 3 AA rosettes Oak Room, or The Orangery which offers seasonal food, perfectly cooked.

Who would like it

Romantics; foodies; anyone who needs a day or two to rejuvenate.

Don't miss

The ESPA super active facial: perfect if you have an event to go to.

Spa type

Hotel spa

Where?

Danesfield House
Henley Road
Marlow-on-Thames
Buckinghamshire SL7 2EY
01628 891881

Signature treatment

ESPA Aromatherapy facial

Brands

Carita
ESPA

Expect to pay

Treatments:
£70 for 55 minutes
Stay: from £245 per night in a double room

Bubble rating

4 out of 5 bubbles

Dart Marina

Dartmouth, Devon

Dart Marina hotel has an impressive location, sitting on the banks of the River Dart; it's particularly good for keeping an eye on your yacht, which you can moor at the hotel. The views immediately outside the spa are spectacular, while inside you'll find a dinky spa offering Elemis delights in just three treatment rooms.

What's on offer

The Dart Marina 'spa' is really more of a treatment rooms than a proper spa; as long as you know this before you go, you'll be happy, as the spa treatments and health-club facilities in themselves are spot-on. Tucked away at the end of the long hotel building, you'll find a pool with a current machine – ideal if the weather's not quite right for swimming at any of the local beaches; a Jacuzzi, sauna and steam room; and a small, but well-equipped gym.

Although small, the Dart Marina spa is run extremely smoothly and efficiently. The spa never felt busy to us, even though, with five of us there, the spa area was actually full to capacity.

We loved

The luxurious pregnancy massage, using lots of cushions and a huge beanbag on the floor; this is incredibly comfortable, and makes it easy for the therapist to give plenty of attention to the whole of your back. The Japanese Camellia oil was incredibly hydrating and smelled good enough to drink.

We didn't love

There's no lolling about in a robe; we didn't see any robes at all, in fact. We also weren't keen on the unisex changing rooms.

Food file

The traditionally-styled Floating Bridge pub serves good quality pub food and has a roof terrace looking out over the river. The River Restaurant is a smarter affair. The Wildfire Bistro & Bar is a midway point between the two. All serve fresh, local produce.

Who would like it

Sailors. Or their wives/girlfriends/partners. There are plenty of sailor-WAGs in Dartmouth for the Royal Regatta each year who would love to spent some quality time in Dart Marina's spa.

Don't miss

The relaxation area: sit on chaise-longue style seats, eat fruit, drink tea, and read magazines before you reluctantly drift back to the real world.

Spa type

Hotel spa

Where?

Dart Marina
Sandquay Road
Dartmouth
Devon TQ6 9PH
01803 837182

Signature treatments

Sensory Stone Heaven and Exotic Visible facial

Brands

Elemis

Expect to pay

Treatments:
£60 for 55 minutes
Stay: from £130 per night in a double room

Bubble rating

5 out of 5 bubbles

Daylesford Hay Barn

Daylesford, Gloucestershire

Smart converted barn buildings house an organic restaurant, upmarket shop, and spa. Daylesford includes a 20-acre market garden, creamery and livestock. But you don't come here for the cows or the utter farm-chic; you come for the sublime and original spa treatments.

What's on offer

Spacious, light-drenched treatment rooms; two voluminous yoga studios; and a dedicated Pilates studio, too.

You can try a great variety of massages: Thai, deep tissue, pregnancy, stone therapy, ayurvedic, Indian head, Balinese, or standby reliable back, neck and shoulders. The custom Japanese REN facial includes ko-bi-do massage.

There are yoga, Pilates and meditation classes, both in groups and on a one-to-one basis.

We loved

The waiting-and-relaxation areas, styled beautifully in white-washed wood and neutrals, with quartz crystals and daisies.

The Bamford Body treatment: a slow and calming massage with elements of shiatsu; we found it serene, indulgent, relaxing and original.

The yoga classes: they take yoga seriously here. You can try everything from Sivananda to yogic cleansing, plus good old-fashioned traditional.

We didn't love

We managed to resist the £1,000+ topiaried box trees on sale in the Daylesford Organic shop. An insight into the clientele they expect to be drifting through their retail opportunities, perhaps.

Food file

The food is fantastic. Our indulgent and delicious lunch hit the spot perfectly. The pea risotto was perfection in green and followed on from a ham-hock terrine flawlessly. Save room for the divine hot chocolate soufflé and home-made vanilla ice cream.

Who would like it

Anyone looking for a calming experience in a tasteful and peaceful environment, with great healthy food on the side.

Anyone looking for an authentic and spiritual relaxation experience.

Don't miss

The Shirodhara treatment; the authentic wooden bed and silver Dhara are impressive even before you begin.

Spa type

Treatment rooms

Where?

Daylesford Organic
Daylesford
Gloucestershire GL56 0YG
01608 731703

Signature treatment

The Hay Barn Signature treatment includes body brushing, Indian head massage, exfoliation, body massage and facial cleansing

Brands

Aromatherapy Associates, Bamford Body, REN

Expect to pay

Treatments:
£65 for 60 minutes

Bubble rating

5 out of 5 bubbles

The Devonshire Arms

Skipton, Yorkshire

This old Yorkshire coaching inn has a sympathetically adapted spa in what used to be the old stable block across the road. The hotel is an ideal destination for walkers, foodies, and romantics. The spa is a cherry on the (gourmet) cake.

Spa type
Hotel spa

Where?
The Devonshire Arms
Bolton Abbey
Skipton
North Yorkshire BD23 6AJ
01756 718142

Signature treatment
The Best bespoke body massage

Brands
Elemis

Expect to pay
Treatments:
£55 for 60 minutes
Stay: from £115 per person per night in a Wharfedale room

Bubble rating
4 out of 5 bubbles

What's on offer

In the hotel, country-house living and log fires. In the spa, a reasonably sized pool, a Jacuzzi, and male and female changing areas, each with a sauna, steam room, plunge pool and showers. The gym is on a mezzanine floor above the pool.

The treatment menu contains all the popular Elemis treatments, plus £20 'taster' treatments. 'Devonshire Days' start at £145, which includes a massage, facial and manicure or pedicure.

Outside of the spa, there are tennis courts and cycles for hire. You can also pick up a fishing permit from reception.

We loved

The well-equipped and reasonably spacious treatment rooms and the friendly and thoughtful staff. The therapists were generous with robes and towels and happy to help whenever they could.

We didn't love

The spa is a bit cramped in places; there's no seating space in the changing area; they have squeezed in rather more facilities than the building can cope with.

Food file

The evening meal is a bit of an occasion at the hotel; our four-course meal rapidly became seven courses with all the little *amuse bouches* and palate cleansers.

Who would like it

Foodies, and people in love – you and your partner can hire the entire spa for two hours' exclusive use.

Don't miss

Food heaven in the Michelin-starred restaurant in the hotel.

Donnington Valley Hotel

Newbury, Berkshire

Donnington Valley is a large, modern hotel next to an 18-hole golf course. It's far enough from the M4 for you not to hear any noise, but close enough to make the hotel an ideal meeting point. The affordable and accessible health club and spa will suit almost everyone.

What's on offer

A good sized pool; a steam room, sauna and Jacuzzi, all at proper high temperatures; and a gym. The pool, gym and café area are on the ground floor, easily accessible to day guests and members; the spa and treatment rooms are on the second floor, completely separate.

In the spa, you can have ESPA and Clarins facials for all skin types. And you don't have to have any old reflexology – try electro-reflexology.

We loved

The spacious relaxation room, which overlooks fields and trees. The cushioned wicker relaxer chairs are comfortable, the lighting subdued, and the music gentle.

The GHD treatment; much more than just a hair treatment, it includes a neck, shoulder, and arm massage.

We didn't love

The separation of the treatment and relaxation rooms on the second floor, away from the pool on the ground floor. It makes the spa experience slightly disjointed.

Food file

The Winepress Restaurant has plenty of local and seasonal food on offer, and one of the best vegetarian menus we've seen.

Who would like it

Golfers' spouses. Anyone who wants to spa at a reasonable price in a non-intimidating atmosphere.

Don't miss

The Aquasun Mineral Treatment, which aims to recreate a day at the beach.

Spa type
Hotel spa

Where?
Donnington Valley Hotel
Old Oxford Road
Donnington, Newbury
Berkshire RG14 3AG
01635 551188

Signature treatment
Natural Magic Holistic Indulgence

Brands
Clarins, ESPA, Moor, Neom, Spa Find

Expect to pay
Treatments:
£68 for 70 minutes
Stay: from £99 per night for a classic double room

Bubble rating
4 out of 5 bubbles

The Dorchester Spa

Mayfair, London

If you're looking for glamour, 1930s elegance and facials that deliver results, head for the Dorchester's treatment rooms on Park Lane for top-notch luxury and service. Take your credit card.

What's on offer

The wow factor, thanks to a £3.2 million refurbishment. White, white and more white. Glamorous champagne-pink tiles. Receptionists in smart black uniforms. Locker keys attached to a faux-pearl bracelet. Two jewel-like glass walls of tiny shelves bearing 1,760 bottles of nail colour. A very large, nicely hot steam room and a choice of ten different facials, including a bespoke one for men. Wonderfully comfortable treatment beds. A stunning blue-and-white relaxation room.

What is rumoured to be the most effective anti-jet-lag massage around. Body treatments including wraps and exfoliations. A caviar manicure with age-defying masque and a massage designed to speed up the production of collagen and plump your skin. A rather grand hairdressing salon and a proper barber's shop, too.

We loved

Everything. Just the way The Dorchester does luxury. Oh, and there's a safe in each locker so you don't have to worry about where to put your pearls.

We didn't love

The Dorchester Spa is expensive, of course. But we think it's worth it.

Food file

In the relaxation room, we felt very pampered with a delicious lemon-and-lychee drink and warm hazelnut biscuits. In the 'Spatisserie', you can have sushi, salads or wraps for lunch, one of The Dorchester's award-winning afternoon teas, champagne or a spa cocktail.

Who would like it

Anyone who wants (or needs) to look like a Hollywood starlet; anyone so famous that they need a discreet, paparazzi-free spa; anyone looking for a glamorous and luxurious spa experience in central London. Ideal for a special treat.

Don't miss

The Carol Joy London facial. This range uses golden millet oil and diamond dust, which reflects the light and brightens the skin. A treatment to book before a big event. Your skin will look great for days.

Spa type

Hotel spa

Where?

The Dorchester Spa
Park Lane
London W1A 2HJ
020 7319 7109

Signature treatment

The Signature Massage, including hot stones

Brands

Aromatherapy Associates
Carol Joy London
Kerstin Florian
Vaishaly

Expect to pay

Treatments:
£95 for 55 minutes
Stay: from £450 per night in a superior double

Bubble rating

5 out of 5 bubbles

Dove Spa Bromley

Bromley, Kent

Sparkly-fresh and very white treatment rooms, which sit within the large Virgin Active Building in Bromley. You do not have to be a gym member to visit, though.

Spa type
Treatment rooms

Where?
Dove Spa Bromley
Virgin Active, Baths Road
Bromley
Kent BR2 9RB
0844 800 2151

Signature treatment
A skin diagnostic and
bespoke facial

Brands
Dove Spa
Elemis
Mama Mio

Expect to pay
Treatments:
£56 for 60 minutes

Bubble rating
4 out of 5 bubbles

What's on offer

There are no pools or water facilities at Dove, apart from the showers in the changing rooms, and in some of the 10 treatment rooms. You can pay to use the health-club facilities in the Virgin Active gym, which include a 25-metre pool, steam room and sauna.

There is a skin consultation area, manicure stations, and a funky, grey-and-white tiled pedicure area with padded white leather seats.

Treatments include facials, dermabrasion, wraps, body scrubs and massages, holistic therapies, Indian head massage, reflexology and beauty treatments.

We loved

The helpful and knowledgeable staff. The unique touch of beautiful sarongs to wander about in.

We were brave enough to try the colonic hydrotherapy, and our therapist was soothing, knowledgeable and reassuring.

We didn't love

The peace of the chill-out area (behind a partition wall) is easily disturbed.

Food file

None.

Who would like it

Bromley locals and gym members. Anyone looking for professional treatments at a good price. The regulars can't praise the relaxing atmosphere enough.

Don't miss

The chance to take sensible dietary advice on board.

Dove Spa City

Aldgate, London

Dove Spa City is more of a salon than a spa, but if you're looking to fit a pick-up or a chill-out into your busy schedule, you'll like these urban treatment rooms.

What's on offer

Seven clean and bright treatment rooms and a relaxation area to use after your treatment. A high-tech multi-dermascope that measures your skin's moisture, elasticity and melanin levels. This allows your therapist to diagnose your skin type and prepare an appropriate treatment.

You can have a 30-, 45-, 60- or 75-minute bespoke facial, or a small range of Dermalogica facials. Dove also offers non-surgical face lifts, and dermabrasion. Body treatments include Swedish, aromatherapy and deep-tissue massage, along with wraps and colonic irrigation. There are Mama Mio treatments for mothers-to-be, and treatments for well-groomed City chaps, too.

We loved

The warm welcome by the friendly staff. The Dove Spa Professional products, a luxury range not to be confused with the everyday Dove brand. Our bespoke facial. The value for money.

We didn't love

Dove Spa is very small, so we didn't come away with that 'aaaah' spa feeling.

Food file

Water. After 4pm, the area around Dove Spa virtually shuts up for the night. When we came out feeling really hungry, there was not a sandwich in sight.

Who would like it

City professionals of both sexes. There's no pool or heat experiences, so not for you if you're seeking a full-on spa day.

Don't miss

Your Personal Skin Profile.

Spa type

Treatment rooms

Where?

Dove Spa City
12 Gravel Lane
London E1 7AW
0844 800 2154

Signature treatment

A skin diagnostic and bespoke facial

Brands

Dermalogica
Dove Spa
Mama Mio

Expect to pay

Treatments:
£62 for 60 minutes

Bubble rating

4 out of 5 bubbles

earthspa

Belgravia, London

Beautiful Belgravia treatment rooms decked out with a designer's eye, offering holistic treatments and beauty quick fixes to well groomed locals. A mere dash across the road from Victoria station so out-of-towners needn't miss out.

What's on offer

A range of massages, body wraps and facials, alongside complementary therapies such as reiki and reflexology. You can also choose from a nice range of beauty treatments, including waxing, eyebrow maintenance, manicures and pedicures. Plus, earthspa offers professional intuitive readings ('Allow your life to be magical!') and a set of packages to help you unwind or revive.

We loved

Our heavenly Pure Lochside facial and the divine massage in the Back to Earth package. Our soft skin and unwound shoulders afterwards.

The beautiful treatment room: olive-green walls with a dark slate-style floor, a large mirror with a dark-wood frame, dimly lit with large deep-red candles and twinkly tea-lights. The room was dotted with gold bowls containing feathers and rose petals, and beautifully arranged fresh flowers in little vases. The massage couch had its mechanics covered in a tasteful brown cover so we didn't have to concern ourselves with such work-a-day matters.

The small, yet perfectly formed relaxation area: it's the epitome of shabby chic. There's a large dark wicker basket laden with a variety of magazines. Candles and ornate mirrors abound.

Did we mention the divine massage?

We didn't love

The cold floor on bare feet!

Food file

Water with lemon and lime, and herbal teas. The tea arrives on a silvery tray with biscuits.

Who would like it

Local Belgravians looking for a beauty quick-fix. If you're looking for a long, lazy spa day, this isn't the place for you, as earthspa doesn't offer a true robe-and-lounger experience. For a top-quality treatment in fabulous treatment rooms, though, earthspa is spot on.

Don't miss

The Pure Lochside facial and the top-notch massage.

Spa type
Treatment rooms

Where?
earthspa
Chantrey House
4 Eccleston Street
Belgravia
London SW1W 9LN
020 7823 6226

Signature treatment
earthspa Stone massage using hot basalt and cool marble stones

Brands
Algologie
Dermalogica
Pure Lochside

Expect to pay
Treatments:
£68 for 55 minutes

Bubble rating
5 out of 5 bubbles

Eastthorpe Hall

Mirfield, West Yorkshire

If you're looking for nurture in the midst of nature, pack your robe and head to Mirfield. This small, welcoming day retreat offers holistic treatments with an emphasis on well-being and relaxation. The perfect place to chill and relax, and return to the world invigorated.

What's on offer

A range of holistic and therapeutic treatments. Many visitors – all women on the day we were there – seem to have therapy rather than beautification in mind. They come to the twinkly rooms and the garden for me-time, for curling-up-in-a chair-in-the-garden-with-a-book time, for emotional strengthening, and for time out from their busy lives. Eastthorpe offers tiger-clam lava-shell treatments, including back, neck and shoulder and full body massages, as well as manicures and pedicures. Massages and holistic facials are their most popular treatments.

Guests bring their own bathrobes and slippers, so there is a mix of styles, which makes the place feel quite different from a spa where everyone is in the regulation-issue robe.

We loved

The welcome ritual: a short hand and foot massage designed to make people relax and ready for their day.

The Eastthorpe holistic facial: it contained more gentle massage than we had ever experienced in a facial before.

We didn't love

We always ask ourselves if we would change anything to make a place perfect. Eastthorpe does what it intends to do perfectly. However, this place won't suit everyone. If angels irritate you, you'd be better staying away.

Food file

Lunch was sea bass, lentils, quinoa and creamed parsnip. All organic and all delicious and we ate every bit. After our treatments, we had pavlova in the orangery and then some herbal tea in the garden.

Who would like it

Eastthorpe would appeal strongly to a nervous spa person, as it offers a very personal service. There is no residential option, which means that most visitors are local. You can arrange bed and breakfast nearby if you want to stay.

Don't miss

In the summer, you can have treatments in a Mongolian Yurt.

Spa type
Day spa

Where?
Eastthorpe Hall
Health & Beauty Spa
Mirfield
West Yorkshire WF14 8AE
01924 498507

Signature treatment
Eastthorpe Holistic Facial includes back, scalp, hand, arm and foot massage

Brands
Darphin
Dr Lewinn
Karin Herzog

Expect to pay
Treatments:
£60 for 60 minutes

Bubble rating
5 out of 5 bubbles

Eden Hall Day Spa

Newark, Nottinghamshire

Comfortable and friendly, and not at all intimidating, Eden Hall does what it sets out to do very well. It's a large and accessible spa with keen pricing and good facilities. Take a friend and spend an enjoyable spa day à deux.

What's on offer

The Aqua Detox Centre, with a steam room, hot room and sauna, as well as experience showers, and an ice cave. There's also a 25-metre salt-water pool with powerful water jets that switch on at intervals for further muscle easing.

For a treatment, choose from a good range, including an Elemis Well Being massage or a Thalgo Purity Ritual facial.

We loved

With about 140 guests a day, Eden Hall handles the numbers very well. The changing rooms have plenty of comfortable seating, it's spotlessly clean – not easy when it's so busy – and all the staff are attentive and friendly.

The good, complex back massage that focuses on really helping you unwind and relax; by the end of an hour, we were limp and ready to fall asleep in one of the rocking chairs.

We didn't love

They don't supply flip flops or slippers and, in fact, recommend you go barefoot.

Though that isn't too much of a pain as there is under-floor heating everywhere.

Experienced Eden Hallers bring their own slippers.

Food file

The Seventh Heaven restaurant offers a monthly menu using locally grown produce. The Juice Bar serves up cake alongside the fresh juices.

Who would like it

Friends. This is not the place to go on your own for peace and solitude. It's a gossipy, girlie place. Almost everyone was in pairs or groups. Lots of people seemed to be regulars.

Don't miss

The huge and stunning conservatory; once crammed with plants from the farthest corners of the empire, now it's filled with wicker chairs and sofas, and people chilling out, drinking smoothies and reading.

Spa type
Day spa

Where?
Eden Hall
Elston Village
Newark
Nottinghamshire NG23 5PG
01636 525555

Signature treatment
Eden full body massage incorporating hot stones

Brands
Elemis
Spa Find
Thalgo

Expect to pay
Treatments:
£56 for 55 minutes

Bubble rating
5 out of 5 bubbles

EF MediSpa

Kensington, London

When gravity comes to call, you need specialist help. If you're not ready for the knife, stop at EF MediSpa first. This glass-fronted corner shop in the very trendy Kensington Church Street offers 'intelligent skin care', as it helpfully says on the sign outside.

Spa type
Treatment rooms

Where?
EF MediSpa
29 Kensington Church
Street, London W8 4LL
020 7937 5554

Signature treatment
EF MediFirm
anti-ageing facial

Brands
AD Synergy, Cosmedix,
Dermaquest, SkinCeuticals,
SkinMedica, SKINN for men,
Susan Posnick, Young blood

Expect to pay
Treatments: from £95
for 60 minutes; the EF
MediFirm anti-ageing
facial is 60 minutes
plus consultation time,
and costs £475

Bubble rating
4 out of 5 bubbles

What's on offer

White and spartan treatment rooms with a reassuringly clinical atmosphere. You can choose from a whole range of treatments from Botox to colonic hydrotherapy; dermal fillers; bodysculpting; new breast enhancement solutions; pain-free laser hair removal; and Fraxel laser. All treatments begin with a private consultation so the treatments are tailored to you and you alone.

There's also a Laser Cosmetic Dental Suite on site.

We loved

The EF MediFirm anti-ageing facial, which it uses a combination of radio frequency and lasers. It aims to stimulate collagen production in your skin; it's the collagen that gives your skin its firmness and plumpness. We were sceptical, but after comments about how lovely we were looking, a course of six was suddenly tempting...

We didn't love

There's lots of doing here but not a lot of time-out; there's certainly no floating about in a robe.

Food file

The spa can order in organic snacks from nearby Ottolenghi or Whole Foods Market.

Who would like it

Those who want the age to stay away.

Don't miss

Vaser Lipo – an advanced procedure that removes unwanted body fat.

Elemis Day Spa

Mayfair, London

One of the flagship Elemis Day Spas, these treatment rooms are in Mayfair, just along from a couple of cocktail bars and restaurants. The glass-fronted boutique spa fits perfectly into this elegant part of London.

What's on offer

Surprisingly enough, Elemis spa treatments; these include a good range of anti-ageing treatments, and skin-specific and skin solutions facials.

There's an Exotic Steam Rasul to try, which would be great for a spa indulgence with a partner or friend.

We loved

The Elemis East-meets-West theme: wooden floors and furniture, Indonesian fabrics and ornaments abound, and there are gorgeously scented oil burners and Elemis goodies in abundance around the sink in the bathroom.

The divine scent of the Elemis Frangipani Monoi Moisture Melt, which is superb for your dry bits.

We didn't love

There is no pool or sauna; it's definitely more a treatment rooms than a day spa, despite the name.

Food file

Herbal tea, water. Café bars next door.

Who would like it

Anyone who likes Elemis products, of course! Apart from that, the location makes it perfect for shoppers.

Don't miss

The brand-new Elemis offering, the Cooling Hot Stone Body Facial, which is far more harmonious and relaxing than the title sounds.

Spa type

Treatment rooms

Where?

Elemis Day Spa
2–3 Lancashire Court
Mayfair
London W1S 1EX
0870 4104210

Signature treatment

Elemis Cooling Hot Stone Body Facial

Brands

Elemis

Expect to pay

Treatments:
£80 for 60 minutes

Bubble rating

4 out of 5 bubbles

Fawsley Hall

(Grayshott Studio Spa and Gym), Daventry, Northamptonshire

A fascinating Tudor Great Hall with a small, intimate spa that's well designed, spotlessly clean and offers good treatments and facilities. And fantastic food.

What's on offer

In the old Coach House of an historic hotel reached through countryside crafted by Capability Brown, a light, bright spa. There are six en-suite spa bedrooms, six treatment rooms, a 17-metre indoor pool (just right for a few lengths), sauna and steam room, poolside shower, outdoor hot tub, nail-bar area, relaxation room and a gym with Nautilus equipment.

Treatments include Guinot Hydradermie facials that use galvanic current to carry the plant-based ingredients deep into your skin – great for anyone worried about wrinkles. We adored our Aromatherapy Associates massage with heated volcanic basalt stones, ideal if you're stressed and need help to relax. That's us, then!

We loved

Our bright and airy bedroom above the spa, ideal for tripping from room to spa in your robes.

We didn't love

Erm… no, can't think of a thing. Be warned though: the spa is small, and won't suit you if you like your spa space.

Food file

The spa café serves a range of healthy salads and light snacks. For straightforward food, eat in Bess's Brasserie. For fine dining with a strong outlandish streak, book a table at Equilibrium. Anyone for chamomile tea, mint and vodka dipped in liquid nitrogen and served as a palate cleanser? Do not attempt Equilibrium after a day in the spa because it takes about three hours to eat the six courses and you may fall asleep before the end.

Who would like it

Friends who want to spa gently together; couples who want a country-house hotel weekend and time to spa; anyone who wants a more intimate spa experience; groups, who can take over the whole spa.

Don't miss

A nice cup of tea in the Great Hall, where you can admire the vast fireplace with the coats of arms of the Knightley family (who built the first hall), Richard the First, and 26 of his knights. The huge soft beds in the spa rooms, so white and fluffy we found it hard to leave them.

Spa type
Hotel spa

Where?
Fawsley Hall
Fawsley, Daventry
Northamptonshire NN11 3BA
01327 892000

Signature treatment
Aromatherapy Associates renew rose anti-aging facial

Brands
Aromatherapy Associates
Guinot

Expect to pay
Treatments:
£50 for 55 minutes
Stay: from £175 per night in a standard room

Bubble rating
5 out of 5 bubbles

Fistral Spa

The Bay Hotel, Newquay, Cornwall

The Bay Hotel is almost at the far end of the Pentire Esplanade in Newquay. It's an unimposing three-storey modern hotel, directly opposite Cornwall's famous Fistral Beach, one of the UK's finest surfing spots. The spa is altogether more upmarket than the outside promises, and is a real little gem with friendly, caring staff.

Spa type
Hotel spa

Where?
The Bay Hotel
Pentire, Newquay
Cornwall TR7 1PT
01637 852221

Signature treatment
The Essential Fistral treatment: back, neck and shoulder massage, express facial, pink hair and scalp mud and a scalp massage

Brands
ESPA

Expect to pay
Treatments:
£45 for 55 minutes
Stay: from £35 per night in an economy room

Bubble rating
4 out of 5 bubbles

What's on offer

An 11-metre pool, and suitable spa music is piped through this area – you can even hear it underwater. There's a decent-size steam room and a wooden-benched sauna, both satisfyingly hot, and at the other end of the pool is a Jacuzzi. There's also a reasonably-sized gym with a good array of machinery.

As well as the whole range of ESPA facials, massages and wraps, there are treatments specifically for men, mums-to-be and, of course, surfers, on offer, too.

We loved

The treatments and the imaginative packages that the spa has put together.

Chilling on the wonderfully comfy loungers and healthy little snacks in the relaxation room after our spa treatments.

We didn't love

The changing rooms betray their health-club origins – you need a pound coin to operate the locker and the only product available for washing purposes is a generic pump dispenser of 'wash'.

Food file

The view from the Bay View restaurant is terrific; the food is standard hotel fare.

Who would like it

Surfers. Silver surfers. Hotel guests. Newquay ladies who lunch.

Don't miss

The Ocean Dreams package: a surfing lesson at Fistral beach in the morning, lunch, and an ESPA surfers massage treatment in the afternoon.

Floatworks

Thrale Street, London

Our motto at The Good Spa Guide is 'It's always nice to have a bit of a lie down'. What better way than in a deliciously relaxing floatation session? If you're looking for hush, calm and a break from your day-to-day concerns, go float at Floatworks.

What's on offer

Floatation! In a warm, hushed and welcoming environment. There are nine floatation tanks, each in a private room with a shower, and two hairdrying rooms. Floatworks isn't a traditional spa – no lounging about in robes – but there are two therapy suites offering complementary therapies and massages.

The expert staff are passionate about floatation. Treatments are taken in an i-sopod, a floatation tank designed and built by Floatworks. The white curvaceous pods have an inviting blue glow inside.

The tank is filled with strongly salty water on which you float effortlessly while your brain switches off, leaving you in a dream-like state. There's plenty of headroom, definitely not claustrophobic. It felt amazing, like floating in space! Afterwards, we felt very relaxed.

We loved

Apart from the other-worldly sensation of floating in ten inches of water, you mean? Well, it's incredibly good value. We were also reassured by the help button in the tank in case of spa emergency.

We didn't love

We would have liked a few more soft touches and a mirror to check our appearance before emerging. Also, there's no relaxation room.

Food file

There is none.

Who would like it

Stress bunnies; anyone who wants to meander happily around their inner landscape for an hour or so.

Don't miss

A fantastic, unusual experience.

Spa type
Treatment rooms

Where?
Floatworks
1 Thrale St
London SE1 9HW
020 7357 0111

Signature treatment
i-sopod floatation treatment

Expect to pay
Treatments:
£48 for 60 minutes

Bubble rating
4 out of 5 bubbles

Formby Hall Golf Resort and Spa

Formby, Merseyside

A good-value spa in a large, modern hotel on England's 'golf coast', with friendly staff, good facilities and interesting treatments. You can choose from a range of Phytomer treatments, including facials, wraps, hot stone therapy, and massages, including a four-hands massage. The locals love it!

Spa type

Hotel spa

Where?

Formby Hall Golf Resort and Spa
Southport Old Road
Formby
Merseyside L37 0AB

01704 875 699

Signature treatment

Deep intense prestige facial

Brands

Phytomer

Expect to pay

Treatments:
£60 for 60 minutes
Stay: from £145 per night in a standard double

Bubble rating

4 out of 5 bubbles

What's on offer

A large and very blue 20-metre swimming pool with a wave-shaped ceiling, a Jacuzzi, and a steam room. A bright and airy gym. A separate spa area with seven treatment rooms, manicure stations, yoga studio and laid-back relaxation room.

You could also rasul with a friend or treat yourself to a Leighton Denny mani or pedi. In the 'Elegance Suite', we had a very pleasant Phytomer hot stone facial, using the gentle Phytomer Fleurs products; we left feeling relaxed, with brighter skin.

We loved

The extremely helpful and friendly staff, who went the extra mile for us. The great value for money.

We didn't love

The fact that, though good, the facilities are a little disjointed. It feels a bit like *The Crystal Maze*, with rooms along corridors, codes for doors, stairs to negotiate and a relaxation room that seems curiously adrift from the treatment rooms.

Food file

A bistro for lunch; later we had fresh mushroom soup and a cooked-just-right steak in the hotel restaurant.

Who would like it

Golf widows; ladies who lunch in Southport; anyone who needs a little pampering or some R&R.

Don't miss

'Thermal Heaven', a beige-tiled steam room and a wooden sauna, in the spa area: both quite compact but nicely hot.

lookfantastic.com will take you
spa and away....

Robed up and revelling in some rare relaxation – now how about some retail therapy? Imparting a little home-spun luxury into your daily routine, lookfantastic.com offers the complete pampering hair and beauty shopping experience. An online boutique, lookfantastic stock their shelves with all the hair and beauty brands any spa connoisseur worth their weight in bath salts will know and love. So whether you like to unwind to the tune of **Elemis**, you favour your **Clarins** over your **Thalgo**, or your beauty boudoir boasts an abundance of **Decleor** – there's something for every product junkie from the budget beauty queen to the trend savvy fashionista - over 8000 products to be precise.

Among their gorgeous spa brands, including **Ole Henriksen, Caudalie, Thalgo, Balance Me, NEOM** and **St Tropez**, they also have an envious collection of make-up, fragrance and electrical products, all at incredible prices.

Peruse their online shelves and relive the spa experience at home, share your beauty know-how with them via their blog, enter 'The Beauty Room' for the latest hair and beauty features, or simply shop 'til your weary linen slipper-clad feet drop. Shopping with lookfantastic.com is pure, unadulterated bliss*.

Find out more at **www.lookfantastic.com**

*Back rub not included

Over 8000 products at great prices!

lookfantastic
Online luxury hair & beauty

The Forum Spa
The Celtic Manor Resort, Newport, Wales

The Celtic Manor Resort is a large complex of a modern luxury hotel, traditional manor house, health clubs, conference facilities and golf courses just off the M4. Home to the 2010 Ryder Cup, Celtic Manor offers impressive health-club facilities and a peaceful ambience in its treatment rooms.

What's on offer

A health club with a large and light pool area; the ceiling above the pool is domed and painted with a deep blue sky. There is also a separate small children's pool and a huge bubbly spa bath. In the changing rooms, where the walls are decorated with Roman maidens disporting themselves carrying jugs of water etc, you'll find a steam room, sauna, cold plunge pool and large Jacuzzi-style bath. For the active, there's a large gym with good equipment.

Treatments include a nice range of facials, some massages, scrubs and wraps, treatments for men, waxing, tanning, tinting, manis and pedis, dry floatation and the signature rasul mud rituals.

We loved

Slathering each other with mineral muds in the rasul on a Monday afternoon; opportunities for mud merrymaking under some twinkly stars in Wales indoors don't come around too often.

We also loved our facial, the view from the relaxation room in the spa (green trees and just a bit of the M4), and having a very elegant dinner at Rafters,

the restaurant in the clubhouse especially built for the 2010 Ryder Cup.

We didn't love

The children splashing around the bubbly jets in the pool outside their allocated swim time.

Food file

Snacks, juices and smoothies in the café next to the pool. Sophisticated dining in Rafters and buffet breakfast in the Olive Tree; we recommend the eggs benedict.

Who would like it

Celtic Manor is a great place for families but the spa means you can duck out of the vacationing for a little hard-earned me-time. It also makes a good choice for a spa day if you are lucky enough to live nearby, as the range of facilities and professional treatments offer plenty to keep you happy.

Don't miss

Swimming on your back in the pool and pretending you're under a real sky.

Spa type
Hotel spa

Where?
The Celtic Manor Resort
Coldra Woods
Newport NP18 1HQ
01633 413 000

Signature treatments
The Rasul mud ritual
Mineral scalp treatment
with dry floatation
Hot tub experience

Brands
Elemis, Clarins

Expect to pay
Treatments:
£70 for 50 minutes
Stay: from £198 per night
in a Superior Double room

Bubble rating
5 out of 5 bubbles

Four Seasons

Hook, Hampshire

Within this classic English manor house on a beautiful lush green estate, you can find an English country spa experience. There are plenty of water and thermal activities on offer, as well as exclusive treatments and delicious food.

What's on offer

There are 18 treatment rooms including self-contained Couples and Single VIP treatment rooms. We loved the Cherish couples ritual – a three-hour relaxation marathon. Some specially-designed ESPA treatments incorporating poultices made from herbs in the hotel's walled garden. These include a chamomile and sage massage, lavender and rosemary back treat, and herbal hand and foot rituals.

When it comes to water-based facilities, there is plenty to keep you busy: a 20-metre pool with a domed glass ceiling; an outside hydrotherapy pool; a clear quartz crystal sauna and an amethyst crystal steam room; there are single-sex heat experience rooms.

We loved

The unnerving-sounding four-hand Purva Karma massage (yes, two therapists!) – it's a sensual onslaught that will leave you positively drunk with relaxation. After a Purva Karma treatment, you'll feel seriously spoilt, like some Greek Goddess. Or at least a Greek C-list celebrity.

Children are welcomed to their room with a personalised chocolate plaque, Barbour-clad teddy and child-size bath robe; plus, any junior guests' names are spelled out in bath sponges, in their room. This creates no end of excitement.

We didn't love

Seeing our seagull-dropping-coated Ford standing out somewhat amongst the gleaming Lotuses and Aston Martins.

Food file

The Seasons restaurant offers a varied cuisine, of a high standard, and includes a large amount of locally sourced products. It's more a question of food metres than food miles.

Who would like it

Parents, particularly, as the hotel is very family friendly. We can't really think of many people who wouldn't like it.

Don't miss

A treatment using herbs from the hotel's own garden.

Spa type
Hotel spa

Where?
Four Seasons Hotel
Dogmersfield Park
Chalky Lane, Hook
Hampshire RG27 8TD
01252 853000

Signature treatment
Soothing Chamomile
and Sage massage

Brands
ESPA
Four Seasons

Expect to pay
Treatments:
£90 for 60 minutes
Stay: from £235 for a
Garden standard double
room

Bubble rating
5 out of 5 bubbles

Fredrick's Hotel Spa

Maidenhead, Berkshire

Fine dining is taken just as seriously as pampering at Fredrick's. For starters, there is their beautiful private floatation room. Add a relaxing Thalgo facial, classic cuisine, and a pinch of excellent customer service and you have the recipe for a perfect 5-bubble spa day.

What's on offer

A beautiful private floatarium tiled in midnight blue and gold; the dark ceiling twinkles with lights. An inside-outside pool with several hydrotherapy stations; access the outside pool by swimming through glass doors suspended just above the water. There is also a sauna, steam room, ornate foot baths and a Kniepp shower.

You can try a wide variety of Aromatherapy Associates and Thalgo facials and body treatments, or be more adventurous with a rasul or mud wrap, a dry floatation hydro massage bath treatment, or hot stone massage.

We loved

The glass of champagne when you check in. The high-ceilinged wooden-panelled relaxation room; it has just four cream leather reclining chairs and large glass double doors that open onto a patio area. The place has an executive, up-market feel about it.

Fredrick's limit spa guest numbers to eight, so the facilities never feel overcrowded.

We didn't love

The décor has a definite nod to the 1980s, which may not be to everyone's taste.

Food file

Fresh fruit, iced herbal tea and a boule of fruit sorbet in the relaxation room. Classic cuisine with a contemporary twist in the formal restaurant. After a selection of *amuse bouches*, enjoy a light and almost fluffy cream of broccoli soup, a succulent sea-bass fillet with seafood ravioli and a passion-fruit soufflé to die for. Breakfast is taken equally seriously and is well worth sacrificing a lie-in for.

Who would like it

People who value good customer service and being treated like an individual, not a number. Spa-goers who like to combine good food with pampering.

Don't miss

The inviting indoor/outdoor pool, heated to a cosy 38 degrees. Arrive early to use the hydrotherapy features. The pictures on Fredrick's website don't do the pool area justice.

Spa type
Hotel spa

Where?
Fredrick's Hotel
Shoppenhangers Road
Maidenhead
Berkshire SL6 2PZ
01628 581227

Signature treatment
Dream Bath (a couples treatment, with a customised bath, essential oils and a glass of champagne)

Brands
Aromatherapy Associates
Thalgo

Expect to pay
Treatments:
£70 for 60 minutes
Stay: from £129 per night in a double room

Bubble rating
5 out of 5 bubbles

Galgorm Resort & Spa

County Antrim, Northern Ireland

We haven't stopped talking about this spa – a short drive from Belfast – since we visited it. We think you'll love Galgorm's dreamy spa experience and 163 acres of idyllic, picturesque woodland as much as we did.

What's on offer

Galgorm has rolling, lush green lawns, dramatic views of the River Maine and a beautiful waterfall.

Lovely changing rooms with little touches of decadence. A thermal spa experience with infinity hydrotherapy pool and outdoor hot tub – we especially liked the humid, subtly scented Herb Caldarium room. Eleven treatment rooms, a mud Serail chamber, Cleopatra bath, and hammam. Fantastic showers with Aromatherapy Associates products. A split-level fitness suite, not huge, but with state-of-the-art Matrix cardio and resistance equipment.

Facials, massage, scrubs and wraps for both women and men, holistic therapies including reflexology, head massage and ear candling, and a Finishing Touches menu with tanning, waxing, and hand and foot treatments. All at a fair price, too.

We loved

The fantastic staff and luscious surroundings: nothing was less than excellent. Our treatments in the stunning double treatment room, the Parisian Suite. Our fantastically relaxing Real Aromatherapy Experience, a stress-busting combination of 'Swedish and neuromuscular massage' and the seriously impressive Mohom Indigo Healing Art treatment.

We didn't love

We did wonder whether there would be enough loungers when the spa was booked to capacity. Then we found out it *was* booked to capacity...

Food file

We could have had a laid-back meal of 'North Coast' seafood chowder, pan-seared salmon or chicken bang-bang in Gillies Bar and Grill, but opted for a formal dinner in the River Room Restaurant, with its panoramic views of the River Maine, a superb menu and accommodating staff.

Who would like it

Anyone looking for a luxurious spa experience, on your own, with a friend, your partner or a group.

Don't miss

Slide into the outdoor hot tub, sip champagne and gaze over the forest.

Spa type

Hotel spa

Where?

Galgorm Resort & Spa
136 Fenaghy Road
Galgorm, Co. Antrim
Northern Ireland BT42 1EA
028 2588 2550

Signature treatments

Eve Lom Experience, Enrich body treatment, Total aromatherapy indulgence

Brands

Aromatherapy Associates, Eve Lom, Ytsara

Expect to pay

Treatments:
£60 for 55 minutes
Stay: from £105 per night in a standard double

Bubble rating

5 out of 5 bubbles

Gleneagles

Auchterarder, Scotland

Gleneagles is one of the most perfect spas we have visited. The serene atmosphere and excellent facilities can unwind you to the point of being horizontal. From the changing rooms to the vitality pool, every detail has been carefully thought through in this elegant and luxurious spa.

What's on offer

In the health-club area: a 20-metre lap pool for serious swimming, a pool for splashing about in, plus an outdoor hot pool with whooshy jets; a sauna and steam room and a reasonable-sized gym, quite bright, with plenty of equipment.

In the spa: a large and hot steam room; a small vitality pool; a sauna; 20 treatment rooms offering a whole range of ESPA treatments, several of which are ayurvedic-inspired. No kind of mani, pedi, waxing or spray-tan frippery, though; the emphasis is on well-being from start to finish.

We loved

The spa and health club each have a separate entrance. As soon as you push open the heavy wooden doors into the spa area, you know you've arrived on Planet Spa: shimmering walls, subdued lighting, wafting music... You can loll about relaxing on the various sofas and loungers, or splash in the pool, without intrusive noise or, dare we say it, people. The spa never felt crowded, as the only people allowed in it are those who have actually booked a treatment.

The changing rooms have been divided into three areas of lockers. Each area has its own seating, mirror, hairdryer, moisturiser and so on. This helps to keep a sense of privacy and intimacy.

They collect your used linens from a discreet corridor around the edge of the spa; your peace is never disturbed by a therapist pushing a trolley of damp towels through your changing-room bliss.

We didn't love

A bit of a shortage of magazines in the relaxation area. That was it!

Food file

Chilled bottles of Voss water in the heat area; healthy bento boxes and snacks in Deseo if you're having a spa day.

Who would like it

World leaders (the G8 summit was held at Gleneagles in 2005).

Don't miss

The relaxation area, set out as a courtyard, with a little 'fire' to sit around.

Spa type
Hotel spa

Where?
Gleneagles
Auchterarder
Perthshire PH3 1NF
01764 694332

Signature treatments
Purva Karma
four-handed massage
Ama Releasing Abhanga

Brands
ESPA

Expect to pay
Treatments:
£80 for 55 minutes
Stay: £410 for a classic room

Bubble rating
5 out of 5 bubbles

Grand Jersey Hotel and Spa

St Helier, Jersey

This recently refurbished spa, plushly resplendent in brown velvet and grey slate with hot pink details, is a twilight cocoon of a spa offering a relaxing experience and good value treatments in a highly individual setting.

What's on offer

A classic, upmarket hotel, all marble floors and dramatic lighting, overlooking the bay and Elizabeth Castle. Its basement spa has stone steps round a central turret, a bit like a medieval castle (there is separate access for those with mobility problems). Changing rooms with grey slate floors and banks of dark wooden lockers. A 15-metre pool, heat experiences, and relaxation room. A large Jacuzzi and a big steam room with black marble seats and twinkly lights. Two experience showers – much oohing and aahing in the Caribbean Rain and Mist. A small, reasonably equipped gym (the spa is a health club as well).

Six treatment rooms, with two doubles. A range of Elemis treatments, with some for men, as well as Swedish massage, reflexology, and beauty treatments. Our Elemis deep rhythmic pressure massage was very deep indeed – the drum music matched the treatment, somewhat.

We loved

The cheerful, attentive staff. The bravery of plush and velvet in a spa: a refreshing change from white, neutrals and wood.

We didn't love

The atmosphere is a tad dark and gloomy and the relaxation area could be quieter. Also, although everything was fresh and clean, there was a bit of a musty smell at the Jacuzzi end of the pool.

Food file

In the relaxation area, there are herbal teas, iced water and little chocolate brownies. Tassili is the hotel's the fine-dining restaurant. At dinner, the blue-cheese beignets and John Dory were delicious and beautifully presented. At the lavish buffet breakfast, perfectly polite chefs served us perfect poached eggs.

Who would like it

Anyone staying in the hotel; anyone who loves twilight; both men and women.

Don't miss

The steam room. It's quite something, entertaining and energising. Spa-ing over, visit the champagne bar where you can try around 100 different types of champagne while enjoying the ocean views.

Spa type
Hotel spa

Where?
Grand Hotel (St Helier)
Esplanade
St Helier
Jersey JE4 8WD
01534 722301

Signature treatment
Holistic total body care with hot stones

Brands
ESPA

Expect to pay
Treatments:
£55 for 60 minutes
Stay: start from £150 for a superior inland view room

Bubble rating
5 out of 5 bubbles

Grayshott Spa

Hindhead, Surrey

This traditional spa retreat, with a health-farm feel, offers a great range of treatments in a peaceful, rural location; there are 47 acres of lush, well-maintained grounds complete with lake. A spa break at Grayshott is a particularly good option for anyone looking to kick off a lifestyle change, as advice and activities abound.

Spa type
Spa retreat

Where?
Grayshott Spa
Headley Road
Hindhead
Surrey GU26 6JJ
01428 602000

Signature treatment
The Grayshott Classic massage

Brands
Aromatherapy Associates, Guinot, ila, Thalgo

Expect to pay
Treatments:
£50 for 40 minutes
Stay: from £395 per person for a two-night De-Stress break

Bubble rating
4 out of 5 bubbles

What's on offer

Grayshott offers everything from massage to reiki, osteopathy to sleep consultation, facials to wraps, hammam scrubs to a cut and blow-dry. There's dietary and lifestyle advice. And then there are the (paid-for) classes: try yoga, Pilates, tai chi, or personal training. The indoor pool has a hydrotherapy pool. The outdoor pool is, thankfully, heated.

If getting in the swing is more your thing, you can play a round on Grayshott's nine-hole golf course. After all that activity, relax in the on-site cinema.

We loved

Having a sociable Zenspa Pedicure side by side with a friend in large comfortable chairs. An auto-massage setting adds to your relaxation.

Our lovely Oriental Wisdom treatment used Eastern massage techniques; Tui Na and shiatsu moves combine with body oils, blended with Chinese herbs.

We didn't love

The sauna, steam room and plunge pool missed out in the recent refurb.

Food file

Fresh and healthy, with the option of two dining rooms for a bit of variety.

Who would like it

Grayshott is suitable for all ages, including anyone wanting to visit on their own.

Don't miss

Grayshott's Tennis Academy, with indoor and outdoor courts, and a 'resident professional'.

THALGO
LA BEAUTE MARINE

The original marine spa brand

"Thalgo is an excellent marine brand - its wraps and facials really work" You Magazine (Mail on Sunday)

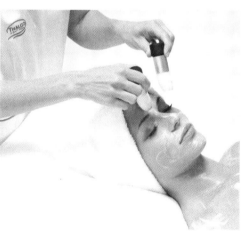 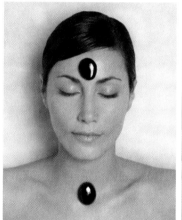 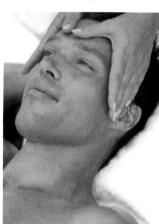

Thalgo is known by spa-goers the world over for the incredible results of its facials, body treatments and products based on marine ingredients, which are known to have beneficial properties due to the body's remarkable affinity with the sea.

Discover our classic marine algae body wrap, high performance slimming treatments, a relaxing yet highly effective facial, or one of our pampering spa rituals.

Thalgo can be found in top spas and beauty salons in more than 90 countries worldwide, and some of the best spas in the UK including Stobo Castle, Hoar Cross Hall, Grayshott Spa, St David's Spa and many more.

To find your nearest Thalgo spa or beauty salon, call 0800 146041 or email enquiry@thalgo.co.uk

Shop online at **www.thalgo.com**

Good Spa Spy Favourites

Sassy Spy

Age early 30s **Skin type** Normal/combination skin **Spa likes** Luxurious scented candles; hot oil massage; being warm; unusual treatments; fluffy towels; natural light; firm pressure **Spa dislikes** Mould; slamming doors; being walked in on while treatment in progress; therapists with cigarette-laced breath

Best spa experiences this year

A four-hour Energising journey at the very cool eco-hotel and spa **The Scarlet** in Cornwall. The journey included an individual consultation, a bathing ritual, guided chakra meditation, an ayurvedic hot oil massage with poultices, and some deep relaxation time. And soaking in the hot tub, situated on the cliff-top looking out to sea.

My serene spa day at the **Lido** in Bristol which included a heavenly Hawaiian lomi lomi massage, complete with traditional music.

Staying in the Manor House room at **Grayshott Spa**.

Worst spa experiences this year

My feet almost cooking to roasting point in pedi booties; nowhere to sit after my treatment as all loungers occupied; not being told to bring any flip-flops and none provided.

Favourite products

ila Face Mask for Revitalising Skin

My tired, sleep-deprived face experienced a healthy tightening as this dense, creamy face mask slowly hardened. My skin can be sensitive but, happily, didn't react to this face mask. I felt that it was drawing out impurities, and I enjoyed the product a little more every time I used it. A gentle, firming, holistic face mask – satisfying to apply as well as remove. This mask gave me a beaming glow and velvety skin.

The Sanctuary Mela Black Pepper & Ginger body scrub

After experiencing the Mela Holistic Experience at The Sanctuary, I fell in love with this scrub. The smell is divine and after each use my spirits are lifted. Thankfully it leaves my skin soft and tactile, too!

The Organic Pharmacy Carrot Butter Cleanser

A firm favourite on my product shelf. I ensure that I rest it within easiest reach of all. There's a bit of a faff with extracting the cleanser with a spatula 'to protect the organic ingredients' but the Carrot Butter glides on smoothly and easily. Leave the cleanser for a minute to work its magic. Remove gently with a muslin cloth or flannel and hey presto: a silky soft and beautifully clean face!

Guinot Nutri Cellulaire serum

My favourite serum. Faintly fragranced and easy to dispense, I did not want it to ever run out. Its light-weight formula silkily glides on, leaving my combination skin smooth and able to breathe.

Green Street House

Bath, Somerset

Green Street House is very much a house, in a traditional Georgian style, with neutral colours and stained wooden floors, and a homely, welcoming feel. These treatment rooms in the centre of Bath offer a friendly, non-intimidating environment for both spa first-timers and experienced spa-goers.

What's on offer

Treatments, mainly, in six treatment rooms. There's no pool, heat facilities or dedicated relaxation room, but the reception area is comfortable and calming.

You can try Elemis and OXYjet facials, and an excellent range of manicures and pedicures. Green Street House is opposite a sausage shop. You can sort out your barbecue and complexion in one easy trip.

We loved

The fantastic location in Bath's main shopping area. The pretty, apothecary-esque shop is brimming with appealing, gorgeous-smelling beauty products.

The large and light treatment room, with original wooden floor and an Indian cotton throw over the bed.

The attentive and genuine staff; they really know their products as well.

We didn't love

This spa is not for anyone with mobility problems. Green Street House is a five-storey building with treatment rooms over four levels.

Food file

Green Street House can order in delicious delights from a local deli.

Who would like it

Anyone who appreciates a good treatment but doesn't need a full-on spa experience.

Don't miss

What else? The Elemis Cooling Hot Stone Body Facial.

Spa type
Treatment rooms

Where?
Green Street House
14 Green Street
Bath
Somerset BA1 2JZ
01225 426000

Signature treatment
Green Street House tranquillity massage

Brands
Dermalogica
Elemis
REN

Expect to pay
Treatments:
£55 for 60 minutes

Bubble rating
4 out of 5 bubbles

The Harbour Club (Amida Spa)

Chelsea, London

The Harbour Club isn't much to look at from the outside – it's rather like a large green aircraft hangar parked on the end of a row of houses. Once you're inside, the smart, understated interior, refurbished in 2007, makes you realise why this was Princess Diana's health club of choice. You don't have to be a member to visit the Amida Spa.

Spa type
Day spa

Where?
The Harbour Club
Watermeadow Lane
Chelsea
London SW6 2RR
020 7371 7744

Signature treatment
Lava shell massage

Brands
Elemis
Mama Mio
Murad

Expect to pay
Treatments:
£65 for 55 minutes

Bubble rating
4 out of 5 bubbles

What's on offer

An exclusive health club and the modern, beautifully-designed Amida Spa. To use the gym and other sports facilities, you have to sign up as a member. Visit as a spa day guest, and you can enjoy the 25-metre lane pool, a sauna/sanarium, a 'salt-inhale room', an aroma room and a gorgeous hydrotherapy pool.

In the nine treatment rooms, you can try an extensive selection of Elemis facials and body treatments, as well as lava-shell massages, Murad facials and Mama Mio treatments for mums-to-be. Beauty treatments include manis, pedis, waxing, tinting and bronzing. Also on offer are more medical services including osteopathy, physiotherapy, acupuncture, podiatry, hypnotherapy and injectables.

We loved

The well-thought-through adult-only and family areas, with cleverly divided adult, family, and junior changing rooms, means that small kids are kept to the family pool.

We didn't love

There's no relaxation area, so you can't chill out after your treatment. Also, you have to cross the spa reception to get from the changing rooms to the wet spa.

Food file

Salads, pasta dishes, and some more filling options.

Who would like it

Anyone who is willing to pay for the privilege of some privacy and exclusivity.

Don't miss

Swimming in peace in the stylish (and adult only) spa pool.

Harrogate Turkish Baths

Harrogate, Yorkshire

These restored Victorian baths attract spa-goers from all over the globe: the drama of the hot chambers, the sense of communal bathing Roman-style, and the gorgeous colours make a mere visit feel like An Occasion. It's also A Bargain.

What's on offer

From the outside, Harrogate Turkish Baths is a grand grey-stone building. Inside, the Victorian baths are much more impressive; they were restored in 2004. There's a large tiered hot chamber, a cold plunge pool, steam rooms and a relaxation area. You'll also find a relaxation room, with Jacuzzi and shower, a tepidarium, caldarium and laconium. The baths are public baths and can get quite busy.

If you're treating yourself to a treatment, you can enjoy hot-stone therapy, reiki, reflexology, [comfort zone] facials, wraps, and Germaine De Capuccini facials.

We loved

The sheer theatricality of the baths themselves: the huge arched ceiling is painted with great swirls of colour, and the walls and screens are decorated with glazed coloured brickwork.

The spa bargain prices: entrance for the baths starts at just £11.50.

We didn't love

The baths are a bit frayed around the edges.

Food file

Drinks and light snacks in the glass-roofed Winter Garden Lounge.

Who would like it

Spa-goers who know a bargain when they see one.

Don't miss

The single-sex bathing sessions that re-create the feeling of a hammam.

Spa type
Day spa

Where?
Harrogate Turkish Baths and Health Spa
Parliament Street
Harrogate
Yorkshire HG1 2WH
01423 556746

Signature treatment
Monticelli Mud Detox

Brands
[comfort zone]
Germaine De Capuccini

Expect to pay
Treatments:
£44 for 60 minutes

Bubble rating
4 out of 5 bubbles

Hartwell House

Aylesbury, Buckinghamshire

Hartwell House is an elegant grey stone seventeenth-century house with a huge circular drive and parkland suitable for driving through in a carriage. Suddenly we'd stepped into a Jane Austen novel and were visiting our moneyed cousins...

Spa type
Hotel spa

Where?
Hartwell House
Oxford Road, Aylesbury
Buckinghamshire
HP17 8NR
01296 746500

Signature treatment
Clarins Pro-Active Facial
incorporating massage
techniques

Brands
Clarins, ESPA

Expect to pay
Treatments:
£56 for 55 minutes
Stay: £280 per night
for a double room

Bubble rating
4 out of 5 bubbles

What's on offer

A Roman themed pool area with pillars, and sculptures in niches on the walls; a smallish pool with a Jacuzzi and steam room at one end. There are small, single-sex saunas in the changing rooms.

You can have Clarins and ESPA facials and body treatments.

We loved

The grounds are gorgeous. There are acres to explore, so allow time for a good long walk.

Thoughtful waiters not only make you coffee, but bring it over and pour it for you so you don't smudge your manicure.

We didn't love

The spa is not all hushed luxury, as you would expect from such a lovely hotel. The changing rooms felt like health-club changing rooms – quite basic and small.

Food file

There is an AA 3-rosette standard Dining Room. The less formal Buttery is above the spa, serving a lighter menu.

Who would like it

Jane Austen addicts! And romantics... it does feel very special. If you want something rather grand for your hotel experience, then this is the place to go.

Don't miss

Packing your gladrags for dinner in the candle-lit and rather hushed dining room.

Hoar Cross Hall

Yoxall, Staffordshire

Hoar Cross Hall calls itself 'the spa in a stately home'; certainly the building and grounds are stately, while the spa is large and offers much to choose from, even if it is on the busy side. With over 100 therapies on offer, you and your friends could be happily amused for days here.

What's on offer

Two pools; great hot and cold areas with a sauna, steam room, sanarium, hot and cold showers, and water jets. There is plenty of space and plenty of choice as you can choose from over 100 spa therapies. A 'natural healing centre' specialises in complementary therapies.

You'll also find a hairdressing salon; a gym; classes in tai chi, yoga, meditation; tennis, croquet, archery and golf.

We loved

The session with the resident nurse at check-in; there was a time when all trips to a spa began with a health assessment (and the dreaded weigh-in). Few spas offer this now, so Hoar Cross is definitely the place to come if you have health worries.

The half-hour treatment included with each night's stay. The quickie facial left our Spy's skin glowing.

We didn't love

Hoar Cross is not a luxurious spa, and it's pretty busy and crowded. There is a confusing layout. Plus the pools and the dining area are in the basement.

Food file

Hot food at lunch was good but the salads were dull. This was a contrast with the evening food, which was good.

Who would like it

Hoar Cross is a good couples destination, and it's popular with groups of friends as well.

Don't miss

The warm seawater pool.

Spa type
Spa retreat

Where?
Hoar Cross
Yoxall
Staffordshire DE13 8QS
01283 575671

Signature treatment
Hoar Cross Mud
Hydrotherapy Bath
and Salt Scrub

Brands
Clarins, Elemis, ESPA,
Maria Galland, Spa Find,
Thalgo

Expect to pay
Treatments:
£47 for 55 minutes
Stay: from £172 per person
for one night

Bubble rating
4 out of 5 bubbles

Horsted Spa

East Sussex National Golf Resort & Spa, Uckfield, East Sussex

A spacious, immaculate modern complex, where both spa and golf are taken very seriously. We loved its neutral décor and curved walls. We booked the his and hers golf and spa day; stereotypical maybe, but perfect!

Spa type
Hotel spa

Where?
Horsted Spa
East Sussex National
Golf Resort & Spa
Little Horsted, Uckfield
East Sussex TN22 5ES
01825 880185

Signature treatment
ESPA Total Holistic
Balancing incorporating
hot stones

Brands
ESPA

Expect to pay
Treatments:
£55 for 55 minutes
Stay: £170 per night for a
Classic double including
breakfast

Bubble rating
4 out of 5 bubbles

What's on offer

Modern, brick buildings for the hotel, spa and golf complex, and a maze of wooden doors. A 20-metre pool (more geared for swimming than splashing), Jacuzzi, sauna and steam rooms. The spa has nine treatment rooms and another sauna, salt steam room, and a particularly attractive aroma room with aubergine tiles and a scent of eucalyptus. There is also a powerful rain shower and an ambient relaxation room. The décor is simple and neutral with a subtle floral theme. There's a full range of Espa treatments, plus Leighton Denny manicures and pedicures.

We loved

The feeling of space – relaxing in itself; the great design; the friendly and professional staff; the varied treatments.

We didn't love

The swimming pool is large, and good by hotel pool standards. But an ambient spa pool it isn't. There are a few loungers but they seem more for resting between lengths than a dedicated 'activity'.

Food file

Eat in the relaxation room, ordering from the stylish Pavilion Restaurant, which serves delicious lunches from salads to shoulder of lamb, plus evening meals.

Who would like it

Golf fanatics. Anyone who likes good spa treatments in modern surroundings. Anyone who dislikes straight lines (the spa walls are curved wherever possible).

Don't miss

The Espa Holistic Balancing treatment; we were so relaxed, we actually found it difficult to move.

Illuminata

Mayfair, London

Illuminata is a rather grand Roman-styled set of treatment rooms hiding behind an unassuming shop front in South Audley Street. Inside are jewel-like private steam chambers, frighteningly elegant furnishings, marble staircases and stone lions, plus a small but expertly delivered range of treatments.

What's on offer

There are two steam rooms, one jasmine and one eucalyptus, some treatment rooms and a relaxation room. The atmosphere throughout is enhanced by stone lions in the wall with water trickling from their mouths, and a mosaic tiled floor.

You can try a session where you lie on a vibrating bed, they play some music and a therapist massages your head. Or what about a steam in the eucalyptus room followed by a Perfect Bust?

We loved

The private steam rooms: not huge, but they do feel opulent, all tiled in dark blue, with two seats like small thrones and a pedestal that we couldn't really fathom the purpose of but it incorporated more lions, which we liked. You don't get to loll around like a Roman matron in a private steam room often enough, in our opinion.

We didn't love

No face-holder on the massage couch. You either have to turn your head far to the right or left and put your neck out, or go for face down and suffocate.

Food file

Illuminata offers light bites and healthy lunches.

Who would like it

Mayfair mavens. Anyone who's had a stressful day applying for a visa at the American Embassy just round the corner.

Don't miss

The personal steam rooms are quite something. Especially in the middle of Mayfair.

Spa type

Treatment rooms

Where?

Illuminata
63 South Audley Street
Mayfair
London W1K 2QS
020 7499 7777

Signature treatment

Jasmine Steam and Purifying Spicy Earth Salts Treatment

Brands

Carita, Decléor, Shiseido

Expect to pay

Treatments:
£88 for 60 minutes

Bubble rating

4 out of 5 bubbles

Imagine Health and Spa

Knights Hill Hotel, King's Lynn, Norfolk

Imagine is a recently built spa, set within a small walled garden in the grounds of the Knights Hill Hotel. It's small enough to feel quite personal and intimate, and it's clean and pleasant with subdued colours and careful lighting. Apart from the changing rooms, that is...

Spa type
Hotel spa

Where?
Best Western
Knights Hill Hotel,
South Wootton
Kings Lynn
Norfolk PE30 3HQ

Signature treatment
English Rose Radiance
facial with rose quartz
massage

Brands
Babor
Voyar

Expect to pay
Treatments:
£55 for 60 minutes
Stay: from £89 per night for
a standard double

Bubble rating
4 out of 5 bubbles

What's on offer

An indoor heated swimming pool with sauna, steam room and Jacuzzi and a gym, all of which are also used by health club members. A thermal suite: steam room, tropical rain and monsoon shower, crystal chamber and mud chamber.

There are two double treatment rooms, and two single rooms. All have their own showers and are very spacious. There's also a hammam table for massages, and a manicure/pedicure area.

We loved

Booking time and then deciding on treatments on the day. You can book time slots of two hours, three hours, four hours or six hours.

We also loved the warm and fragrant aromatherapy bath, with rose petals, orange slices and a little goat's milk – underwater lighting changes colour as you wallow – and the delightfully minty monsoon shower.

We didn't love

We were alarmed at how run down and frankly smelly the changing rooms were.

Food file

The spa can make a fresh carrot-and-orange juice on the spot in front of you. The only place to eat is in the relaxation area or reception area, which is a bit of a drawback.

Who would like it

Friends who need a day to catch up and relax together.

Don't miss

The warm, wide, stone hammam table.

K Spa

K West Hotel, Shepherds Bush, London

This super-cool spa in a super-cool hotel just off Shepherd's Bush Green offers imaginative treatments and great massages. You could have a great time here exploring all the facilities with a group of friends, and an extremely stylish lunch.

What's on offer

A spacious gym; hydrotherapy pool; 'Snow Paradise'; sanarium, sauna, steam room, footbaths, experience showers, and dry floatation tank; Thai massage room; a 'sun meadow' for light treatments. There's also a dedicated room for manis and pedis.

The Signature Ritual includes exfoliation, hot stone massage, mud mask in the dry floatation bed, plus a private sauna. Lots of Thai-inspired treatments.

The spa also functions as a health club, so the changing rooms are a little on the Spartan side, with just three showers, plus you need a pound coin for your locker.

We loved

Our 'sauna exfoliation hot stone facial massage wrap' turned out to be so dreamy, we didn't want it to end.

We didn't love

You can't get away from the fact that the spa is divided in two by a hotel corridor: treatment rooms on one side, heat areas on the other. It's the equivalent of having the M6 drive through your spa.

Food file

Spa groups go up in their robes to Kanteen, the rather stylish restaurant on the fourth floor, which makes for a remarkable contrast between spa and style.

Who would like it

People who live or work nearby; BBC staff, Olympia exhibition delegates and Notting Hillbillies in general.

Don't miss

The water-bed in the treatment room.

Spa type
Hotel spa

Where?
K West Hotel
Richmond Way
West Kensington
London W14 0AX
0871 222 4042

Signature treatment
K Spa Signature Ritual

Brands
Crystal Clear, ESPA, Ytsara, Germaine de Capuccini

Expect to pay
Treatments:
£75 for 60 minutes
Stay: from £149 for a junior double

Bubble rating
4 out of 5 bubbles

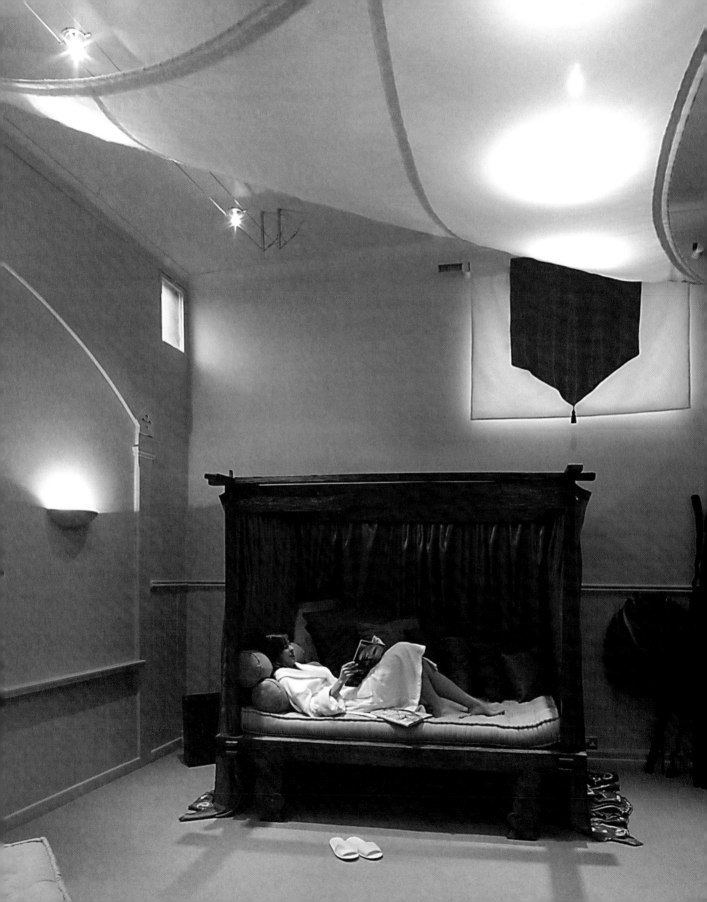

KuBu

Henley, Oxfordshire

In these Balinese-themed treatment rooms in the centre of Henley, you'll find a cool, calm and spacious interior, and a genuinely holistic and treatment-focused approach.

What's on offer

There are three very spacious, wood-floored treatment rooms offering luxurious spa treatments based on Balinese therapies; our room was warm and calming, with a large, original fireplace at one end. Loose, hanging fabric covers the windows, allowing just a little light to come through onto the wooden floors.

KuBu's Ultimate Pampering ritual clocks in at a mighty three hours and 45 minutes of spa indulgence. You can try yoga classes, too, either in a group or in private. You enter the wooden-floored yoga studio through carved wooden doors that were originally part of a Balinese temple.

You can hire the whole spa for a party or group of up to 16 people. Mind you, they'll all be fighting for space on the supremely relaxing day bed.

We loved

The attention to every detail: rolled, fluffy white flannels to dry your hands; rose petals; organic oils; just the right Lavera products for your age and skin type left in the room for you to use.

Our Balinese Boreh exfoliation; a freshly-mixed frangipani paste is massaged, rather than scrubbed into your skin. The therapists at KuBu have regular treatments themselves so that they 'stay in touch' with customers, and it shows.

We didn't love

The parking; Henley is a bit of a residents' permit and short-term-parking nightmare with a lot of one-way streets. Phone in advance and the staff will suggest good options and directions for you.

Food file

Delights from the local deli if you book KuBu's Ultimate Pampering package.

Who would like it

Someone who's looking for a private, exclusive retreat, rather than a busy spa atmosphere.

Don't miss

Sipping champagne and eating freshly made chocolates in a flower-strewn bath as part of the KuBu signature ritual.

Spa type
Treatment rooms

Where?
KuBu
16 Bell Street
Henley on Thames
Oxfordshire RG9 2BG
01491 414130

Signature treatment
KuBu ritual: massage, exfoliation and flower petal bath

Brands
Lavera

Expect to pay
Treatments:
£68 for 60 minutes

Bubble rating
5 out of 5 bubbles

Lake Vyrnwy Hotel and Spa

Llanwddyn, Powys, Wales

Lake Vyrnwy Hotel and Spa sits on a hillside above the vast atmospheric lake itself, with pines and water as far as the eye can see. The spa is a recent addition to the hundred-year-old hotel. Relax in the thermal suite, and enjoy excellent treatments and amazing lakeside views in stunning Snowdonia. A Welsh one to watch.

Spa type
Hotel spa

Where?
Lake Vyrnwy Hotel and Spa
Llanwddyn
Nr Welshpool
Powys SY10 0LY
01691 870692

Signature treatment
Ytsara Body Oil Ceremony

Brands
Pevonia
Spa Find
Ytsara

Expect to pay
Treatments:
£60 for 60 minutes
Stay: from £138 per night
in a double garden room

Bubble rating
5 out of 5 bubbles

What's on offer

You reach the spa from the main hotel, so you don't have to brave the elements – very important in North Wales. The main thermal suite is a large room with a huge window giving a wide view of impressive Lake Vyrnwy. There's no swimming pool, but there is a Jacuzzi, sauna, heated tepidarium loungers, rasul chamber, salt steam room, two experience showers and an ice fountain.

Good value treatments, professionally delivered, include Thai-inspired Ytsara treatments, Pevonia spa treatments and Escutox, a 'natural alternative to Botox'. Chaps can try a Skinfit Facial For Him.

We loved

The welcoming oriental-style treatment rooms draped with deep purple-and-gold fabric. We're very keen on Ytsara natural products and holistic approach, so had the Ytsara Thai Herbal Energizer, a body treatment combining shiatsu pressure point and traditional massage.

We didn't love

The changing area lets the spa down a little; it's neither luxurious nor comfortable.

Food file

All spa packages include a light lunch at the friendly hotel restaurant. In fine weather, dine on the terrace overlooking the lake.

Who would like it

Anyone looking for a sense of space, escape or a complete change of scene. Nature lovers. A good place to take your friend or mum.

Don't miss

The scenery. Admire the amazing views as you relax.

Landmark Hotel

Marylebone, London

A minimalist hideaway in a large, traditional five-star hotel in fashionable Marylebone that provides good value treatments and a fabulous lunch. Inside the hotel you can take tea to the accompaniment of a grand piano, once you've recovered from the rather chilly pool...

Spa type
Hotel spa

Where?
Landmark Hotel
222 Marylebone Road
Marylebone
London NW1 6JQ
020 7631 8000

Signature treatment
Landmark Signature Ritual:
exfoliation, massage,
hot stones and facial

Brands
ESPA

Expect to pay
Treatments:
£75 for 60 minutes
Stay: £550 for a night in
a standard double room

Bubble rating
4 out of 5 bubbles

What's on offer

A 15-metre swimming pool; a whirlpool and sanarium by its side; small steam rooms in the changing areas; and a small but well-equipped gym.

ESPA delights include the indulgent Spa Me Rotten: an overnight stay with aromatherapy massage, chocolate-dipped strawberries, champagne and your very own ESPA candle.

We loved

The professional and perfect ESPA full body massage, and the candle-lit

relaxation area, which has a code on the door so only those having treatments can get in or out, which keeps it peaceful.

We also liked the can-do, helpful and professional attitude of all the staff.

We didn't love

The surprisingly cold pool. Plus, the top half of the steam room was hot but the bottom half wasn't. We considered standing on the bench to reach the steam, but weren't brave enough.

Food file

Lunch comes down to you in the relaxation area so you can stay in your robe, and is a bento box, beautifully presented.

Who would like it

People staying at the hotel, obviously, but also those who live or work locally; it's a good value spa experience.

Don't miss

If money is no object, you may like to consider booking chauffeur transfers there and back.

The Lanesborough

Hyde Park Corner, London

Whether you're on your own or a celeb who just wants to be alone, The Lanesborough's intimate, exclusive Spa Studio is the place to go for comfortable, hushed privacy.

What's on offer

A small, classy spa studio in an imposing luxury hotel in central London. All is calm and quiet at this bijou spa – more luxurious treatment rooms than spa, as there's no pool or water facilities and the gym is only available to hotel guests. Just three treatment rooms and a rather nice large loo with good lighting.

The treatment rooms are some of the grandest in London, with high ceilings, marble floors, floor-to-ceiling wooden doors and lights that change colour.

A wide range of facials and body treatments from two of the great names, La Prairie and [comfort zone], with a good selection for men, including a Gentleman's Wet Shave, and beauty treatments including Leighton Denny hand and foot treatments. Pricey, but we think it's worth it.

We loved

The sheer privacy of the whole experience and the sense of hushed luxury. The brilliant 'privacy button' to buzz when you're ready for your treatment, so you don't dread being discovered halfway to the treatment table in one-sock-on one-sock-off glory.

We didn't love

There is nowhere to sit and unwind after your treatment. We would have liked to have our cool drink in a lounger rather than an upright chair in reception.

Food file

The afternoon tea after your spa experience is well worth it. A conservatory, piano music, and a tea sommelier, no less. We adored our jasmine tea and the wonderful array of tiny elegant cakes and scones.

Who would like it

Ladies who Lanesborough; celebs looking for a private spa experience; anyone feeling frazzled and harassed; jetsetters after a long flight; men – the spa is sophisticated and quite masculine; busy business people who want some pampering in privacy.

Don't miss

The fantastic Serail Spa Massage Ritual (it's even better *à deux*), which involves being coated with 'medicinal' muds, steamed in the serail chamber, then a full body massage.

Spa type

Hotel spa

Where?

The Lanesborough
Hyde Park Corner
London SW1X 7TA
020 7259 5599

Signature treatment

La Prairie Caviar
Firming Facial

Brands

[comfort zone]
La Prairie

Expect to pay

Treatments:
£85 for 60 minutes
Stay: from £558 per night
in a standard double room

Bubble rating

5 out of 5 bubbles

Lansdowne Place Hotel

Hove, East Sussex

Lansdowne Place is a huge Regency hotel just off Hove seafront. It's grand and imposing, and decked out in a funky, quirky style. Dark, lavish fabrics and oriental touches abound. The basement spa complements this boutique hotel beautifully. It's an opulent cocoon of spa.

Spa type
Hotel spa

Where?
Lansdowne Place Hotel
Lansdowne Place, Hove
East Sussex BN3 1HQ
01273 732839

Signature treatments
Holistic Total Body Care
with Hot Stones; full body,
face and scalp massage

Brands
ESPA

Expect to pay
Treatments:
£47 for 55 minutes
Stay: from £69 per night in
a standard double room

Bubble rating
4 out of 5 bubbles

What's on offer

Eight treatment rooms including two generously sized dual treatment rooms. There's a sauna and steam room and a Jacuzzi is on its way. You can also visit a contender for The World's Smallest Gym.

You can have the full range of ESPA treatments, plus complementary therapies or microdermabrasion.

We loved

The lavish purple spa reception: there's a grey slate floor, and dark wood shelves laden with purple-packaged ESPA products. Tea-lights twinkle within amethyst candle holders. A pretty fish tank is set into the front of the reception desk.

The dark-wood vintage lockers in the changing room that lock with a reassuringly large brass key, and the suitably steamy steam room with a pleasant eucalyptus and mint aroma.

We didn't love

Changing rooms are on the small side with only one loo. We had to wait both times we needed to use it.

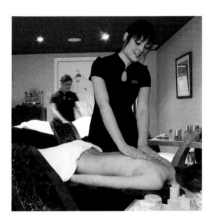

Food file

Fresh fruit and teas in the relaxation area; lunch and traditional afternoon tea in the stylish hotel dining room.

Who would like it

The rich décor is stylish without being girly. It appeals to both sexes, so Lansdowne Place is a good choice for couples.

Don't miss

Each of the eight treatment rooms has a different coloured ceiling – try them all!

Le Kalon

Bentley Hotel, South Kensington, London

This upmarket hotel with a white Victorian façade is home to the only authentic hammam within a 5-star luxury hotel in London. Le Kalon offers a delight: a traditional spa experience in the heart of the city.

What's on offer

Gorgeous, carefully chosen Karin Herzog treatments. You can have chocolate facials, manicures, pedicures, and Le Kalon's own massage treatments. There's a gym. And the glorious hammam...

We loved

Being told this is a proper hammam doesn't give you a feel for the size of the place. It is a large room, all in white marble. In the middle is a large marble slab, where you lie for your massage after the heat has relaxed you.

The steam heat is hot. You may not think that you'll enjoy pouring a bowl of cold water over your head, but you will. With enthusiasm. And the massage is doubly relaxing for being carried out in the steam.

Even if you're staying in the hotel, you have to make an appointment to use the facilities, so the spa is not crowded and you get a sense of privacy.

We didn't love

There's no pool, so if you don't like or can't have heat treatments, this is not the spa for you.

Food file

Spa guests can order food and drink from the hotel's room service menu.

Who would like it

Anyone who enjoys an authentic spa experience, especially if you like to spa with friends.

Don't miss

The marble hammam is the star. There are terrific treatments on offer in the fantastic hammam. And did we mention that there's a hammam?

Spa type

Hotel spa

Where?

Bentley Hotel
Harrington Gardens
South Kensington
London SW7 4JX
020 7244 5371

Signature treatment

Hamam Le Kalon:
a traditional Turkish experience using black-olive soap and thermal clay mask

Brands

Karin Herzog

Expect to pay

Treatments:
£80 for 60 minutes
Stay: Room rates for overnight stays from: £219

Bubble rating

5 out of 5 bubbles

Forget everything you know about candles. Forget everything you know about bath oils and body products...

At NEOM we have created the most incredibly powerful, organic range of luxury bath & home products that all work as treatments to make you feel more relaxed, more energised or even just a whole lot happier depending on the treatment you choose.

Experience our cult, beauty-editor favourite candles to vitamin packed anti ageing body oils, deeply pampering bath oils in precious glass bottles and organic room mists. We even have organic hand/body washes and lotions for a touch of everyday organic luxury.

www.NEOMorganics.com

NEOM

LUXURY ORGANICS

Lido Spa

Clifton, Bristol

A day-spa oasis of calm and tranquillity, with great attention to detail, top-notch treatments and divine food. There are six treatment rooms, a shimmering heated outdoor 24-metre infinity pool and, rather excitingly, a Victorian spa tea room.

What's on offer

No room for poolside loungers here, but the cubicles with retro-stripey curtains will make you think you've stepped back in time. The relaxation room, sauna and steam rooms all have windows overlooking the pool. There's a unisex boudoir, with marble-topped dressing tables.

A range of holistic facials, massages, scrubs and wraps, using ila products.

We loved

The Lido Lomi Lomi Hawaiian full body massage. The treatment, said to heal the body of ills and the mind of bad thoughts,

uses yummy oil containing kukui nut, ylang ylang, ginger and rose geranium. We followed it with a Rainforest Rejuvenation facial, and reached Nirvana. Seriously.

We didn't love

We would have liked a water machine near the sauna and steam room. Members of the public are allowed into the Lido to eat, so if you're the only one in a robe, you might feel a little out of place.

Food file

They're passionate about food at the Lido. There's a glass-walled poolside bar and a restaurant above. We had a delicious breakfast of homemade granola, natural yoghurt and fresh fruit. The tempting lunch menu offers fresh local produce

Who would like it

Anyone looking for a day of peace and quiet, on their own or with a friend.

Don't miss

The crystal clear infinity pool. They've used reclaimed wood in the renovations, including the barrel showers that line the pool.

Spa type
Day spa

Where?
Lido
Oakfield Place
Clifton
Bristol BS8 2BJ
0117 933 9530

Signature treatments
Lido Lomi Lomi Massage
The Perfect Hawaiian Ritual

Brands
ila

Expect to pay
Treatments:
£50 for 60 minutes

Bubble rating
4 out of 5 bubbles

Loch Lomond Golf Club

The Spa in the Walled Garden
Rossdhu House, Luss, Scotland

Opulence and Scottish hospitality at its grandest, in extensive grounds. An exclusive, tranquil ESPA spa offering a serene and soothing experience in a simply stunning setting. Once reserved solely for members, the spa is now open to mere mortals.

What's on offer

The impressive secluded spa building blends beautifully into the natural surroundings. Separate 'journeys' for men and women. Tasteful, minimal vitality pool and heat areas in black slate with twinkling gold mosaic tiles and a view of the gardens. Very hot, beautifully finished crystal steam room, a good size sauna and a 'lifestyle shower'. Excellent and spotlessly clean changing rooms.

A wide range of ESPA treatments, including massages, wraps and facials. (The Pre-Golf warm-up massage uses hot golf balls to target your driving muscles!) There's a gym, and you can also have a fitness assessment, book some personal training, or do Pilates and yoga.

We loved

The showers in the treatment room: large, warm, private, and each with its own little area to hang your robe. Our Dosha Specific Advanced Ayurvedic Hot Stone Massage and Body Wrap with blue marine mud. Our therapist diagnosed our dosha (mix of energies) so she could choose the right oil for the massage – energising peppermint, eucalyptus and rosemary.

We didn't love

The disappointing snacks in the relaxation room – our requested blueberry muffin turned out to be chocolate, and we think it may have been microwaved.

Food file

We had dinner in the Spike Bar, in the main house. All the food was freshly cooked and tasty (we wanted to take a vat of the spiced olives home with us). We were staying in The Point, a lakeside lodge, where we took cereals and juice from the kitchen, and watched the wind rippling across the loch and acres of trees.

Who would like it

Serious golfers (the club hosts the Scottish Open); members and their friends; anyone.

Don't miss

The walled garden itself. This was once the kitchen garden and contains a large palm house and extensive lawns. Mary Queen of Scots wrote her love letters in Rossdhu Castle, the ruins of which overlook the 18th green. Impossibly romantic.

Spa type
Hotel spa

Where?
Loch Lomond Golf Club
Rossdhu House
Luss G83 8NT
01436 655315

Signature treatment
Loch Lomond Experience

Brands
ESPA

Expect to pay
Treatments:
£80 for 60 minutes
Stay: Spa residential experiences start from £580 for double occupancy; includes dinner, bed and breakfast

Bubble rating
5 out of 5 bubbles

Lucknam Park Hotel and Spa

Colerne, Wiltshire

A country house surrounded by 500 acres of lush parkland. We loved everything about this new spa in a quintessentially English country house hotel – the friendly staff, the pool, the thermal suites, the idyllic, rural surroundings, the effective treatments and the great food. A true all-round 5-bubble experience.

Spa type
Hotel spa

Where?
Lucknam Park Hotel and
Spa
Colerne
Wiltshire SN14 8AZ
01225 740537

Signature treatment
De-Stress Botanical Oil &
Herbal Back Therapy

Brands
Anne Sémonin
Carita

Expect to pay
Treatments:
£75 for 60 minutes
Stay: from £295 per night in
a standard room

Bubble rating
5 out of 5 bubbles

What's on offer

A large new, gleaming spa building. A handsome, inky blue, 20-metre pool with submerged lighting. A beautifully lit inside-and-outside hydrotherapy pool. Thermal suites including Japanese Salt and Amethyst steam rooms, tepidarium and large sauna. Single-sex sauna and steam room. A good gym, two outdoor tennis courts and 5-a-side football pitch.

There are nine treatment rooms, and a good range of treatments, including specific treatments for men and 'Little Misses'.

We loved

Our Carita Ideal Hydration facial. We were amazed at our soft skin, which lasted a couple of weeks. Good value, despite the top-end price.

We didn't love

The strange metallic taste in our mouths from the Pro-Lift machine. But it didn't last long.

Food file

The spa's Brasserie offers both traditional dishes and a lighter menu – marinated smoked salmon with spiced aubergine, or lemon and ginger poached chicken with mango and avocado yoghurt. For fine dining, there's the Michelin-starred Park restaurant in the main hotel.

Who would like it

People who enjoy the finer things in life; anyone looking for a friendly country hotel with a good sized spa.

Don't miss

The outdoor part of the hydrotherapy pool; subtly lit by night, it's magical.

Lush Spa

Chelsea, London

A subterranean spa reached through a secret door at the back of a busy Lush shop in London's King's Road. These dramatically different treatment rooms offer just one treatment: the Synaesthesia massage. Curiouser and curiouser. This is spa as theatre. We loved it so much that we forgot where we were, when we were and who we were.

What's on offer

An imaginative, original, quirky approach to the whole spa experience. The Synaesthesia multi-sensory massage, a blend of 'experiences, music, birdsong, colour, scent and a carefully choreographed massage' is currently the only treatment offered at this spa.

The reception and relaxation area is an other-worldly mix of Severus Snape's kitchen and an old-fashioned tea-room.

It isn't all smoke and mirrors, though: this is a carefully planned spa journey. Behind the theatricality is a solid base of well thought-through massage techniques and aromatherapy wizardry, and fantastically friendly, well-trained therapists.

We loved

The Synaesthesia multi-sensory massage, of course, with dry ice pouring from sconces and orange-lit flowers casting psychedelic shadows on the wall. Our therapist gave us a really invigorating massage, choreographed to Lush's own album, loud, very English folk music with orchestral swoops, bird song and church bells. Afterwards, we felt quite out of it.

We didn't love

We would have liked something fancier than a white ceiling to look at.

Food file

A beautifully presented selection of teas afterwards, and fresh fruit in season.

Who would like it

English eccentrics; jaded spa bunnies looking for a new experience; Lush fans.

Don't miss

The lovely herb garden, complete with topiary hedges.

Spa type
Treatment rooms

Where?
Lush Spa
123 Kings Road
London SW3 4PL
020 7349 9648

Signature treatment
The Synaesthesia multi-sensory massage

Brands
Lush: B Never Too Busy To Be Beautiful

Expect to pay
Treatments:
£125 for 90 minutes

Bubble rating
4 out of 5 bubbles

The Spa at Luton Hoo

Luton, Bedfordshire

An historic Grade-I listed mansion in over 1,000 acres of landscaped parkland and gardens. The Adams stable buildings, which surround a central courtyard, are home to the golf house, the spa and leisure facilities. A luxurious hotel where the service, the spa and the leisure facilities are first-class.

What's on offer

Clean and modern changing rooms that feel spacious. The showers contain products from The Spa at Luton Hoo signature range. Comfortable loungers around an 18-metre infinity pool. A vitality pool with sauna, steam room, caldarium and experience showers. Six cosy treatment rooms with a relaxing atmosphere. The fitness studio and gym are well equipped.

The treatment menu is simple but well chosen, using their own or Circaroma organic products. You can have facials, body treatments including polishes and wraps, and alternative therapies, such as reflexology, reiki, and Indian head massage. There are finishing touches, too: hand and foot treatments; manicures and pedicures; waxing.

We loved

The staff. Nothing was too much effort, they were friendly and professional but never intrusive. The spa has a real sense of tranquillity and peace. Our signature 5 Senses facial; the organic flowers and herbs in the spa's own range of products felt genuinely nourishing to the skin.

We didn't love

The fact that couldn't spend a lot more time here.

Food file

Very delicious ginger tea in the relaxation room, where the refreshments station had a range of herbal teas, fresh juices, water, fresh and dried fruits. For dinner, we visited the 2 AA-Rosette Wernher Restaurant. Originally a State Dining Room, the walls are panelled with marble and covered with enormous tapestries.

Who would like it

Who would *not* like it? Luton Hoo is especially good for those who like to combine activity with relaxation: there's an 18-hole golf course, tennis courts, mapped walks, clay-pigeon shooting, fishing and boating, as well as the spa.

Don't miss

The fleet of golf buggies that will taxi you around the estate or just to the spa. The spectacular gardens. Packing some formal dress for the restaurant.

Spa type
Hotel spa

Where?
Luton Hoo Hotel, Golf & Spa
The Mansion House
Luton
Bedfordshire LU1 3TQ
01582 734437

Signature treatment
Luton Hoo Spa 5 Senses Body Signature Treatment

Brands
Circaroma

Expect to pay
Treatments:
£75 for 55 minutes
Stay: from £220 per night in a deluxe double room

Bubble rating
5 out of 5 bubbles

Mandarin Oriental

Knightsbridge, London

A confidently understated London luxury hotel spa, which offers spa perfection within easy reach of Harvey Nicks. The opulence lies in the standard of service and attention to detail. The Mandarin Oriental is a soothing oasis of calm in the shopping jungle of Knightsbridge.

What's on offer

Although the spa is subterranean and doesn't have any natural light, it doesn't feel in any way dingy – more private and secluded. The granite floor and dark wood and horsehair walls are decorated with tea lights and the odd cymbidium flower.

There are separate facilities for men and women, including a Vitality pool with warm mineral water and hydrotherapy stations, an amethyst crystal steam room and a sanarium.

Treatments include the shiatsu-inspired Ginger Ritual, the Life Dance Massage, Balinese massage, shiatsu, reflexology, oriental scrubs and wraps.

We loved

The standard of service: used towels are removed in the blink of an eye, blankets and flowers are precisely rearranged within moments of someone vacating their relax-ation bed. Yet it seems intuitive; there's no therapist watching over you.

One of the most relaxing relaxation rooms of any spa we have been to. The subdued lighting in the room discourages the reading of magazines, as if even this minor activity is too demanding and therefore to be discouraged. And anyway, there's the ergonomic bed and personal music system to be played with. Oh, and the subtle colour therapy lighting in the fireplace to be enjoyed.

We didn't love

Be prepared for the dimly lit changing rooms. Memorise the position of every-thing in your locker – or bring a torch.

Food file

Water, tea, juice and fruit.

Who would like it

Ladies who shop – preferably at Harvey Nichols; anyone who has high standards and demands the best; anyone who wants a treat.

Don't miss

Book two hours of Advanced Time and decide your treatments on arrival. Top-end rates, but in terms of location, ambience, and spa perfection – it's worth it.

Spa type
Hotel spa

Where?
Mandarin Oriental
66 Knightsbridge
Knightsbridge
London SW1X 7LA
020 7838 9888

Signature treatment
Oriental Harmony
four-hand massage

Brands
Mandarin Oriental (by Aromatherapy Associates)

Expect to pay
Treatments:
£155 for 80 minutes
Stay: from £455 for a Courtyard king room

Bubble rating
5 out of 5 bubbles

Matfen Hall

Matfen, Tyne and Wear

Matfen Hall hotel is a lovely Victorian house in huge grounds. Here you will find excellent customer service and a relaxed and well-run spa with great fire and ice rooms.

Spa type

Hotel spa

Where?

Matfen Hall
Matfen
Newcastle upon Tyne
Tyne and Wear NE20 0RH
01661 886500

Signature treatment

[comfort zone] exfoliation, back massage and facial

Brands

[comfort zone]

Expect to pay

Treatments:
£55 for 60 minutes
Stay: £185 per night for
a standard double room

Bubble rating

4 out of 5 bubbles

What's on offer

A good spa with golf on the side. The spa building looks as if it's a converted stable block from the outside, but inside everything is bright and light. There is a 16-metre swimming pool and spa pool which are UV filtrated to cut down on chlorine.

The fire and ice rooms are great fun. Sit in the cool blue salt/ozone room, press the button and fine salt spray descends: it feels like a fresh breezy day at the seaside. Cross into the herbal sauna and warm up gently. Cover yourself with ice at the ice fountain. Step into the steam room and from there go on to the circular shower where you can choose cold mist or summer rain.

We loved

The whole place is wonderfully peaceful. The grounds are lovely, the countryside fantastic. And we adored feeling truly pampered the whole time we were there.

We didn't love

Not being able to read the fire and ice instructions without our glasses on.

Food file

Most day escapes include a welcome drink and two-course lunch.

Who would like it

Golfers, naturally, get-away-from-it-all-ers, and romantics looking for a break with some pampering thrown in.

Don't miss

The [comfort zone] treatments in spacious and candlelit treatment rooms.

May Fair Spa

Radisson Edwardian May Fair, London

These subterranean treatment rooms are in a five-star hotel in the heart of fashionable London (Mayfair, obviously). You come here for the results-driven treatments rather than the pool, as there isn't one. Small, a little pricey, but very classy.

What's on offer

The May Fair hotel is very swish and modern but has old-fashioned customer-service values. In the small spa, you'll find a hammam room; a compact gym with plenty of equipment and personal trainers. The steam room is a great size and the heated ceramic loungers in the dimly lit relaxation room are more comfortable than they look. No pool, though; you'll be disappointed if you need one to spa.

The wide-ranging and imaginative treatment menu includes: non-surgical facelifts; oxygen therapy; red-vein treatments. The emphasis is very much on the treatment that is right for you, so you are encouraged to book 'time' and discover what would suit you on the day.

We loved

The stylish spa area with water features built into the walls. The rippling water has a very 'spa' effect on you.

The helpful and friendly staff.

We also loved our very, very good Pevonia hot-stone massages. Both done by a man, which was a bit of a surprise, but fabulously relaxing and restoring.

We didn't love

Fairly small changing rooms with a bit of a musty smell; only one bench to put things on. The used towelling spa slippers awaiting us in our lockers.

Food file

The promised 'platter of fresh fruit' in the relaxation room turned out to be green apples. Herbal teas and small dish of refreshing sorbet after your treatment.

Don't miss

The Moroccan Steam Cleansing Ritual. Slather mud over yourself and sit in a twinkly cavern to steam it off.

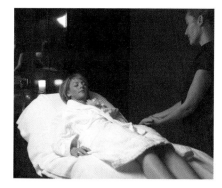

Spa type
Hotel spa

Where?
The May Fair Hotel
Stratton Street
Mayfair, London W1A 2AN
020 7915 2826

Signature treatment
Perfect Peace package, includes tailored facial and Swedish massage

Brands
Biodroga
Dr Murad

Expect to pay
Treatments:
£99 for 60 minutes
Stay: from £195 per night in a superior bedroom

Bubble rating
4 out of 5 bubbles

Moddershall Oaks

Stone, Staffordshire

A luxurious, sociable countryside spa retreat that offers personalised peace, great facilities, friendly fun and great value. All that, and a woodland walk, too.

What's on offer

A spa retreat in a rural location. Great customer service from friendly, courteous staff. A good gym. Ten stylish, comfortable bedrooms. A hot tub looking out onto fields, free-form pool with enough space to exercise and splash about, if not to swim in. Sauna and steam room. Jacuzzi with a good view of the gardens.

A good range of treatments to help you relax, detox or recharge, with treatments for men and mums-to-be, and complementary therapies such as reflexology, Indian head massage and ayurvedic treatments. Manis, pedis, tinting and waxing, and a hair salon too, so you'll go home looking and feeling top-to-toe gorgeous. We found our massage bed a bit uncomfortable but had a wonderfully relaxing float and perfect pedicure. The spa days and spa breaks are worth every penny.

We loved

The location, the facilities and the friendly staff. The little phial of Elemis cooling mint mist that magically appeared on the pillow in our room. If only that happened at home…

We didn't love

The treatment bed. It was the sort where the bottom falls away for the float, but before it did that, it was quite hard and unforgiving. A shame, as otherwise the massage would have been excellent.

Food file

The smart restaurant has a patio area with views over the lake, a good atmosphere and swift, friendly service. Local produce is used where possible; our risotto was delicious but you can have anything from baguettes to venison sausages with watercress mash, braised red cabbage, honey red wine and Dijon sauce.

Who would like it

Anyone! But particularly friends or groups, as there are lots of sociable things to do. The atmosphere is 'fun' rather than 'hush'.

Don't miss

The wonderful woodland trail, where you can see deer and pieces of sculpture. The outdoor tennis court. The hot tub with its rural views, where Real Life and its cares feel far away.

Spa type

Spa retreat

Where?

Moddershall Oaks
Moddershall
Stone
Staffordshire ST15 8TG
01782 399000

Signature treatment

Gerard's Oriental Reviver with Bamboo

Brands

Elemis, Gerard's

Expect to pay

Treatments:
£50 for 55 minutes
Stay: from £160 per night in a double five star luxury suite

Bubble rating

5 out of 5 bubbles

New Park Manor Bath House Spa

Brockenhurst, Hampshire

A mixture here: a rather grand and elegant New Forest country house with a modern, purpose-built spa on one side. The overall design of the Bath House Spa takes its inspiration from nature; the emphasis is on the floral, herbal, natural and fresh.

What's on offer

There are six treatment rooms on two wood-panelled floors. You could have a different kind of massage here every day for a month. The Bath House Spa offers detox treatments, fresh organic wraps and scrubs, a range of Bath House facials, manicures and pedicures, along with [comfort zone] face and body treatments.

The 16-metre pool sits behind floor-to-ceiling glass windows with views of the New Forest. There's a small gym, a sanarium, a genuinely hot sauna and steam room, foot baths, experience showers, and a hydrotherapy pool.

We loved

The day spa packages are a genuine bargain. There aren't many places where you could get such good treatments and such a range of facilities for the price. There's simply a relaxing and peaceful atmosphere throughout the spa, carefully nurtured by the spa team.

The modern rooms in the new Forest Wing have LCD TVs in the bathroom so you can watch your favourite soap in the bath!

We didn't love

The changing room is very small, and a little frayed at the edges of the showers.

Food file

Fresh, locally sourced wherever possible and GM-free. The Polo Bar menu does plenty of sandwiches and healthy options. For something a little more formal and indulgent, the oak-panelled Stag Restaurant awaits. The seasonal menu in the spa makes the most of local produce.

Who would like it

New Park Manor is a great choice for a day to catch up with a friend, or for mums and daughters. The spa offers a wide enough range of treatments to keep all ages happy.

A group of 12 can book the whole spa for the day.

Don't miss

The outdoor Canadian hot tub; great fun, hot and very bubbly. There's something special about sitting outside in the frosty air and not feeling cold.

Spa type
Hotel spa

Where?
New Park Manor Hotel
Lyndhurst Road
Brockenhurst
Hampshire SO42 7QH
01590 624964

Signature treatment
Herb and Hay Detox:
a soothing and
detoxifying massage

Brands
[comfort zone], Numbers

Expect to pay
Treatments:
£60 for 55 minutes
Stay: from £155 per night
in a double country classic
room

Bubble rating
5 out of 5 bubbles

Nickel

Covent Garden, London

Looking for express treatments and instant relaxation? Put Nickel's number in your little black book. Once over the threshold, this men-only spa puts you in mind of a rather upmarket pharmacy: its low shelves are amply furnished with a wide selection of skincare products.

Spa type
Treatment rooms

Where?
Nickel
27 Short's Gardens
Covent Garden
London WC2H 9AP
020 7240 4048

Signature treatment
Complete Facial:
a relaxing custom facial

Brands
Nickel

Expect to pay
Treatments:
£60 for 60 minutes

Bubble rating
4 out of 5 bubbles

What's on offer

Five cosy, dimly lit treatment rooms and a manly menu of spa treatments. An array of different massages running from 30 to 90 minutes, as well as a 'love-handle wrap'. You can have facials, brow and eyelash tints, manicures and pedicures, micro-dermabrasion and osteopathy. There is also an extensive range of waxing options.

We loved

The proper grown-up men's massage. The kind of treatment guys expect, with plenty of firm pressure and hard strokes

to encourage blood flow. Our therapist located our problem areas without prompting, and persisted with the knottiest areas of muscle until everything had loosened. The moments of border-line pain were fine. The treatment felt like it actually had some much needed medium-term benefit.

The oils in the massage: gorgeously aromatic, and not a rose in sight.

We didn't love

No musical choices besides Echoes of the Ocean, or whatever it was. The couch was rather too narrow for those with a broad frame.

Food file

Only water.

Who would like it

Any man who enjoys getting pampered. If you do, Nickel is just the ticket.

Don't miss

The punch bags. But don't get stuck into them; they appear more cosmetic than intended for use.

Nirvana Spa

Wokingham, Berkshire

An enormous, maze-like, dedicated day spa that's fresh, clean and functional – more like a good health club with added robes. You'll need a whole day to make the most of the pools, gym and heat facilities at this good-value spa. And they have cake. Spa heaven.

What's on offer

Six pure, natural spring-fed pools, massive pool area, large relaxation room, extensive water and heat facilities. The Ocean Room, where powerful water and air jets deliciously tenderise your weary muscles. A very large, candle-lit tepidarium. Menthol-infused aroma steam room, with twinkling colour-changing stars. Monsoon showers, fitness pool, Jacuzzi, single-sex steam rooms and saunas.

A large, pleasant gym with a wealth of machines. Lots of friendly, attentive and cheerful staff.

Facials (try the Celestial facial with 'pure colloidal gold' moisturiser), manis, pedis, massages and body treatments.

We loved

Floating weightlessly in our Celestial Float in the Celestial Pool with its huge, domed, twinkling roof.

We didn't love

The layout is a little confusing at first. There was no hair conditioner in the changing rooms, and if you forget your flip-flops, you have to pay a pretty penny for some.

Food file

Fresh and filling cold meats, fish and salads in The Garden Café. (Dishes on the menu are not included in your day-spa package. We think that's a bit naughty.)

Who would like it

Locals and members. Men, women, couples and small groups (limited to six people to maintain that spa hush).

Don't miss

Nirvana's unique floatation therapy Celestial Pool, with 100 tonnes of salt and 21 Dead Sea minerals.

Spa type
Day spa

Where?
Nirvana Spa
Mole Road
Sindlesham
Wokingham
Berkshire RG41 5DJ
0118 989 7575

Signature treatment
Nirvana's Personalised Facial

Brands
Celestial Spa Authentic, Clarins, n-spa

Expect to pay
Treatments:
£60 for 55 minutes

Bubble rating
4 out of 5 bubbles

Norton House Hotel and Spa

Edinburgh, Scotland

The original country-house part of Norton House Hotel is very traditionally grand. Think gilt mirrors and large lilies. The newly built spa at Norton House is a dramatic contrast to the comfy old hotel, all glass walls and ultra-ultra-modern.

Spa type
Hotel spa

Where?
Norton House
Ingliston
Edinburgh EH28 8LX
0845 072 7468

Signature treatment
Hand Picked Organic Bliss: foot ritual, meditation and massage

Brands
ESPA, NEOM

Expect to pay
Treatments:
£65 for 60 minutes
Stay: from £109 for bed and breakfast in a standard double room

Bubble rating
4 out of 5 bubbles

What's on offer

A nice array of modern facilities including an 18-metre pool, a steam room and a sauna in a corner of the pool area, plus a hydrotherapy pool. There's a rasul room and a good size gym with all-new equipment and a wide choice of free weights.

You can have all the ESPA treatments, and some alternative treatments such as reiki and reflexology.

We loved

Our ESPA Holistic Back, Face and Scalp Massage with Hot Stones. Our therapist had a nice touch – no fairy fingers here.

The pleasant relaxation room has dimmed lights and wicker loungers to continue your sojourn on Cloud Nine.

There are ample loungers round the pool, and good customer service.

We didn't love

The pool, heat areas and changing rooms felt much like any health club. Not much of a spa 'feel'. The pool felt heavily chlorine-treated. We also didn't love the children splashing about in the hydrotherapy pool.

Food file

Fresh, tasty and delicious salads in the Amber Dining Lounge. 3 AA Rosettes restaurant in the Hotel. Split-pea soup in The Brasserie.

Who would like it

Edinburgh refugees who don't wish to flee too far; mums and daughters for the day.

Don't miss

Ask for Norton House's courtesy car to come and pick you up from the airport.

Old Course Hotel

St Andrews, Scotland

For most visitors to St Andrews, there's only one reason they're there: the Royal and Ancient game of golf. Don't miss the Kohler Waters spa in the Old Course Hotel, though. It's modern and welcoming, using lots of natural materials, and the treatments emphasise 'the therapeutic benefits of water'.

What's on offer

The hotel lies right next to possibly the most famous golf course in the world: the Old Course (as opposed to the New Course, you understand, which only opened in 1895). The spa has a 20-metre pool, a thermal suite with a large hydrotherapy pool, steam room, sauna, and plunge pool. Even if you're staying in the hotel, there is an extra charge for access, unless you also book a treatment. This keeps the area tranquil and spa-focused. There are 11 treatment rooms, two with water facilities.

We loved

Our Sea Lime Sigh, a body treatment of moisturisation and exfoliation, followed by a Kohler experience shower and a final warm coat of body butter. Our male spy found this very soothing, to the point where sleep may have been involved.

Bracing walks along the sandy beach, around the golf-courses and up to the castle; you don't have to play golf to enjoy this interesting town.

We didn't love

The relaxation area felt more like a corridor then a haven of calm.

Food file

Healthy snacks and lunches in the spa; in the evening, the 3 AA-rosette Road Hole Grill offers Scottish food with a view.

Who would like it

Golfers, obviously, and those whose Significant Other is playing golf.

Don't miss

Chromatherapy in the overflowing infinity bath.

Spa type

Hotel spa

Where?

Old Course Hotel
Golf Resort & Spa
St Andrews, Fife KY16 9SP
01334 474371

Signature treatment

H2O Inspiration: a warm oil scalp massage, body exfoliation, Vichy shower, River Bath, moisturiser, and foot massage

Brands

Kohler, Phytocéane

Expect to pay

Treatments:
£87 for 50 minutes
Stay: from £195 for one night in an Eden Parkland room

Bubble rating

4 out of 5 bubbles

ONE Spa

The Sheraton Grand Hotel, Edinburgh, Scotland

ONE Spa is a modern spa attached to a traditional hotel. It offers excellent ESPA treatments, an impressive array of thermal experiences, and a stunning rooftop hydrotherapy pool. Who knew that the best way to see Edinburgh was to sit in some warm bubbly water?

What's on offer

Three floors of modern, light spa: a rooftop hydrotherapy pool; an indoor 19-metre pool; an excellent thermal suite with plenty of different areas to try out – a hammam, laconium, rock sauna, bio sauna, aroma grotto and several large seats where you can rest and cool off. There's also a gym with state-of-the-art equipment.

The treatments include ESPA facials and massages, including the slightly confusingly named 'face and back facial'. If you want to push the boat out, go with the Purva Karma synchronised four-hand massage. All the treatments we've had here have been top-notch, and there's a large and quiet relaxation area to come back to the real world in, too.

We loved

ONE Spa's rooftop hydrotherapy pool; it has inside and outside areas, both with strong massage jets and good bubbly zones. It's amazing to be in the middle of Edinburgh, looking at the city from warm, bubbling water.

The way you can decide which treatments to have on the day by simply booking 'Time'. Your therapist can then create a body treatment programme to suit your specific needs. This is great, as you don't always know when you book whether you'll want skip out soothed or drift out with your energy restored.

We didn't love

The changing area is very much 'health club' rather than spa, with lots of lockers and not really enough seating space. The robes are well washed, too.

Food file

The ONE Spa Café offers light meals and smoothies. Food options in the hotel include the carvery at The Terrace, or modern Italian at Santini.

Who would like it

Almost anyone.

Don't miss

Anything: allow yourself enough time to really enjoy the pools and thermal area.

Spa type
Hotel spa

Where?
Sheraton Grand Hotel
8 Conference Square
Edinburgh EH3 8AN
0131 221 7777

Signature treatment
ESPA Time experience: a sequence of body therapies

Brands
ESPA

Expect to pay
Treatments:
£75 for 55 minutes
Stay: from £140 for bed and breakfast in a standard double room

Bubble rating
5 out of 5 bubbles

Good Spa Spy Favourites

Salubrious Spy

Age 30-something **Skin type** Combination **Spa likes** Outdoor pools; clean everything; a generous fluffy robe; 'real' non-robotic therapists **Spa dislikes** Paper spa knickers; communal flip-flops; enforced macrobiotic dining; periods of abandonment during treatments; teeny-tiny lockers; anything including the word 'detox'

Best spa experiences this year

Swimming in – and lounging by – the idyllic outdoor pool on a bonus sunny morning at **The Grove**. Ordering a smoothie from the poolside bar made me feel like I was on holiday.

Experiencing the smorgasbord of hydrotherapy pools at the impressive **Pennyhill Park**.

Meeting one of the friendliest and most genuine therapists I've ever met while having a treatment at **Dove Spa**, Reigate.

Worst spa experiences this year

Being abandoned for five minutes while having a wrap in a chilly room listening to a scratched *Sounds of the Andes* CD. Not my idea of relaxation!

Favourite products

Aromatherapy Associates Enrich hair oil

I just adore the scent of Aromatherapy Associates products and this one is no exception. The scents of ylang-ylang, geranium and rosemary go so well together that I was instantly won over and wanted more. The oil can be used either as a 20-minute treatment or an overnight quencher. I could feel that it had worked some moisturising magic when I washed the oil out of my highlighted hair.

REN's rose otto bath oil

A perennial favourite. I've tried many other bath oils since but none hits the decadent, fragrant spot for me in the way this queen of oils does.

Balance Me's Rose Body Balm

Another established favourite. I love its upmarket feminine packaging and subtle but luxurious rose aroma. The balm is a solid wax that melts into a smooth balm when applied to warm skin. Not thick enough to clog, but reassuringly present. Perfect for smooth summer legs, soft hands and feet, or pretty much anything/anywhere else for that matter. This is a luxurious and petro-chemical-free alternative to the ubiquitous Vaseline.

The Organic Pharmacy's Antioxidant Face Gel and Face Firming Serum

I love everything about these products from the subtly stylish glass containers to the divine sweet-citrus fragrance of the gel. Using the gel and the serum together, as recommended, also makes the experience feel more pampering than just applying moisturiser. Worth saving up for.

Oxley's at Underscar

(Blue Fish Spa), Keswick, Cumbria

Wander lonely as a cloud in the direction of this small, good-value spa, where you can work out, swim, and chill in Wordsworth country. The nineteenth-century buildings have been converted into upmarket time-share properties in this stunning Lake District location. (Luckily, you don't have to own a time-share to use the spa.)

What's on offer

A light and airy pool area with pool, Jacuzzi and sauna, and a very clean gym.

Li'Tya and Decléor facials and body treatments, along with traditional massage, and Li'Tya massage rituals 'inspired by traditional Australian Aboriginal techniques...'. Manis, pedis and beauty treatments, lush-sounding Li'Tya hand and feet treatments. For men, there's a Wet Shave facial or a 'Man'icure.

We loved

The good deep massage we'd asked for, using subtle lavender and chamomile oils, in a large, airy treatment room.

We didn't love

Despite the notices advising people to rehydrate, there's no water-cooler in the pool area and you have to go out to reception in your slippers to get a drink. We would have liked a warmer welcome and guided tour.

Food file

Elevenses in the quiet café, where there's a wide range of herbal teas and an

espresso machine. For lunch, we enjoyed a Greek salad and light, refreshing sea-bass fishcakes. The staff were very attentive. A great pity the café looks onto the car park, not the lovely Lake District beyond!

Who would like it

Women in pairs (a big group could wreck the calm; there are only 11 loungers). Walkers – an intense massage after a brisk walk on the fells would be great.

Don't miss

Walking in the stunning countryside.

Spa type
Day spa

Where?
Oxley's at Underscar
(Blue Fish Spa)
Underscar
Applethwaite
Keswick
Cumbria CA12 4PH
017687 71500

Signature treatment
Dreaming spa day

Brands
Decléor
Li'Tya

Expect to pay
Treatments:
£41 for 60 minutes

Bubble rating
4 out of 5 bubbles

Pavilion Spa

Cliveden House, Berkshire

There aren't many spas that can claim to have changed the face of British politics, but Cliveden is one. This most luxurious of country-house hotels has a spa in its walled garden that's not quite up the sumptuous standards of the house, but the treatments are excellent and splashing about in the outdoor pool unmissable.

Spa type
Hotel spa

Where?
Cliveden House
Taplow
Berkshire SL6 0JF
01628 607177

Signature treatment
Honey and Mango wrap

Brands
Carita
Terraké

Expect to pay
Treatments:
£70 for 55 minutes
Stay: from £255 for bed and breakfast in a Club room

Bubble rating
4 out of 5 bubbles

What's on offer

The hotel is imposing and elegant, built on cliffs above the River Thames, with formal and extensive parterre gardens. In the spa, you'll find an 18-metre ozone-treated indoor pool and a slightly disappointing Jacuzzi. In the walled garden is a heated outdoor pool and two Canadian hot tubs. It was in this garden that Stephen Ward and Christine Keeler first met; their liaison later triggered the infamous Profumo scandal of the 1960s.

Elsewhere in the hotel you can find a small gym, an exercise studio, and indoor and outdoor tennis courts; add the extensive possibilities of walks in the grounds, and you can be active during your spa stay, too.

The treatments on offer include a range of Terraké and Carita facials and massages, plus manis and pedis.

We loved

The spa staff are young, friendly and happy to help when asked. We were enamoured of our Carita Pro-Lifting facial, promising and delivering an instant face-lifting effect.

We didn't love

The indoor pool, which needed some TLC, and the small changing rooms.

Food file

In the spa, there is a conservatory serving healthy smoothies and snacks.

Who would like it

Everyone who could afford it.

Don't miss

The sybaritic pleasure of sitting in the hot tubs in the walled garden is priceless.

Peak Health Club and Spa

(Jumeirah Carlton Tower), Knightsbridge, London

Everything you could want from a health club and spa, in a grand but unpretentious five-star London hotel. On the second floor, an inviting 20-metre pool, Jacuzzi, sauna and steam rooms. On the ninth floor, a spa with sweeping views across the city.

What's on offer

The spa has six treatment rooms and a pleasingly lengthy spa menu including Pevonia facials, men's treatments and an appealing range of body treatments and wraps. A large, very modern gym with Techno-gym equipment, polished floors, more lovely views and a good ambience, and a state-of-the-art golf simulator area.

We settled on an expert Peak manicure and Environ Prescriptive facial. We were intrigued by the algae mask, which solidifies and peels off in an exact replica of your face.

We loved

The top quality. The professional, highly qualified therapists. The surroundings.

We didn't love

The lack of a relaxation room – the Club Room is great, but hardly spa-hushed. The massage rooms are reached through the gym, and the pool, Jacuzzi and sauna are seven floors down, which makes the spa experience a little disjointed (lots of glass doors and entry buzzers).

Food file

We had a tasty, nutritious buffet lunch in the Club Room, gazing at panoramic views of London. Other options are the tranquil Chinoiserie, the traditional Rib Room and the Champagne Lounge.

Who would like it

Hotel residents and moneyed Sloane Street visitors (some of the spa treatments are pretty expensive, but they're definitely worth every penny). Anyone looking for an upmarket urban health club/spa retreat with all the trimmings in central London.

Don't miss

The glorious views across the city.

Spa type
Hotel spa

Where?
Peak Health Club and Spa at Jumeirah Carlton Tower
Cadogan Place
Knightsbridge
London SW1X 9PY
020 7235 1234

Signature treatment
'Tangle me up' Voya facial and massage

Brands
Environ, Pevonia, Voya

Expect to pay
Treatments:
£80 for 60 minutes
Stay: from £200 per night in a superior room

Bubble rating
4 out of 5 bubbles

Pennyhill Park

Bagshot, Surrey

Pennyhill Park Hotel is a 19th-century, ivy-clad mansion with landscaped gardens and lily-ponds. The spa facilities are fantastic, the treatments tremendous and the customer service spot-on. There's 45,000 square feet of spa to explore. That's why they give you a map.

What's on offer

The thermal suite is huge: 11 rooms of varying temperatures, humidity and scents. Pennyhill has not one, not two, but eight pools. There's a Jacuzzi, hot tubs in the garden, and a large, well-equipped gym with windows overlooking the lawns. A sprung-floor studio next to the gym offers classes – and there's a good range of these, including aqua-Pilates, several forms of yoga, and body conditioning.

They have 21 therapy rooms, so there's unlikely to be a crush. Li'Tya treatments and rituals incorporate Aboriginal massage techniques. Outside the spa, there's a nine-hole golf-course, tennis court, jogging trail and croquet. You can also indulge in archery and clay-pigeon shooting.

We loved

The feeling of space; even if you're staying at the hotel, there's an extra charge for use of the spa. This policy keeps the spa exclusive. It is never crowded and you can always make the most of what's on offer, unwinding in your own time and at your own pace.

We didn't love

Nothing. You won't want to leave.

Food file

Café Themis has a casual atmosphere; people lounge around in their bathrobes tucking into salads, smoothies and home-made soup. And chocolate cake. This spa has a definite self-indulgent side.

At The Latymer, the food is excellent, and the focus is on seasonal produce from around Surrey. There are rich touches to the dishes, such as foie gras.

Who would like it

Anyone who wants to feel completely relaxed and never bored. There are enough facilities on offer to get blissed out and stay blissed out.

Don't miss

The ozone-treated ballroom pool, a 25-metre pool large enough for some serious swimming. If you like to swim on your back, you'll charmed by the underwater music.

Spa type

Hotel spa

Where?

Pennyhill Park Hotel & The Spa, London Road, Bagshot, Surrey GU19 5EU
01276 471774

Signature treatment

'The Dreaming' using Li'Tya products: foot soak, body polish, mud wrap, exfoliation, body massage, scalp massage, mirri facial

Brands

Li'Tya, Terraké, The Spa

Expect to pay

Treatments:
£90 for 60 minutes
Stay: from £175 per night in a Traditional Guestroom

Bubble rating

5 out of 5 bubbles

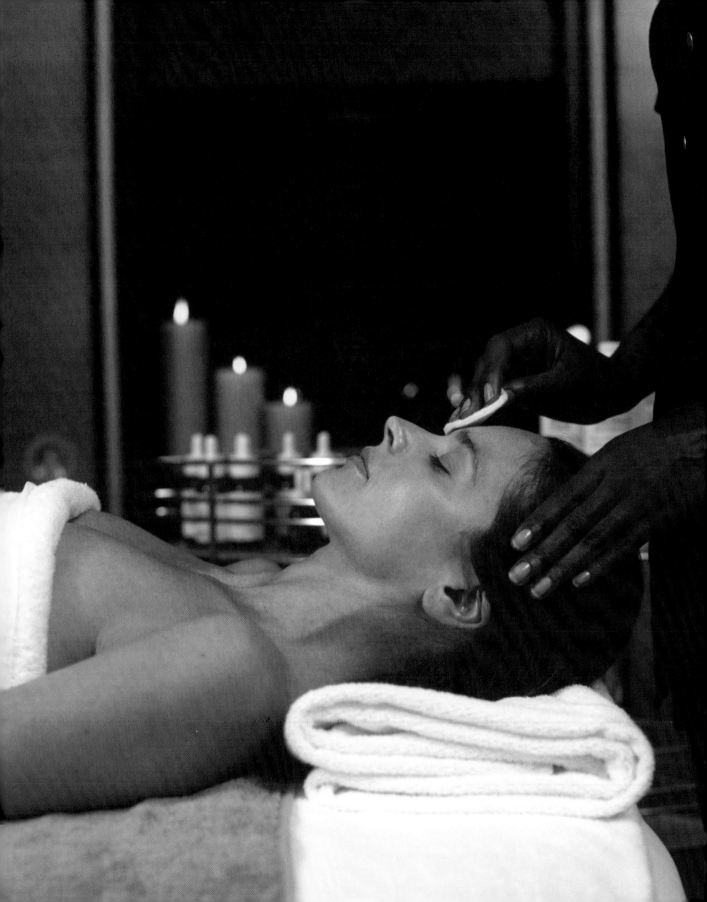

Petit Spa

Malmaison Hotel, Birmingham

Malmaison's red and black theme is appropriate for a building that was once Birmingham's main post office. These days, the Mailbox is an upmarket shopping centre, complete with Harvey Nicks and the Malmaison hotel. Petit Spa is a dinky delight of a city spa offering great Elemis treatments.

What's on offer

There's no swimming pool, but you can enjoy a large whirlpool bath, a sauna, a steam room, a couple of circular showers and a small gym. The lighting is subdued and the finishes all good quality and very clean: black slate tiles around the whirlpool bath, wooden flooring throughout.

Elemis facials, massages and body rituals, plus Elemis manicures and pedicures, treatments for men, and the usual spa beauty treatments. You can choose from a small range of holistic therapies. The Exotic Thai day includes a Lime and Ginger body exfoliation, hot stone massage and facial.

We loved

Our Elemis anti-ageing facial; the 'tri-enzymes' in the Elemis range make such a difference to your skin.

We also loved, as always, the abundance of clean fluffy towels.

We didn't love

The lack of body lotion or moisturiser in the changing area; most spas have *some*.

The spa gets so booked up. We've stayed at Malmaison a couple of times before on business and never managed to use the spa. You need to book a good three weeks in advance for weekends.

Food file

The Brasserie serves a seasonal menu of modern European food, with lighter salads and a grill as well, plus a separate 'homegrown and local' menu.

Who would like it

Malmaison is the ideal destination for anyone who wants to combine shopping, spa-ing and a good night out. The bar area is buzzy and lively. The hotel is great for couples and for friends who want a fun weekend away.

Don't miss

The huge leather reclining seats in the relaxation area. They have a massage setting if you need any more after your treatment. With only five chairs, you might have to wait for a turn, which is a bit of a shame as they are so good.

Spa type
Hotel spa

Where?
Malmaison Hotel
1 Wharfside Street
Birmingham
West Midlands B1 1RD
0121 246 5008

Signature treatment
Elemis exotic coconut rub and milk ritual wrap

Brands
Elemis

Expect to pay
Treatments:
£60 for 60 minutes
Stay: from £160 per night in a standard room

Bubble rating
5 out of 5 bubbles

Portland Hall Spa

Southport, Lancashire

A Moroccan-themed spa in what was once a synagogue with original stained glass windows that give this spa a rococo air. A very particular offering, which won't suit everybody. There are few frills here, but if you like unique professional treatments and lounging about on sofas, you'll love Portland Hall.

Spa type
Day spa

Where?
Portland Hall Spa
17a Portland Street
Southport
Lancashire PR8 1LR
01704 537733

Signature treatment
Spa ritual for two special

Brands
Elemis

Expect to pay
Treatments:
£55 for 60 minutes

Bubble rating
5 out of 5 bubbles

What's on offer

A friendly welcome in an imposing building. A small, very basic changing room, no gym, swimming pool or steam room, just a very private experience. A small, candle-lit spa pool with five tall, narrow windows, a small wooden sauna and brightly coloured rasul. You don't share the spa pool with anyone, so your experience here is time-tabled.

This is mainly an Elemis day spa, with plenty of facials and massages in warmly decorated treatment rooms. Also on offer: Kimia treatments, Universal Contour Wrap inch-loss programme, the Spa Jet, which uses infra-red heat and

water massage to reduce cellulite or ease stress. Reiki, reflexology, hand and foot treatments, tanning, waxing and tints. You can also have your hair washed and dried after your treatments (book this in advance).

We loved

Our fantastic Kimia facial; this treatment incorporates a relaxing back massage.

We didn't love

The wooden floors. The traffic past your treatment room can be noisily distracting.

Food file

Our buffet lunch of carrot and coriander soup, salmon and chicken was freshly prepared on the premises.

Who would like it

Anyone looking for a little peace, privacy and proper me-time. People who fancy no-frills spa-ing.

Don't miss

The small art gallery downstairs, exhibiting originals by local artists.

Radisson Edwardian

New Providence Wharf (East River Spa), Canary Wharf, London

This newish hotel perched on the edge of the River Thames, has a shiny, delightfully fragrant spa that is a wonderful haven in the hectic world of Canary Wharf. High quality therapists offer terrific treatments. A trip here will brighten the dullest of days.

What's on offer

The spa (the only spa in Canary Wharf) and gym are reached by an impressive bridge – you know you've arrived when you get to a Buddha and a divine fragrance. Well-stocked, atmospheric changing rooms. Stone oven sauna, ice fountain and experience showers, and twinkling crystal steam room with pleasing, gargantuan quartz crystal. Swanky new Technogym. There is no pool.

Treatments on offer include Pevonia, Algotherm, and Kimia products, skin analysis and a good range of facials. Crystal Clear microdermabrasion, oxygen therapy, CACI treatments, eye treatments, Botox and Restylane. A small range of massages. Try the Cleopatra Bathing Experience, with an 'indulgent selection of exotic, mineralising muds and natural salts' in a private steam room.

We loved

The East River Signature facial, fantastic from start to finish. Our therapist used spa-exclusive Pevonia products, gave us a thorough skin consultation and included a head and neck massage. It left us feeling fabulous, relaxed and rejuvenated.

We didn't love

There is access to a pool next door but you have to get dressed, go outside, cross the road to the pool, then undress again. It also costs money. Nah.

Food file

Lunch in the smart Azura Restaurant, with views over the Thames. We had scallops with baby fennel, and walnut-crusted cod.

Who would like it

Anyone working and living in Canary Wharf.

Don't miss

Chilling out on a warmed marble lounger in the stylish, dimly lit relaxation room.

Spa type
Hotel spa

Where?
Radisson Edwardian
New Providence Wharf
(East River Spa)
5 Fairmont Avenue
London E14 9PQ
020 8820 8123

Signature treatment
East River Spa
Signature Facial

Brands
Algotherm, CACI, Crystal Clear, Kimia, Dr Murad, Pevonia

Expect to pay
Treatments:
£65 for 60 minutes
Stay: from £140 per night in a standard double room

Bubble rating
4 out of 5 bubbles

Ragdale Hall Health Hydro

Melton Mowbray, Leicestershire

The original and still the best dedicated spa retreat, Ragdale Hall is a large, comfortable country house set in attractive gardens and grounds. Ragdale is the John Lewis of spas: good quality, well priced and delivered by people who really know their stuff.

What's on offer

This is a pure spa retreat where the whole point of going is to wander around in your robe all day.

With about 50 treatment rooms and 120 therapists, you can have almost any treatment you have ever heard of. There's a thermal spa, outdoor pool, and gym. Health and fitness classes include yoga, tai chi and dance fitness. Enjoy tennis, volleyball, cycling and boules, talks, demonstrations and workshops.

The new Mind Gym room is fun: puzzles, games, books, brainteasers of one sort or another all gathered together in one room.

We loved

The way the staff park your car for you; they take your luggage to your room and whisk you off to the conservatory for a tea while they check you in. No matter how many times we come here, we're always impressed by the smooth running check-in system.

We didn't love

The dining room décor – it's looking a bit dated.

Food file

There's a three-course buffet lunch, and a three-course dinner for residential guests. Tea and cake in the Verandah Bar. Plenty of healthy options.

Who would like it

Anyone who wants to unwind, relax and enjoy some good treatments. It's not for you if you want to stay up late: most people are off to bed by 10pm.

Anyone who likes to try a range of therapies and treatments; you have a lot to choose from here.

It's not trendy and it's not posh. Fab – you don't have to suck your stomach in when you sit by the pool.

Don't miss

The new thermal spa area; the hot and cold, wet and dry rooms, all offer something different. Fun to use and very popular. So enjoyable, we would have stayed an extra day.

The Decléor anti-ageing face and body treatment is heavenly: two and half hours of bliss.

Spa type

Spa retreat

Where?

Ragdale Hall
Melton Mowbray
Leicestershire LE14 3PB
01664 434831

Signature treatment

NEOM Top to Toe Organic Indulgence

Brands

Clarins, Decléor, Elemis, Li'Tya, Neom, Spa Find

Expect to pay

Treatments:
£51 for 50 minutes

Stay: from £266 for two nights in an economy room for a two-night taster break (includes a 50 minute treatment)

Bubble rating

5 out of 5 bubbles

Good Spa Spy Favourites

Suave Spy

Age 20s **Skin type** Very sensitive **Spa likes** None as I'm still a Spy trainee and they haven't let me out in the world on my own yet! Never mind, I got to stay in the office and review all of the male spa products that arrived this year…

Favourite products

Dermalogica: Daily Clean Scrub

Part of Dermalogica's shave range, their daily clean scrub contains micro-fine silica beads and willow-bark extract to help clear pores and minimize ingrown hairs. I have frustratingly sensitive skin that makes shaving a chore. This scrub prepared me for the best shave I've ever had, leaving me with absolutely none of my usual neck rash. For once, I started the day without looking like I'd jumped through a glass window instead of into the shower.

After scrubbing and shaving for a fortnight with this scrub, I was impressed. Although be warned: if you have sensitive skin, it can irritate a little if you use it too aggressively.

Dermalogica: Daily Defense Block

This block is designed to defend against skin ageing UV rays as well as defeat dryness. I'm still being asked for ID in my mid-twenties so I wasn't expecting or needing a block to slow the ravages of time. However, I get through a lot of moisturiser so I was curious to see what effect I would get.

My face felt like I had a weightless yet protective shield across it for the day, and dare I say it, I looked almost radiant. Actually, let's use a more manly description. I looked 'forcefully incandescent' or 'aggressively resplendent'. Either way, my skin looked and felt good in a masculine way. Use this block, and you'll be ready for another day making fire and hunting wild beasts. Or walking confidently into the office. Your choice.

Willow Organic Men's Moisturising Aftershave Balm

As shaving is a practice carried out first thing in the morning when I'm barely awake, an after-shave product which is easy to find, grip, and use without engaging one's brain too much is always welcome. The square and sturdy Willow bottle proved a winner on that front, with a pump top that can both take a bleary thump and dispense a perfect amount.

When first applied, the balm gave a refreshingly cold tingle, which died down slowly to a pleasant waking glow. The fragrance was just right, long lasting but not overpowering.

Willow Organic Men's Black rice soap

It looked as attractive as it sounds: a grey bar with a very subtle 'garagey' smell. In actual use, however, the soap

came into its own. The bar fitted well into my palm, and made a smooth lather without being too oily or slippery. The orange fragrance emerged with the lather.

The soap felt so good that it made heavily perfumed and coloured products seem even less attractive. In short, I will happily continue to use this effective soap. I have also discovered an interest in soap ingredients which was previously dormant.

The Refinery

Mayfair, London

The Refinery is located opposite Claridges; it doesn't get more old-school posh than this. The entrance to the treatment rooms is suitably discreet, and the opening hours and location are designed to accommodate busy London gentlemen so they can pop in after work or during a lunch break.

What's on offer

All the treatments you would expect from a traditional gentleman's barber, such as wet shaves, haircuts, waxing, and manly manicures and pedicures, plus some more unusual ones, such as scrubs, wraps, threading, and eyelash and brow tinting. There is a range of male-specific facials on offer, including microdermabrasion, and also several varieties of massage; exclusive to The Refinery is their own rebalancing hot stone body treatment.

We loved

The new Refinery well-being treatment – a holistic face and body treatment with a circular trip around the body, extending our muscles; a deeply relaxing foot massage with abrasive gloves and aroma oils; manipulation of pressure points: overall, a nice sense of weightlessness and surrender, like being on a very gentle fairground ride. Wonderfully therapeutic.

We didn't love

We were tempted to hit the shops immediately afterwards; after all, a fresh and glowing complexion needs some (expensive) new clothes to match.

Food file

You don't go here for the food.

Who would like it

Any man who has ever enjoyed a good shave, or scrubbed up before they went out, would enjoy a few hours of grown-up grooming here.

Don't miss

The traditional wet shave featuring aromatic hot towels.

Spa type

Treatment rooms

Where?

The Refinery
60 Brook Street
Mayfair
London W1K 5DU
020 7409 2001

Signature treatment

The Refinery Signature Face and Body treatment: back cleanse, exfoliation and massage, scalp massage and facial

Brands

Aromatherapy Associates, Dermalogica, Kyoku for Men, Refinery

Expect to pay

Treatments:
£80 for 60 minutes

Bubble rating

4 out of 5 bubbles

The Ritual Rooms

Marylebone, London

As far as we know, The Ritual Rooms are London's only private hair and beauty rooms. Situated in a quiet, exclusive area minutes away from the hustle and bustle of Oxford Street, you can have your hairdo and spa too, without leaving the room.

What's on offer

Book time for your spa treatments and have your hair attended to at the same time, in the same private space. You book for the minutes you spend rather than the specifics of your treatment, allowing you flexibility and avoiding hidden extras.

A whole range of face and body rituals, including made-to-measure facials, detoxifying or hydrating wraps and cellulite treatments. The Ritual Rooms also offer treaments for mums-to-be, and there's a full range of hair cut-and-colour services.

We loved

The Ritual Rooms' contemporary boudoir style, and the comfortable relaxation area, with two brown leather recliners and a good stash of magazines.

One of the most comfortable massage beds we'd ever experienced, with linen covers and a gorgeous dark brown, faux-fur throw.

Combining our anti-stress back therapy with a cut and blow dry using Keratase

and Bumble and bumble products; we felt fantastic every day for a week because our hair looked great, and somehow the back therapy felt more beneficial because of our overall lasting sense of satisfaction!

We didn't love

Nothing; it felt great to be there.

Food file

Water was presented on an oriental tray with a lily and some miniature chocolate treats. Try blackcurrant sorbet after your treatments. Lunch or afternoon tea can be ordered from a nearby Italian deli if you're staying for a half or full day package.

Who would like it

Anyone working nearby who wants to make the most of their precious me-time. Anyone who is fed up with having their hair done in a noisy, very public salon.

Don't miss

The massage room that transforms into your own private hair salon.

Spa type
Treatment rooms

Where?
The Ritual Rooms
13 New Quebec Street
Portman Village
London W1H 7RR
0207 724 3884

Signature treatment
Signature facial ritual

Brands
Aromatherapy Associates
Skinceuticals

Expect to pay
Treatments:
£75 for 60 minutes

Bubble rating
5 out of 5 bubbles

Rookery Hall Hotel

Nantwich, Cheshire

Rookery Hall is an attractive country house in landscaped grounds with a stud farm next door. How much more county set can you get? The hotel is a romantic destination offering comfortable rooms, very good food, and a light, airy, delightfully spacious spa.

What's on offer

The spa at Rookery Hall is in a separate building that was once the stables. A large, glass-roofed pool occupies what was the central courtyard, with the treatment rooms around the sides. Everywhere is light and airy. There's a gym and huge hydrotherapy pool, sauna and crystal steam room, too.

When it comes to treatments, you can enjoy a good range of ESPA and Clarins facials, massages and wraps; a rasul mud treatment; an interesting Hopi ear candle and express facial combination. Our massage and facial were exceptional.

We loved

The relaxation room with soft, subdued lighting, eight comfy beds and a water wall, lit from the top. The sound of running water lulls you into a deep daydream.

The serenity of the spa; there were plenty of other people around on our visit, but we hardly noticed them. We always found space in the lounge and relaxation room.

The Spa Hostess who greets you, checks your consultation forms, makes sure you have everything you want, knows where you need to go, and brings you drinks.

We also loved the 38 acres of parkland to walk in; take time for a long country stroll before dinner to work up an appetite.

We didn't love

As the spa is in what was the stable block, you have to walk across the courtyard to get to it. If you set out at 6.30am to swim, you'll need a hat, coat and gloves to brave the frosty air. Go prepared.

Food file

A spa brasserie serving healthy snacks and main meals, plus teas, coffees, alcoholic drinks and smoothies. There is formal dining in the hotel.

Who would like it

You'll want everyone you love (and even those you just like) to try this spa.

Don't miss

The heated towel rails in the treatment rooms, so your robe is nice and warm after your rendezvous with relaxation.

Spa type

Hotel spa

Where?

Rookery Hall
Main Road
Worleston, Nantwich
Cheshire CW5 6DQ
01270 610016

Signature treatment

Hand Picked spa experience: exfoliation, skin brushing, hot stone massage, facial

Brands

Clarins, ESPA

Expect to pay

Stay: from £140 bed and breakfast in a Classic double room

Bubble rating

5 out of 5 bubbles

Royal Crescent Hotel

(The Bath House), Bath, Somerset

A serene, natural-feeling spa attached to a beautiful period hotel in Bath's most exclusive Georgian crescent. The key ingredients here are tranquillity and quiet. Your soul will be soothed and your skin will be smoothed, in The Bath House.

What's on offer

This is a very unusual spa, set in a stone coach-house building with huge arched windows that let in the light. Bath stone, wood and bamboo are all used effectively to create a spa that feels part Roman bath house, and part monastic retreat.

Almost half of the building is taken up with a 12-metre pool, heated to body temperature. There are hot and cold wooden plunge tubs, a sauna, and a steam room.

Treatments include a Tranquillity massage and a Sagami algae body wrap. The Earth and Stone Treatment uses nutrient-rich mud to stimulate a sluggish lymphatic system. There's a good range of complementary therapies, including Watsu, lymphatic drainage, and reflexology.

We loved

One of the best massages we'd ever had (take it from a confirmed massage junkie); the fabulous views across the city of Bath.

We didn't love

The bitter coffee served at breakfast. Even asking for a second pot didn't help.

Food file

Interesting modern English cooking: plenty of choice on the menu, and all the dishes were carefully balanced and with interesting additions.

Who would like it

Anyone who wants to feel special. Anyone who wants to step back in time into a Jane Austen novel. Anyone who wants a really romantic place to stay.

This is an unusual spa. If you come expecting glitz and glamour, you will be disappointed. But if you come looking for a place to rest and unwind, to find some tranquillity and to recharge, you will be happy.

Don't miss

The divine strawberry and neroli sea salt scrub.

The food – it's exceptionally good. Try crab tortellini served with cauliflower purée. It's made with two pastas so the twisted tortellini is black and white.

Spa type
Hotel spa

Where?
Royal Crescent Hotel
16 Royal Crescent
Bath
Somerset BA1 2LS
01225 823333

Signature treatment
The Bath House Treatment: bathing, exfoliation and massage

Brands
[comfort zone]
Numbers

Expect to pay
Treatments:
£60 for 60 minutes
Stay: from £215 for bed and breakfast in a Classic double room

Bubble rating
5 out of 5 bubbles

Royal Day Spa

Tunbridge Wells, Kent

Feel like a queen in Tunbridge Wells at this subterranean royal cocoon of a spa. Excellent therapists, imaginative, unique and dreamy treatments and facilities – and one of our very favourite swimming pools.

What's on offer

Their glass-doored and fabulous pool-room is minimal in style, and partially lit by lanterns; here you'll find the jewel in Royal's crown: a large, dark-tiled 18-metre salt-water swimming pool. There's a spacious and well-equipped gym. Personal trainers are always available to talk you through the use of the equipment and answer any questions.

There's a mineral-infused Moor Mud Jacuzzi that's big enough for six, a marble-benched rose quartz steam room, and yoga and Pilates classes.

Glorious 'royal' themed treatments include the Dirty Royal facial for problem skin, an Overdone The Polo massage, or The Emperor's New Clothes exfoliation.

We loved

The 'bedroom': a relaxation room with a real difference. Lounge on a wall-to-wall bed with a mattress that moulds to your body, and piles of deep cushions, opposite a large wooden table laden with books and hip magazines. Snuggle up under a blanket and relax with a peppermint tea and *Dazed and Confused*.

The light and bright Ballroom studio with antique French doors and mirrors, and tall windows.

We didn't love

Not living in Tunbridge Wells. We'd love to be a member.

Food file

Lunch or tea is taken in the glamorous Ballroom. Choose from a selection of picnic hampers or delicious afternoon teas designed exclusively for Royal Day Spa by celebrity chef Richard Phillips. Probably some of the best spa food we've ever tasted – and plenty of it, too.

Who would like it

People who are into clean, organic products. Treat yourself and a friend, or just go on your own, when you need a genuine hideaway.

Don't miss

The impossibly glamorous salt water swimming pool. We've been to Royal three times, and each time we just couldn't get enough of the pool.

Spa type
Day spa

Where?
Royal Day Spa
12 Vale Road
Post Office Square
Tunbridge Wells
Kent TN1 1BP
01892 616191

Signature treatments
Smelly Royal Body: aromatherapy massage and ko bi do facial

Brands
Aromatherapy Associates, Mama Mio, HRH (Herbals for Her, Royal Day Spa's own range), REN

Expect to pay
Treatments:
£66 for 60 minutes

Bubble rating
5 out of 5 bubbles

the runnymede-on-thames

Egham, Surrey

Not one, but two delightful spas, nestling in a modern hotel which looks onto the River Thames. Runnymede's tip-top main spa has everything you need for a perfect spa day. Aquitaine, their private spa, offers secluded and fun spa treats for up to eight people.

What's on offer

A large and light 18-metre main pool with a good-sized steam room and sauna adjacent, a children's pool, outdoor pool, and a Jacuzzi; a gym; and a studio with a wide range of classes – Bhangra, anyone? For treatment treats, you can try a Guinot hydradermie facial or holistic aromatherapy massage, pre-natal pampering, and complementary therapies such as osteopathy. There's a very good range of teen treatments for spa-goers aged from 13–17, too.

We loved

The quiet relaxation room in which spa guests can chill; there is a separate lounge in which health-club members can compare their work-out routines.

The wonderful ESPA hot stones facial: the warm stones are just the right temperature and are placed at key points on your body to help the facial be more effective. It feels like lying on a pebbly beach when the sun is shining and the pebbles are hot.

The Aquitaine group day-spa suite: it's luxurious, fun and very well organised and designed; very popular, too.

Plenty of fluffy towels – one of our absolute 'musts' for a good spa.

We didn't love

The long flight of stairs down to Aquitaine; these would defeat anyone with mobility problems.

Food file

Salads, sandwiches, jacket potatoes, and more indulgent treats such as cakes and pastries in The Garden Room.

Who would like it

Friends who want to spend a day being cosseted and catching up; anyone wanting to celebrate a special birthday in style; work groups who want to do some team bonding; mothers and daughters, sisters, best friends.

Don't miss

Hiring Aquitaine for the day; enjoy music, gossip, treatments in the dual treatment room, and plenty of food and drinks. You can also go upstairs and use the pools and other facilities, or take a walk along the riverbank.

Spa type
Hotel spa

Where?
the runnymede-on-thames
Windsor Road
Egham
Surrey TW20 0AG
01784 220973

Signature treatment
Aromatherapy full body massage and facial with hot stones

Brands
Clarins, ESPA, Guinot

Expect to pay
Treatments:
£55 for 55 minutes
Stay: from £195 for bed and breakfast in a standard double room

Bubble rating
5 out of 5 bubbles

The Sanctuary Spa

Covent Garden, London

This well-loved, women-only London spa is a bit of a labyrinth – The Sanctuary is huge and spread out over five floors – but worth the money (except for the sandwiches). The range of pools, facilities and treatments on offer is pretty special for a day spa in central London.

Spa type

Day spa

Where?

The Sanctuary
12 Floral Street
Covent Garden
London WC2E 9DH
01442 430 330

Signature treatment

Mela Holistic Experience

Brands

Aromatherapy Associates
La Sultane de Saba
Sanctuary

Expect to pay

Treatments:
£65 for 50 minutes

Bubble rating

4 out of 5 bubbles

What's on offer

A ravishing range of fun and frolics.

There are two pools: the atrium pool is quite shallow and has the famous swing; the more serious exercise pool is in the basement. There's also a hammam, sauna and sanarium, and two relaxation lounges, plus a Sleep Retreat where the bed gently vibrates.

There's a huge range of treatments on offer. A Skin Spa also offers micro-dermabrasion and glycolic peels.

We loved

The pretty boudoir-style mirror-lined dressing room. The lovely hot hammam complete with a ceiling of fairy lights. The warm, dimly lit, fragrant treatment room. Our Mela treatment, which was expertly executed and nothing short of divine. Everywhere is comfy, warm, clean and appealing. This is a good-value spa.

We didn't love

The fact that we forgot our flip-flops and the only choice was to go barefoot or buy some from the spa shop. It is a busy spa, so be prepared for that.

Food file

Pan-fried sea bream on shredded cabbage and pancetta, plus rocket and parmesan shavings with balsamic vinegar. Yum. Rather pricey sandwiches.

Who would like it

If you've not been to a spa before, The Sanctuary is an excellent place to start. It's also a fun place to go with friends.

Don't miss

The evening combination packages; a facial and manicure in just 25 minutes!

Sanook Spa

Courthouse Hotel, Soho, London

'Sanook' means 'Enjoy yourself' in Thai. The tiny bijou spa in the basement of this central-London hotel gives you a rare private space in the heart of the capital where you can enjoy yourself with ease.

What's on offer

The Thai theme lends Oriental tranquillity to this bijou spa, and the dim lighting and hushed atmosphere is a delightful contrast to the busy Soho streets above.

There's a small, warm, dimly lit pool; a pocket-sized bright, light sauna; a compact exercise room; and a glass relaxation room over the swimming pool. There's also a wide and imaginative range of treatments for such a small spa. When you book time at Sanook, you book the whole spa, so you get a sense of luxury and privacy: this is all for you!

We loved

The fact that you have the spa to yourself is absolutely gorgeous. Sitting in the glass room over the swimming pool was relaxing and certainly very different. The reflection of light off the water gives the room a very peaceful ambience.

We didn't love

Small can be good, but Sanook is so small you bump into things.

Food file

Fruit, water and teas in the spa.

Who would like it

Anyone who needs to stay in central London and build some downtime into the busy-ness.

Don't miss

Call in advance to book a treatment and time in the spa. Even use of the swimming pool is booked by appointment.

Spa type

Hotel spa

Where?

Courthouse Hotel
DoubleTree by Hilton
19–21 Great Marlborough Street
London W1F 7HL
020 7297 5555

Signature treatment

Hot stone massage

Brands

Dermalogica

Expect to pay

Treatments:
From £60 for 60 minutess
Stay: from £199 per night in a standard double room

Bubble rating

4 out of 5 bubbles

Good Spa Spy Favourites

Swedish Spy

Age 40s **Skin type** Combination/normal skin **Spa likes** Deep, slow touch, warmth; great treatments and flawless bedside manner – goes without saying; being greeted well and seen off in style **Spa dislikes** Being slightly chilly; failure to attend to the proper theatrics of a spa experience – I want to be in a bubble of bliss and have no interest in being reminded about the outside world in any sense whatsoever

Best spa experiences this year

A toe-curlingly good scalp massage that was delivered with genuine care, exquisite sensuality and absolutely no hurry.

Worst spa experiences this year

Being left to see myself out via dull, brown, cramped and confusing corridors after a most cursory end to an otherwise fair treatment.

Favourite products

Aveda Green Science Firming Face Cream

A gorgeous face cream that gives my skin the nourishment it needs whatever the season. This is not due to heaviness; the cream absorbs beautifully and leaves no oil-slick on your skin. The cream has a fresh, slightly herbal fragrance that I have grown to like. Best of all, I can literally feel this product working!

Eve Lom Rescue Mask

A great product with a deservedly great reputation – no news to old spa hands. This mask feels and smells like it means business in a firm, yet subtle way. Wonderfully toning. Purifying. Yep, this product does what it says on the tin.

MAC Fluidline gel eyeliner

This product is magic. A little glass pot with thick gel eyeliner to apply with a brush (I prefer a small angle brush as it gives great control over line width.) You can use it to make 50s-style sharp eyes, or softly smudged. It is easy to get right. Slight mistakes are easily corrected. It stays put. It comes off easily with normal eye make-up remover. It comes in six colours. What's not to like?

Neals Yard Nourishing Orange Flower Daily Moisture

A light lotion that I have become strangely addicted to over the past few months. It feels fresh to apply in the morning and moisturises the skin surprisingly well, while smelling divine (provided you like Neroli).

Aromatherapy Associates Enrich Massage & Body Oil

This oil is well presented in a tall, frosted-glass bottle with a smart dispensing top.

Gorgeous, warm fragrance. Lovely texture. I have greedily used it all over myself, including my face. Yum, yum.

Savana urban spa

Westbourne Grove, London

A white and airy Temple of Calm in the middle of noisy London town. Savana urban spa's speciality is its mix of complementary therapies and massage with beauty treatments and indulgence. Imaginative options for group spa days, too.

What's on offer

A very wide range of treatments, indulging both inner and outer beauty. Massages include ayurvedic, hydrotherm, Thai, seated, manual lymphatic drainage. There's baby massage and couples' massage workshops as well. You're spoilt for choice when it comes to manicures and pedicures.

Choose from 15 complementary health therapies including homeopathy, hypnotherapy and Bach flower remedies. The spa also offers yoga, private meditation and personal training.

We loved

Savana's mix of complementary therapies and indulgent beauty treatments; there aren't many spas where you can combine reiki with a Hollywood.

The wonderful massage combining Thai, shiatsu and deep-tissue massage techniques. The added extras, including a mineral mud masque for your spine.

It's great to hang out in London treatment rooms that are flooded with natural light, rather than lurking in a dimly-lit basement.

We didn't love

There's only one really dinky toilet and two changing rooms.

Food file

Large jugs of fresh lemon water. Fruit juices. Bowls of apples.

Who would like it

Anyone looking for beauty treatments with a well-being twist.

Don't miss

Savana's Happy Lunch Hours: the spa equivalent of a Formula One pit stop.

Spa type
Treatment rooms

Where?
Savana urban spa
45 Hereford Road
Westbourne Grove
London W2 5AH
020 7229 8300

Signature treatment
Sea breeze body wrap: full body massage, seaweed wrap and mini-facial

Brands
Crabtree & Evelyn, Eminence Organic, Green People Organic, REN, Savana

Expect to pay
Treatments:
£75 for 55 minutes

Bubble rating
4 out of 5 bubbles

The Scarlet

Mawgan Porth, Cornwall

Their only desire is to make you happy at this stylish, adult-only holistic spa in a new eco hotel 10 minutes from Newquay, built on a stunning cliff-top location, with every window facing seawards.

What's on offer

No mobile phones (they won't work here!). Deliciously hot eucalyptus-infused steam room, 13-metre pool, hanging relaxation pods, wet treatment room, hammam and rasul. Six changing rooms, each with monsoon shower and ayurvedic tri-dosha products, and a large relaxation room. The outdoor freshwater pool, glistens pure and clear in the sunlight, the heated cliff-top baths look across the bay and there are two luxuriously tented treatment rooms.

The ethos here is that an hour's treatment is not enough to experience restoration, so there are seven three- or four-hour spa 'journeys' (from restoring to uplifting) and 'beyond journeys' that include facials, hammam and rasul treatments.

A genuinely happy place, with jovial staff – you can even take the dog for walks.

We loved

The commitment to being eco without compromising on luxury.

Every second of our Bespoke Journey, from the consultation with our bubbly therapist to the seaweed bath, guided chakra meditation and energising ayurvedic massage. We emerged calm, awake and chilled. Happy, too, as we lay in a state of contented bliss in the relaxation room, watching the sun set.

We didn't love

Having to leave.

Food file

Michelin-starred chef Ben Tunnicliffe's food is fresh, tender and tasty. We had delicious lemon sole and seared scallops, then monkfish, mussels, bacon and avocado; also on the menu were bouillabaisse fish stew, confit of rabbit, and breast of Cornish duck with shallot puree. Vegetarian options are available.

Who would like it

Anyone interested in eco tourism, contemporary design, light and space; foodies; people with money; those looking for something different. The spa and restaurant are open to non-residents, too.

Don't miss

The outdoor heated hot tubs and the hanging relaxation pods.

Spa type
Hotel spa

Where?
Scarlet Spa
Scarlet Hotel
Tredragon Road
Mawgan Porth
Cornwall TR8 4DQ
01637 861861

Signature treatment
A bespoke 'spa journey'

Brands
Tri-Dosha
Voya

Expect to pay
Treatments:
£175 for 4 hours
Stay: from £180 per night
in a just right room

Bubble rating
5 out of 5 bubbles

Scin

Notting Hill, London

A Notting Hill boutique spa with an über-modern, pure white interior, which mirrors the spa's approach: a no-nonsense menu of treatments using the latest ranges of clean, organic products.

Spa type
Treatment rooms

Where?
Scin
27 Kensington Park Road
Notting Hill
London W11 2EU
020 3220 0121

Signature treatment
Scin Spa De-Stress Facial

Brands
Dermalogica
Mama Mio
Suki
This Works

Expect to pay
Treatments:
£65 for 60 minutes

Bubble rating
4 out of 5 bubbles

What's on offer

Four treatment rooms and a hydrotherapy pool tucked into an alcove. A pristine white waiting room/nail bar. The treatment menu offers straightforward but effective treatments, cutting out fussy treatments such as wraps in favour of facials and body massages.

We loved

The effective full body massage, using organic essential oils. The natural product ranges on offer are interesting; some of the brands, such as Suki and Taer Icelandic, are not the usual names that you find in spas or beauty counters.

We didn't love

The limited space; Scin is more salon than spa. One treatment room has to have the massage bed placed diagonally for it to fit.

There's nowhere to put your clothes and accoutrements in the changing room, just a hanger on the back of the door.

Food file

Herbal tea. No lunch facilities but plenty of upmarket cafés nearby.

Who would like it

Anyone who wants to avoid chemical nasties. It's a great spa for busy city dwellers but, as it's so compact, this is really a place to drop in for that essential massage or pick-me-up facial rather than a full day of indulgence.

Don't miss

The organic massage; Scin have a specially designed couch for pregnant bumps so that mums-to-be don't have to miss out on this treat.

The Scotsman Spa & Health Club

The Scotsman Hotel, Edinburgh, Scotland

A health club and spa in an impressive hotel in the former home of The Scotsman newspaper. This historic hotel is a great place to go to combine an active health club day with a spa treat.

What's on offer

Open-plan spa reception with exposed pipes and big-screen TV, mezzanine with wicker tables. Dramatic, dimly lit 16-metre pool in stainless steel and slate. Tropicarium, Arctic shower, Tropical shower, small sauna, Jacuzzi and large steam room. Refreshing showers, which spray jets of water at every level of your body. Large, busy, well-equipped gym.

In the spa, a wide range of treatments, including facials, massages, wraps, manicures, pedicures, waxing, tanning, acupuncture and cupping.

We loved

The excellent massage using Thalgo products. We don't know if it really 'replicated the movements of the sea', but we certainly drifted off on waves of pleasure.

We didn't love

The health-club atmosphere dominates, and this means the spa suffers: the changing rooms are functional rather than luxurious, and the pool is a busy hotel pool, with generous children's swimming times.

Food file

In the spa: paninis, sandwiches and salads in the mezzanine. Dinner in the Scotsman's North Bridge Brasserie, once the newspaper's reception room, was fresh and delicious, with generous portions of asparagus starters and lamb mains.

Who would like it

Anyone looking for a health club with a treatment on top.

Don't miss

The massage chair, tucked behind a screen in the mezzanine.

Spa type
Hotel spa

Where?
The Scotsman Spa
The Scotsman Hotel
1 Market Street
Edinburgh EH1 1DF
0131 622 3800

Signature treatment
Writers Block facial

Brands
Mama Mio
Skinceuticals
Thalgo

Expect to pay
Treatments:
£60 for 60 minutes
Stay: from £180 per night
in a double room

Bubble rating
4 out of 5 bubbles

SenSpa

Careys Manor Hotel, Brockenhurst, Hampshire

Why fly to Thailand? Lose the spa miles and go to the New Forest instead. Thai-themed SenSpa has impressive hydrotherapy facilities and high-quality treatments, using their own natural and organic products.

What's on offer

A large, bright main pool, plus a very impressive hydrotherapy area, over two floors. A large hydrotherapy pool with several different areas, including submerged loungers with underwater jets, and there's a spacious and nicely hot sauna and steam room, an ice room and experience showers. Upstairs, a slightly less busy laconium and tepidarium.

A small but equipment-packed gym. Studio classes. Treatments using SenSpa's own organic range, made locally in the New Forest.

We loved

The lovely Kasui facial, using the SenSpa Organic Therapy range. The manuka honey mask has a gorgeous smell and feels very kind to your skin while doing it some antiseptic good.

The relaxation area, thoughtfully divided in two: the main area, which has soft seats and sofas; and a smaller, more serious relaxation area through a door, where you're asked to remain silent while people recover from their treatments on loungers.

We didn't love

There were times when we felt there were more people than facilities. We had to queue for a vacant shower, and the showers themselves are a bit basic.

The hydrotherapy areas are noisy rather than peaceful, and a bit bedecked with abandoned towels late in the day.

Food file

The Zen Garden restaurant in the spa provides perfect spa eating from breakfast to lunch to snacks. The two-AA-rosette Manor Restaurant is quite a formal experience for the evening, with organic food and some local produce. Blaireau's brasserie offers French cuisine.

Who would like it

Anyone who has neither the time nor the budget to actually go to Thailand.

Don't miss

The Thai massage – all the therapists are trained in Thai massage and many of the staff are from Thailand.

Spa type
Hotel spa

Where?
Careys Manor
Brockenhurst
Hampshire SO42 7RH
01590 624467

Signature treatment
Sen Fusion full body massage

Brands
Living Nature, SenSpa
Organic Therapy, Willow

Expect to pay
Treatments:
£72 for 60 minutes
Stay: from £99 per night in a standard room

Bubble rating
5 out of 5 bubbles

Sequoia Spa

The Grove, Watford, Hertfordshire

Appearance is paramount at this 'groovy grand' country house spa. It's ideal for a top-end golf and spa break. The plush velvet loungers and full range of ESPA treatments will send you to spa paradise.

What's on offer

A full range of ESPA treatments including an ayurvedic-influenced shirobhyanga; Indian Head massage; Purva Karma four-handed massage; holistic treatments; aqua aerobics; Pilates; and body pump classes.

There's a good-sized swimming pool, tiled in black mosaic, with a separate large Jacuzzi and showers at one end. Heat experience rooms include a crystal steam room, sauna with twinkly lights and a 'blitz therapy' shower.

The Grove is home to one of the top new golf courses in the UK. If golf's not your bag, there are good outdoor tennis courts, an outdoor pool and a croquet lawn.

We loved

Booking a two-hour 'Time' slot, to allow us to decide what treatment we were in the mood for on the day. A good option if you prefer to go with the flow.

The softly lit relaxation room, with plush, individually-controlled velvet loungers, and the modern but quirky décor of the hotel, with a clear perspex four-poster bed giving our room a sense of space and light.

The impressive children's facilities; The Grove has an Ofsted-rated nursery, and there's a dedicated children's pool.

We didn't love

The dark swimming pool does give the spa a rather cool feel. One of the other guests described the pool area as 'slightly intimidating' when we were there.

Food file

Choose from The Glasshouse restaurant with its buffet-style cuisine and lively atmosphere; The Stables, which has more of an up-market country pub feel; and 3-rosette Collette's for fine dining.

Who would like it

The golf course offers a rare opportunity for any level of golfer to experience a championship course on a pay-and-play basis; so, perfect for a top-end golf *and* spa break.

Don't miss

The 25-metre outdoor pool housed within the Grove's huge Walled Garden, complete with its own poolside bar.

Spa type
Hotel spa

Where?
The Grove
Chandler's Cross
Watford
Hertfordshire WD3 4TG
01923 294294

Signature treatment
The Sequoia Signature Massage

Brands
ESPA

Expect to pay
Treatments:
£90 for 55 minutes
Stay: from £225 per night in a standard double room

Bubble rating
5 out of 5 bubbles

Good Spa Spy Favourites

Sybaritic Spy

Age 50s **Skin type** Dry **Spa likes** Warm treatment beds; fragrant steam rooms; therapists who listen to what you say; unexpected treats such as back massages that start with hot towels on your feet **Spa dislikes** Small towels; crowded changing rooms; black mould in the showers; therapists who sniff; anyone who doesn't take my allergy to lavender seriously — until I'm actually sick on them!

Best spa experiences this year

The Carol Joy London facial at The Dorchester spa. My skin looked fantastic and I felt ten years younger without going under the knife. The glamour of The Dorchester spa helped. At the other extreme, a day at the Aqua Sana Spa at CenterParcs Sherwood Forest was a budget delight: wonderful facilities, great treatments, and lovely staff.

Worst spa experiences this year

Stepping into the water in a Japanese spa to find it was piping hot, and not being able to screech for fear of offending the locals who take their spa-ing very seriously

Favourite products

Spa SPC Decadent Rose toner

This is a light spritzer toner. You just spray it on the skin after cleansing and before moisturising. The smell is fantastic: roses lightened by the addition of aloe vera. I find many toners harsh, but the SPC toner is gentle and feels good on my dry and slightly sensitive skin. Makes a good body spray in the summer when the temperature is too hot for perfume.

Germaine de Capuccini Exfoliating Scrub

This scrub is a smooth white cream with very well defined granules; it doesn't leave my skin feeling sore or tight as many scrubs do. It worked wonders on the areas of congestion on my chin and on the blocked milia on my forehead. I loved the menthol smell and the way it left my skin looking much brighter.

Waterfall 24-hour moisturising lotion

This lotion contains calendula, aloe vera and chamomile, and the combination soothes and hydrates my skin very effectively. It also lasts; most moisturisers sink into the skin in a few minutes, but this one left my skin feeling smooth and soft – if not quite for 24 hours, then certainly for hours rather than minutes. The lotion is also light and easy to apply.

Espa 24-hour eye complex

Another 24-hour product! I am either a) very rushed and can only use products once a day or b) have reached the stage where my skin needs all the help it can get. Actually it's both a and b! If I were very brave, I might consider having cosmetic surgery on the skin above my eyes as this area is getting horribly baggy. However, I'm a cosmetic coward so, instead, I have started using this nourishing eye cream which makes my eyes look a whole lot better.

Jo Malone grapefruit shower gel

This smells wonderful, lasts forever, and is just exactly what you need first thing in the morning: a wake-up jolt without the downside of that extra cup of coffee.

Serenity in the City

Edinburgh, Scotland

Dramatic, Japanese-inspired red and black treatment rooms: black walls, mood lighting, and brilliant touches of red in fabrics and furnishing make Serenity in the City feel lavish – a sharp contrast to the white, clinical ambience of some spas.

What's on offer

Six treatment rooms with two rooms for couples, both with walk-in showers. There's a Zen Lounge relaxation room, express treatments, and medi-spa treatments on request.

We loved

The Leighton Denny Pristine Pedicure, which includes a lot of massage of your feet and lower legs. We had been pacing the streets of Edinburgh the day before, so our feet were in need of some TLC. The colour lasted impressively well, too.

No hard sell of the products.

We didn't love

We had to ask the staff to take our coats and bags away when we arrived.

The waterbed in the relaxation room wasn't warmed, so it was too cold to stay on it for more than a second, and there's something slightly pompous about a city-centre treatment rooms offering you a 'Lifestyle Recommendation' sheet on the basis of a pedicure.

Food file

Tea or juice in the Zen Lounge.

Who would like it

Anyone who's been lost in Jenners; office workers; anyone for whom manicures, pedicures, tinting, tanning, shaping and waxing really are 'essentials' in life.

Don't miss

Should the urge take you, you can also book the spa for your exclusive use with up to 15 guests.

Spa type
Treatment rooms

Where?
Serenity in the City
9a Castle Street
Edinburgh EH2 3AH
0131 226 7459

Signature treatment
Serenity Wellbeing Massage

Brands
Elemis

Expect to pay
Treatments:
£60 for 55 minutes

Bubble rating
4 out of 5 bubbles

The Serenity Spa

Seaham Hall, Seaham, County Durham

Impressive and expansive, cool and classy Seaham Hall will appeal to everyone who can afford it. There is plenty to occupy you, with a whole day of warming up and cooling down if traditional spa-ing is your thing. Plus an elephant to greet you as you walk through the underground tunnel from the hotel to the spa.

What's on offer

A large, ozone-treated pool in a light, glass-walled part of the spa building. At the far end of the pool, you will find a sauna, a steam room, a sanarium, two cold plunge pools, and a rather splendid hydrotherapy bath. When you get in and turn it on, it's like Vesuvius. There's also a gym with a variety of equipment.

There are many treatments on offer, including massages, body treatments, facials and wraps. As the spa also offers teen treatments, all ages and tastes are well catered for.

We loved

The fabulous underground walkway from the hotel to the spa: a huge carved elephant greets you on the other side. It's a brilliant and inspired way of joining the hotel to the spa.

You can check out of your room, leave your luggage with Reception, then enjoy the spa for the rest of the day. Nice.

We didn't love

No face-holder on the couch during our otherwise lovely Aroma Stone Therapy,

so you have a choice: turn your head to 90 degrees for the entire treatment, or suffocate.

No spin-dryer in the changing rooms! You'll have to cart your sodden cossie around with you.

Food file

The Ozone café in the spa serves drinks and snacks throughout the day. You can have the first two courses of your lunch here, and come back for dessert later. In the evening, you can have a rather grand dinner in Michelin-starred The White Room.

Who would like it

Seaham Hall will appeal to everyone who can afford it. The Serenity Spa will appeal to everyone else. It offers excellent value for a spa escape.

Don't miss

The outdoor hot-tubs. Try them with the person you love and a glass of champagne.

Just lounging about by the side of the pool and enjoying the view.

Spa type
Hotel spa

Where?
Seaham Hall
Lord Byron's Walk
Seaham
County Durham SR7 7AG
01915 161400

Signature treatments
The Serenity Spa Signature Hot Stone Back Ritual

Brands
Elemis, Karin Herzog

Expect to pay
Treatments:
£60 for 50 minutes
Stay: from £250 for bed and breakfast in a Cool/Classic room

Bubble rating
5 out of 5 bubbles

Shymala Ayurveda

Kensington, London

The focus on authentic ayurvedic treatments and techniques sets Shymala Ayurveda apart. So many spas use ayurvedic terms in treatments that have little to do with ancient Hindu medicine. Here, you get the real deal, and in an elegant, bijou West London townhouse.

What's on offer

Choose from a range of traditional Indian ayurvedic therapies, from Udvartana (a body firming therapy) through to a full 21-day Panchakarma detox programme. There's a yoga studio, too. Regular spa treatments are offered, as well, so you can still get a body polish and manicure if you fancy it.

The cosy little heat area downstairs has a small steam room, shower and sauna, which, while compact, are stylishly decorated. Great for a couple of spa guests to make the most of their relaxation time.

We loved

The décor. It's simply gorgeous: a mixture of traditional Indian and contemporary European design with imported carved wooden furniture from Kerala, vividly coloured and embroidered fabrics, and walls in cerise and gold. A glass-topped table in the lounge area displays herbs and spices used in ancient ayurvedic medicine, and there are modern touches such as the vertical water feature in the hall. The overall effect is a spot-on effort at Eastern vibrancy in the urban West.

The 15-minute pre-treatment ayurvedic consultation with Shymala's own ayurvedic doctor includes an analysis of your dosha plus suggestions for a suitably dosha-nurturing eating plan.

The Sundari Abhyanga massage: as soon as the therapist begins to drizzle warm, fragrant oil over your shoulders, you may start to melt into the bed.

We didn't love

Being advised to avoid coffee, chocolate and ice cream.

Food file

A healthy vegetarian lunch if you book a day package. Otherwise, tea and dried fruit.

Who would like it

Shymala Ayurveda is feminine and bijou: just right for a quiet afternoon relaxing with your mother, daughter or best friend.

Don't miss

Ask the spa to reserve time in the heat area if you want to make sure it isn't full when you get there.

Spa type
Day spa

Where?
Shymala Ayurveda
152 Holland Park Avenue
London W11 4UH
0207 348 0018

Signature treatment
Panchakarma Detox

Brands
Pukka
Sundari

Expect to pay
Treatments:
£100 for 60 minutes

Bubble rating
5 out of 5 bubbles

Slieve Donard

Newcastle, County Down, Northern Ireland

This spa has the wow factor. Every inch of it is stylish, spacious and sumptuous, and the surroundings are spectacular. A perfect oasis of peace and pampering.

What's on offer

An imposing Victorian hotel – with a tower! – in six acres of grounds, a spectacular mountain in one direction, miles of golden beaches in the other. Impressive reception area with marble floor, glass chandelier and traditional Irish peat fireplace.

Two floors of spa (The Active Floor and The Treatment Floor). A 20-metre swimming pool with amazing floor-to-ceiling views of the coastline. Amethyst steam room, rock sauna and drench showers. Spacious gym with modern Technogym equipment. Zen Studio classes including yoga and tai chi.

Over the floating glass bridge to spa reception and 16 treatment suites with mood lighting and sensory showers. Spacious, contemporary changing rooms with underfloor heating – a decadent touch. Male and female relaxation rooms, snug and personal, warm and cosy, a cocoon of pure restfulness.

ESPA treatments, including Super Active facials, hot stone therapies and ayurvedic treatments. Lots of wraps, massages and envelopments. Mostly for Men treatments, manicures, pedicures and waxing.

We loved

The ESPA Super Active facial. Not cheap, but worth it. Your only problem is which to choose: Repairing and Restoring? Toning, Lifting and Firming? We went for Calming and Soothing, so wonderful we drifted off… Afterwards we could almost feel our skin glowing.

We didn't love

The fact that we can't live in this spa forever.

Food file

Delicious snacks and smoothies in the Horizon Juice Bar, or dine on Cobb salad or fresh Kilkeel prawns while enjoying magnificent views towards the Mountains of Mourne in the Lighthouse Lounge.

Who would like it

Any individual, any couple and any group.

Don't miss

The hotel's own private gate onto the beach.

Spa type
Hotel spa

Where?
Slieve Donard
Downs Road
Newcastle
County Down
Northern Ireland
028 4372 6166

Signature treatment
Chakra balancing
with hot stones

Brands
ESPA

Expect to pay
Treatments:
£70 for 55 minutes
Stay: from £160 per night
in a classic double room

Bubble rating
5 out of 5 bubbles

LAVASHELLS ®

The warmth of the Tropics in the Palm of your Hands™

The Hottest New Massage Treatment

The Lava Shell Massage is the UK's hottest new treatment delivering a magical and healing experience. This deeply comforting body treatment uses recycled, naturally self-heating Tiger Clam shells from the sun kissed shores of the Philippines. As the marine polished sea shells glide smoothly over the body, you will instantly drift into a blanket of warmth, falling into a state of utter relaxation and calm thanks to the comfortable warming temperature.

During the massage, the shells are worked over the palms, arms, neck and shoulder area, with the focus of the massage surrounding pressure points. Deep tissue work on these tension areas such as the feet, back and shoulders, ease away all muscle tension, knots and stress points, unblocking an energy flow and releasing a sense of balance to the entire body and mind. The heat and massage motions in this treatment are also excellent for aiding digestion, acting as a holistic colonic cleanse, as well as strengthening pelvic floor muscles, releasing emotional stress and helping with problems like IBS and menstrual cramps.

The Lava Shell Massage can be found in the top spas and salons nationwide including The Grove, Ragdale Hall, Calcot Manor, Marriott Hotels, David Lloyd and Bannatyne Spas.

To find your nearest Lava Shell spa or beauty salon call 01869 338890 or visit www.sharedbeautysecrets.com

SHAREDBEAUTYSECRETS
surrender to the elements
Telephone 01869 338890 **Mobile** 07815 786201
Email info@sharedbeautysecrets.com **Website** www.sharedbeautysecrets.com

Sofitel London Heathrow

Terminal 5, Heathrow Airport, London

What a find! This small but chic spa is so relaxing and professional, it's easy to forget you are next door to one of Europe's busiest travel hubs.

What's on offer

A large, grandly designed hotel with a surprisingly quiet, clean, contemporary ESPA spa. Large, comfortable treatment rooms, relaxation room in pale brick, five treatment rooms, small but clean and well-stocked changing rooms. A fair-sized gym full of the latest equipment. No swimming pool, but there is a quiet, exclusive hydrotherapy area with a vitality pool, and a nicely hot sauna and aromatherapy steam room.

Relaxing ESPA massages, as well as facials, wraps, manis and pedis, and treatments for men and for mums-to-be.

We loved

That all the staff went out of their way to ensure that we were having a good time – a real art of the spa.

We didn't love

Small things. We were a little chilly in the relaxation area. The showers have glass doors, which can be disconcerting. And, although the spa is small, it is easy to get lost; more signs to the pool, gym and reception would be welcome.

Food file

We ate in the Brasserie Roux, headed up by Michelin-starred chef Albert Roux himself. We'd go out of our way to eat this high-quality gourmet food again.

Who would like it

Travellers, especially those felled by jet lag or cursed with lost luggage. Business people looking to de-stress while travelling. Anyone can visit the spa, so those living or working locally, too.

Don't miss

If you only have one spa treatment, you can't go wrong with the Advanced Back, Face and Scalp treatment with hot stones.

Spa type
Hotel spa

Where?
Sofitel London Heathrow
Terminal 5
Heathrow Airport
Hayes, Middlesex TW6 2GG
020 8757 7741

Signature treatment
Sofitel Spa Signature ritual

Brands
ESPA

Expect to pay
Treatments:
£60 for 60 minutes
Stay: from £79 per night in a standard double room

Bubble rating
4 out of 5 bubbles

So SPA, Sofitel St James

London

So SPA in St James is a stylish London hotel spa with a French twist. Attention to detail is key: your 'spa butler' will tailor everything in your spa experience to your preference. Lighting, music, fragrance...

What's on offer

In the discreet and peaceful spa, glass and metalwork panels and the bright pinks, purples and yellows of velvet upholstery complement the restored original features.

Choose from Carita or Cinq Mondes treatments; the spa menu plays with the theme of French gastronomy and presents the massages, facials and finishing touches on offer as 'starters', 'mains' and 'desserts'. No pools, but the double treatment room with a small hydro-pool is perfect for friends or partners; there is also a treatment room with a Kohler chromatherapy bath if you fancy an aromatic soak beforehand. You can have a traditional hammam ritual, too – a slathering of rich, black mineral soap before a steam, then an invigorating scrub to finish.

The pedicure stations are regal, plush thrones fit for the most majestic of toes.

Small but clean changing rooms, and three loungers, each with noise-reduction headphones, in a quiet relaxation room.

We loved

The staff: impeccably polite, professional and friendly. The single most comfortable bed we have ever had a treatment on. The hot stones in our facial. The 'martini and manicure'; the cocktails are designed to match the colours of the OPI polish. The very relaxed and very chic atmosphere.

We didn't love

That we can't go more often. So SPA doesn't fit into everybody's budget for regular spa visits, but certainly isn't overpriced given the level of service.

Food file

After our treatment, our cleansing white peony tea arrived on a little tray with a flapjack. In the restaurant, foie gras and duck for indulgence; salmon and salads if you want to stick to healthier options.

Who would like it

Perfect for a couple, or two friends who want a relaxing day out.

Don't miss

Your spa butler, of course. Also, try to treat yourself to lunch in Brasserie Roux or a classic afternoon tea in the pretty Rose Lounge.

Spa type
Hotel spa

Where?
So SPA by Sofitel
Sofitel London St James
6 Waterloo Place
London SW1Y 4AN
020 7747 2204

Signature treatments
So Rejuvenating Facial Treatment
So Exhilarating Body Massage

Brands
Carita, Cinq Mondes

Expect to pay
Treatments:
£85 for 60 minutes
Stay: from £211.50 per night in a superior room

Bubble rating
5 out of 5 bubbles

Solent Hotel and Spa

Fareham, Hampshire

A modern, well designed spa. Pale colours, wide corridors, and subdued lighting soothe the busy business traveller. Just off the motorway, so it's easy to find, but cleverly screened by trees and meadows. Forget your journey and concentrate on the serious business of spa.

Spa type
Hotel spa

Where?
Solent Hotel
Rookery Avenue
Whiteley, Fareham
Hampshire PO15 7AJ
01489 880027

Signature treatment
ESPA Holistic Aromatherapy
Back Face and Scalp
treatment

Brands
ESPA
VitaMan

Expect to pay
Treatments:
£54 for 55 minutes
Stay: £140 per night
in an Executive double

Bubble rating
4 out of 5 bubbles

What's on offer

A pool, with a steam room and sauna; a monsoon shower; a hot tub. There's also a well-equipped gym and studio with a great range of classes.

You can have hydrotherm massage and ESPA 30-minute taster treatments. Very useful if you are there on business and can't spare much time.

We loved

The comfortable relaxation area with doors onto a small terrace area, overlooking a meadow; plenty of space and stacks of up-to-date glossy magazines to get lost in.

The ESPA Back Face and Scalp treatment: heated pads keep you warm and help hold your body in a good posture. Ideal for long treatments when your lower back can feel stiff.

We didn't love

The robes are those synthetic ones, which feel cuddly soft but they do cling to the body in all the places you would rather they didn't cling to.

The pool area is a bit dark, and the pool is not very large (on average seven or eight breaststrokes for a length).

Food file

Water, juices, coffee, fruit and pastries.

Who would like it

Anyone travelling on business who wants to take a few hours out.

Don't miss

The double treatment room with its own private terrace and hot tub.

Spa at 51

Westminster, London

They make it very clear what they offer at Spa at 51: 'spa treatments and fitness facilities'. And that's what you get in these classy hotel treatment rooms. Spa at 51 is an excellent place to go for treatments for any sort of Big Day.

What's on offer

Treatments, mainly; there's a teeny steam room and small sauna in the changing rooms (so single-sex), but no pool. The gym is a good size for a hotel spa, though.

For treatments, you can choose from the full range of Anne Sémonin facials, including the must-have Eternal Youth, as well as facials specifically designed for men. Also on the menu is a pregnancy massage that uses specialised cushions so mums-to-be can lie face-down in a safe and supported way.

We loved

The spa reception area: elegant and spare, brightened by some gorgeous – and real – orchids.

Our Anne Sémonin back treatment and massage; this was a gloriously de-stressing spa treat. The treatment also includes the most glamorous disposable knickers you'll ever see: they come in a silver box.

We didn't love

The changing rooms were a bit Spartan. The area had a definite 'health club' rather than 'spa' feel. Also, the tiny steam room.

Food file

Lunch in Bistro 51 at the hotel; we can recommend their chicken satay and delicious Caesar salad.

Who would like it

Anyone staying in the hotel or apartments, or going to a garden party at nearby Buckingham Palace.

Don't miss

The steam cupboard (it's so tiny, you just might). Also, the treatments with active algae that warms up and bubbles.

Spa type
Hotel spa

Where?
Spa at 51
51 Buckingham Gate
Westminster
London SW1E 6AF
020 7963 8307

Signature treatment
L'Expérience Anne Sémonin signature facial

Brands
Anne Sémonin, Osmium

Expect to pay
Treatments:
£70 for 60 minutes
Stay: prices start from £339 for one night in a deluxe suite

Bubble rating
4 out of 5 bubbles

Good Spa Spy Favourites

Single Spy

Age Young at heart. Oh, alright then, 50s **Skin type** As the therapists like to say: 'mature' **Spa likes** Warm floors when you put your bare feet upon them; heated treatment beds; soft towels; attention to detail, so that your treatment room looks and smells beautiful when you arrive in it **Spa dislikes** Cold floors when you put your bare feet upon them; therapists who use your treatment time to write up a list of product 'recommendations' that they hope you will later buy

Best spa experiences this year

Sipping peony tea in the relaxation area after a divine massage at **Spa Intercontinental** in London. Chilling out (twice!) at **The Sofitel**, **Heathrow**, before early flights at Terminal 5: I love the massage, the pool and loungers, and the can-do willingness of all the staff there. The Woodland Walk at **Moddershall Oaks** in Staffordshire, plus chilling out at their lakeside. My feet say: the foot-sander blitz at **Cowshed**, **Clarendon Cross**, as well as the three-week pedicure at **Zen Lifestyle** in Edinburgh – that bright pink really did stay bright pink for the advertised time.

Worst spa experiences this year

Going into a jimjilbang in Korea and not being able to read any of the signs, so completely clueless as to what to do (hence dashing about naked); going to an onsen in Japan and realising (and doing) the same. Going to too many UK spas where I was cold. Massage may make *you* warm, therapists, but *we* come in not warmed up!

Favourite products

ESPA Fitness bath oil

A refreshing and comforting bathtime experience. I love this oil's spicy tang, from the essential oils of clove, rosemary, peppermint, eucalyptus and Indian bay that it contains. I enjoy all of the ESPA bath oils, but this one always makes me energised for the day.

Pure Lochside Revitalising face treatment oil

I was unsure about facial oils until I met this one. Pure Lochside products are made in Scotland from natural ingredients from plants – no parabens, mineral oil or petrochemicals here. This honey-coloured oil also contains the 'exclusive Pure Lochside Anti-Ageing Complex', whatever that may be, as well as antioxidants and vitamins. It contains organic orange blossom and rose otto, too, so smells divine. The oils are made in small batches to ensure both freshness and effectiveness. Not only does my skin instantly feel softer, but the aroma is very therapeutic and makes me smile. A product that's kind to you and kind to the earth.

Tri dosha Kapha face cream

When you want a face cream, don't you want it to be suited to your dosha – your unique mix of vata, pitta and kapha energies, which is the basis of the ayurvedic approach to health? I'm a kapha type, so this product was prescribed for me. I found the cream easy to use, good for moisturising when travelling, and instantly absorbed – my skin drank it in. It's a little on the pricy side, but it left my skin feeling 'balanced', as promised.

The Spa at County Hall
Westminster, London

Tranquillity, relaxation and indulgent luxury in the heart of London, plus breathtaking views across the city from every window. The location could not be more impressive, even on a traditional rainy day. Feel your stresses vanish at this oasis of elegance.

What's on offer

A 25-metre swimming pool (a serious find in the centre of London) with floor-to-ceiling windows. Sauna, steam room and Jacuzzi. Dedicated manicure and pedicure area. Small, calming relaxation room. Over 6,000 square feet of gym, full to the rafters with sophisticated training equipment.

Decléor facials, massages, eye treatments, tanning treatments, Jessica hand and foot therapies, male treatments, and a good range of day packages.

We loved

The Decléor Essentially Yours Aromatic facial, which includes a back massage using aromatherapy oils. The skilled therapist left our skin radiant and smooth as silk. We loved The Jessica Deluxe Manicure, too.

We didn't love

The changing rooms are part of the gym, so smell more of chlorinated health-club than luscious relaxation. We also felt the relaxation room was too small for such a popular spa. And we didn't like having to get dressed and go downstairs for lunch.

Food file

We lingered over a two-course lunch in Leader's Bar. We'd pre-ordered our melt-in-the-mouth grilled salmon, and a brulée with the distinct taste of green tea.

Who would like it

Anyone looking for luxury, relaxation and pampering in busy London, or excellent gym facilities and a top-notch pool.

Don't miss

The best part of the County Hall experience: coming face to face with London's history through every window.

Spa type
Hotel spa

Where?
The Spa at County Hall
Marriott County Hall Hotel
Westminster Bridge Road
London SE1 7PB
020 7902 8023

Signature treatment
Lava shell massage

Brands
Decléor

Expect to pay
Treatments:
£80 for 55 minutes
Stay: from £199 per night in a standard double room

Bubble rating
4 out of 5 bubbles

Spa Intercontinental

Park Lane, London

From the swish seating area to the blissful steam and fabulous treatments, this true spa experience will make you fairly twinkle with delight.

What's on offer

A calm, chic spa in a Hyde Park corner hotel that's unprepossessing from the outside, but plush and golden inside. No pool, no sauna, no crystal steam room, but still offers a true pampering spa experience with an atmosphere that is dedicated 'spa' and very peaceful.

Five ellipse-shaped treatment rooms that make you feel as if you are in a space-age cocoon, each with its own private changing area. Elemis facials, wraps and massages, including treatments for men and for mums-to-be. Manis and pedis, eyebrow shaping and tinting, and waxing, too.

The spa charges by time, not treatment (except for grooming treatments and the VIP suite) so you can choose 'pure time' and let your therapist create a person-alised menu for you on the day. Pretty pricy, but we think it's worth it.

We loved

The supremely enjoyable English Rose treatment journey, designed to leave you feeling Relaxed, Oxygenated, Sensual and Energised. Our therapist climbed onto the bed to reach our deepest muscles, and used Balinese, Thai, and Hawaiian techniques, together with hot stones.

We didn't love

We'd have brought trainers if we'd known there was a separate gym you can use.

Food file

Depending on the package, afternoon tea, spa boxes or a three-course lunch at Theo Randall's restaurant in the hotel.

Who would like it

Business people looking to de-stress. Holidaymakers looking to re-energise. People working in the local area who need either de-stressing or re-energising.

Don't miss

The candlelit black-and-gold-mosaic Temple of Steam. We had the absolutely fab Steam Temple therapy in it, and you haven't lived until you've sat in blissful solitude under the twinkling star-lights, slathering two types of mud over yourself. Obviously, you could do this much better *à deux*.

Spa type
Hotel spa

Where?
Spa InterContinental
InterContinental Hotel
One Hamilton Place
Park Lane
London W1J 7QY
020 7318 8691

Signature treatment
English Rose signature treatment

Brands
Elemis

Expect to pay
Treatments:
£90 for 60 minutes
Stay: from £211.50 per night in a double classic room

Bubble rating
5 out of 5 bubbles

Spa NK

Westbourne Grove, London

These treatment rooms within the huge, brightly lit SpaceNK shop on Westbourne Grove in west London offer effective, professional treatments to keep you looking good. No pool or spa facilities here and no loungers, either, but you can have a little relax on the low-backed chairs (and a shop) after your results-focused treatment.

Spa type
Treatment rooms

Where?
Spa NK Notting Hill
127-131 Westbourne Grove
Notting Hill
London W2 4UP
020 7727 8002

Signature treatment
Spa NK signature massage

Brands
Aromatherapy Associates
Dr Sebagh
Eve Lom
Natura Bissé

Expect to pay
Treatments:
£75 for 60 minutes

Bubble rating
4 out of 5 bubbles

What's on offer

A spacious changing area with lockers and a couple of showers complete with gorgeous Bumble and bumble products. Eight treatment rooms.

Slick and professional therapists. Soft background piano music. Choose from a nice range of specialist facials and body treatments including pregnancy massage, back, neck and shoulder massage, and packages combining facial and body treatments. There are no specific male-oriented treatments, but most treatments are suitable for men.

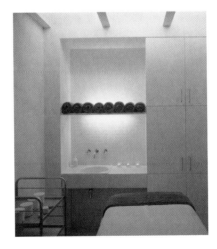

We loved

Our supremely comfortable treatment couch. Our delectable Eve Lom facial complete with warm wax to open our pores before the surprisingly comforting 'extraction' process. The treatment was unexpectedly pampering and we really enjoyed the massage elements. Three weeks later, our skin was still looking so good that we were even skimping on foundation. Impressive stuff. The products – all crying out to be purchased, like the beauty equivalent of a sweet shop.

We didn't love

The shabby shower cubicles.

Food file

Lemon-infused water. Herbal tea.

Who would like it

Execs, shoppers, yummy mummies, and ladies who lunch. Spa NK offers a quiet escape from the bustle of Notting Hill.

Don't miss

The authoritative therapists – they will tell you what your skin requires.

Spa Sirène

The Royal Yacht, St Helier, Jersey

A peaceful, well lit basement spa in a recently refurbished, stylish, bustling luxury hotel. The elegance, luxury and serenity of this spa make up for the lack of sea views. Everything Spa Sirène does, it does well.

What's on offer

Good facilities, with everything fresh and clean. Beautifully done rasul room, hydrotherapy sea-water bath, small, bright gym, spacious changing rooms. Very pleasant 12-metre pool with glistening light lattice and sails covering the ceiling. Children under 16 aren't allowed in, which preserves the spa atmosphere. 'Experience' showers, nicely hot sauna, mosaic steam room with twinkly lights and crystals. Wicker chairs so large you can hide in them. Five treatment rooms named after mermaids.

Phytomer treatments, a marine-based range made in nearby St Malo. Massages, facials and wraps, all with poetic names. Treatments for men and mums-to-be. Manis and pedis using the Essie range, Fleurs make-up, and waxing, tints and tans. Attentive, friendly staff (though a little less selling on the lounger would be good).

We loved

The spa's signature Me Me Me facial treatment, including a very soothing back massage and bubbling sea mud.

We didn't love

The lack of a clock in the pool area, which made those of us booked in for treatments fret a bit.

Food file

Salads, sandwiches and smoothies by the pool. Sirocco, the hotel's elegant dining option, tends towards foie gras.

Who would like it

The spa is only available to hotel residents, members and those spending a certain amount on spa treatments.

Don't miss

Relaxing *à deux* in the hydrotherapy sea-water bath, with champagne and nibbles.

Spa type
Hotel spa

Where?
Spa Sirène
The Royal Yacht
Weighbridge
St Helier
Jersey JE2 3NF
01534 720511

Signature treatment
Me Me Me facial

Brands
Phytomer

Expect to pay
Treatments:
£77.50 for 75 minutes
Stay: from £125 per night in a standard double room

Bubble rating
5 out of 5 bubbles

Spa SPC at Stoke Park Club

Stoke Poges, Buckinghamshire

Spa SPC is within Stoke Park Club, a private members' club. The hotel is a Palladian mansion commanding imposing views over 350 acres of manicured parkland and the greens of the golf-course; the purpose built spa has many fine facilities, and many health club members using them.

Spa type
Hotel spa

Where?
Stoke Park Club (Spa SPC)
Park Road
Stoke Poges
Buckinghamshire
SL2 4PG
01753 717173

Signature treatment
SPC Active Glow facial

Brands
CACI
Crystal Clear
SPC

Expect to pay
Treatments:
£80 for 55 minutes

Bubble rating
4 out of 5 bubbles

What's on offer

A large rectangular pool, Italian marble steam rooms with twinkly lights; a relaxation room; plenty of fluffy towels; a large, state-of-the-art gym. You can also try a fitness class in one of the studios, or some tennis (book in advance).

Many treatments use Stoke Park Club's skin care range, SPC; you can choose from facials, scrubs, wraps, massages and hot stone therapy, with twists for mums-to-be, teens and men; microdermabrasion and oxygen therapy; ghd hair treatments; beauty finishing touches.

Between treatments, you can relax in the spa atrium, which has a peaceful atmosphere and a five-metre-long aquarium to lull you into calm.

We loved

The pool with its ultra-violet cleansing system (no nasty chlorine in your eyes) and its double-height windows. We're also very fond of the SPC skin-care range, especially the rose toner.

We didn't love

Lots of small children in the pool outside the 'splash' times; your 'spa retreat' is unlikely to be enhanced by this.

Food file

A light lunch or brunch is included in all the half-day or day retreats.

Who would like it

Midweek: ladies who lunch. Weekends: ladies who lunch with their partners.

Don't miss

The steam room that is bigger on the inside than it is on the outside.

Sprowston Manor

Norwich, Norfolk

A good-value spa and swimming pool in a large four-star Marriott hotel. While it's not the last word in luxury, La Fontana spa offers good treatments for those with an eye for a bargain.

What's on offer

A large and pleasant 'tropical' hotel pool (think free-form and palm trees) which also has a children's area and a large Jacuzzi; the steam room is also large (some steam rooms in hotels resemble cupboards) and so is the sauna, and both were deliciously warm on our visit. On sunny days, you can sit outside in the walled terrace area. There is a small gym and an 18-hole golf course. The hotel is often used by football teams visiting Carrow Road. Maybe you'll be sharing the pool with an entire team, as we did…

The La Fontana spa offers massages, facials, wraps, facials and manis and pedis. There are specific treatments for mums-to-be and men, and day packages are available for groups, mums and daughters, and couples.

We loved

Some great and professional treatments; Sprowston Manor compares favourably in price with grander spas.

We didn't love

The cold changing rooms on our visit.

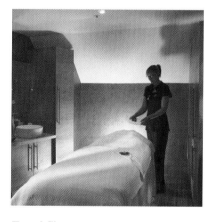

Food file

Herbal teas in The Garden Room, where you can relax before and after treatments. Grander dining in the hotel.

Who would like it

Anyone who enjoys being in a hotel where you can get some exercise, a swim and a steam, and a facial in between meetings.

Don't miss

La Fontana can get busy; to make the most of the treatments, call the hotel, ask for the spa and book in advance.

Spa type

Hotel spa

Where?

Sprowston Manor
Marriott Hotel
and Country Club
Wroxham Road
Norwich, Norfolk NR7 8RP
01603 410 871

Signature treatment

Holistic Back, Face and Scalp: back cleanse, exfoliation, and massage

Brands

Decleor, ESPA, Guinot

Expect to pay

Treatments:
£44 for 60 minutes
Stay: from £118 per night in a standard double

Bubble rating

4 out of 5 bubbles

St Brides Spa Hotel

Saundersfoot, Wales

St Brides is a modern hotel with a high-spec spa that makes the most of its stunning cliffside location; the sea theme reverberates from the beach views in the relaxation room to the marine-based treatments on offer from professional therapists.

What's on offer

A gorgeous thermal suite, with a sauna, a salt infusion room, an aroma steam room, a sensation shower and an ice fountain. All of the heated rooms are of a high standard; there are turquoise mosaic tiles in the steam room, twinkly mother-of-pearl tiles in the infusion room: not a plastic seat in sight. There is no swimming pool, but there is an outside vitality pool with an infinity edge that blurs the boundaries between pool and sea.

Treatments on offer include 'day escapes', and all continue the marine theme with names such as Drifting Tides or Coastal Breeze, with a choice of treatments and use of the thermal suite. There are Algotherm and [comfort zone] facials, LaStone massages, wraps, manis, pedis and eye treatments, and treatments for men to choose from.

We loved

Warming up and cooling down in the thermal suite, then enjoying a wrap treatment in the double treatment room with its dramatic views of sea and sky. We also loved that the spa wasn't crowded; it's not an automatic addition to a hotel stay; you're allowed in if you've booked a treatment or you're willing to pay an extra charge.

We didn't love

Having to leave.

Food file

Herbal teas and water in the relaxation room; local produce freshly cooked in the hotel restaurant in a contemporary environment.

Who would like it

Savvy Welsh spa-goers who know a bargain when they see one; anyone who is looking for marine well-being treatments; couples who will enjoy both the hotel and the dual treatment room. Friends who'll enjoy a shared experience, too.

Don't miss

Booking the thermal suite in advance; it may be maxed out if you leave it till you get there. Splashing about in the outdoor (heated) vitality pool with its views over Carmarthen Bay, even if it is raining.

Spa type
Hotel spa

Where?
St Brides Hill
Saundersfoot
Pembrokeshire SA69 9NH
01834 812304

Signature treatment
Algotherm Sea Salt
Body Treatment

Brands
Algotherm, [comfort zone]

Expect to pay
Treatments:
£65 for 55 minutes
Stay: from £200 per night
for bed and breakfast in
a Good sea view room

Bubble rating
5 out of 5 bubbles

The St David's Hotel and Spa

Cardiff, Wales

This dramatic, modern hotel, built right on the waterfront on Cardiff Bay, is flooded with light and Welsh wonder, and the spa is dedicated to your comfort.

What's on offer

From the hotel, there is a separate lift down to the spa: great idea as you don't have to walk through any public areas dressed only in your robe.

There is a fairly large main pool which is ideal for some serious swimming. There's also a hydrotherapy spa pool with underwater jet beds, a hydrotherapy walk-through corridor with swan neck showers, a large sauna and a gymnasium. The water in the hydrotherapy area contains marine extracts to cleanse and nourish the skin and it feels slightly silky to the touch.

For a treatment, choose from oxyjet oxygen facials; a chakra-balancing ritual with hot stones; a Thalgomince pregnancy pamper to smooth away stretch-marks; Beauty-Tox cellulite busting; personal training sessions. Add a Jet Blitz to your treatment and be blasted with high-pressure water.

We loved

The waiting room with glass walls overlooking the bay; loll about here and help yourself to herbal tea and snacks of cranberries and dried bananas.

The professional, relaxed and friendly staff. A lot of attention has been paid to getting all the details right.

The heavenly hotel rooms: St David's is a five-star hotel and it shows.

We didn't love

Although the treatment rooms are a good size, you can hear people out in the corridor and voices drifting into the room.

Food file

Waves is on the first floor and provides food and waterfront views for spa guests, as well as an outside terrace; there's also an all-day poolside butler menu. Formal dining and great food in the Tides Grill.

Who would like it

Anyone. Any business person, especially those travelling alone.

Don't miss

Looking out of the window while swimming in the pool. It's built on the same level as the bay outside. You might see a sailing boat passing you by.

Spa type
Hotel spa

Where?
The St David's Hotel and Spa
Havannah Street
Cardiff CF10 5SD
029 2045 4045

Signature treatment
The St David's Ritual
hot stone massage
and facial (we loved it!)

Brands
ESPA, OXYjet, Thalgo

Expect to pay
Treatments:
£65 for 60 minutes
Stay: from £99 bed and
breakfast per night in a
Classic King room

Bubble rating
5 out of 5 bubbles

Stobo Castle Health Spa

Stobo, Peeblesshire, Scotland

A short stay in a Scottish Castle is always bound to cheer you up. Add in relaxing spa treatments, a swimming pool and delicious food, and you're going to float home. Stobo is a deeply romantic as well as healthy place to stay.

What's on offer

A 25-metre ozone-treated pool with glass walls and infinity edges so you feel as if you're swimming up and down in a Scottish glen; there's also a large hydropool, a poolside steam room, and heat experiences in the changing rooms.

Each day offers a varied range of activities: usually a light walk, a more strenuous walk, aquarobics, and a variety of classes in the studio. Try the Dance of the Dragon, a fun yet challenging class we enjoyed, based on tai chi.

You can choose from a very wide range of spa treatments. Book in for fitness analysis and personal training, and one-to-one yoga and Pilates in the gym.

We loved

Driving through the green grounds and up the winding road to get to the castle. You already feel as if you're leaving the stresses and strains of the world behind. The setting is something that sets Stobo apart. Each time we visit, we are struck by how beautiful the place is. We love watching the Scottish hills through the gym window as the sun goes down.

When you're staying, lunch is included on the day of departure. This means you can enjoy the spa, eat, read the papers in the drawing room with your coffee... it's a delightful delay of your return to the real world.

We didn't love

Spa slippers are not provided and you'll have to fork out for some at the shop if you are so remiss as to forget your own.

Food file

While the choice is not wide, the food is fresh, often locally sourced, and all beautifully cooked.

Who would like it

People looking to dip out of the business of life for a while; anyone who wants a quick spa fix for the day.

Don't miss

The Cashmere Suite. It's an utterly fabulous and luxurious place to stay, with cashmere on the beds, on the sofas, on the walls... we had trouble prising The Spies out.

Spa type
Spa retreat

Where?
Stobo
Peeblesshire EH45 8NY
01721 725300

Signature treatment
The Ritual Vie facial, massage and body exfoliation

Brands
Castle Care, Darphin, Mary Cohr, Phytomer Thalgo, Vie

Expect to pay
Treatments:
£72 for 55 minutes
Stay: from £125 per person per night, sharing in a Castle Lodge room

Bubble rating
5 out of 5 bubbles

Sura Detox

Dolton, Devon

Lose weight, rest, relax and tune out in idyllic surroundings while being attended to by caring therapists. Something between a wellness spa and a medi-spa, Sura Detox provides a holistic approach and one-to-one consultations on how to change your life.

What's on offer

A delightful, picturesque, remote Victorian farmhouse with luscious gardens in a magic dell, 45 minutes' drive from Exeter St David's station. Welcoming cottages in converted barns and outbuildings. A wonderful warm and loving spirit.

A large, heated pool and sauna complex and communal Green Room. Numerous (optional) therapies, practices and informative talks including aromatherapy, shiatsu, Bach Flower remedies, reflexology, homeopathy, astrology, Miessence facial treatment with organic products, lymphatic drainage, a stunning La Stone massage, mentoring, counselling and life coaching. A reassuring team of caring therapists.

We booked a six-day detox retreat, which included a supervised juice fast and two daily colonic treatments. We left seven pounds lighter, feeling and looking cheerful, energised, bright-eyed and fighting fit. Not cheap but worth every penny.

We loved

Having an excellent massage therapy almost every day. The very relaxing Dynamic Detox. The deep aromatherapy massage with geranium, chamomile and patchouli oils hand-picked just for us. The tougher shiatsu massage – not for everyone, but it induced deep 10-hour sleeps.

We didn't love

The carrot juice. The caffeine-withdrawal symptoms. We did fall over a couple of times (onto the bed) but the staff had told us to expect this and pressed us to drink plenty of water and delicious herbal teas.

Food file

On the last night, you have a wonderful feast prepared for you, all vegetarian and all raw. A mushroom will never taste so good again.

Who would like it

Anyone who wants to lose weight sensibly in an atmosphere of tranquillity, or who just wants to regain a life balance.

Don't miss

The food testing – fascinating. Gentle walks round the estate and surrounding fields with fawns, up the Tarka Trail to the river and ponds.

Spa type
Spa retreat

Where?
Sura Detox
Ham Farm, Dolton
Devon EX19 8QT
08456 343 895

Signature treatments
Juice fast, Detox massage

Brands
Miessence, Raw Gaia

Expect to pay
Treatments:
£55 for 60 minutes
Stay: £850 each for a week long Sura Detox retreat, based on two people sharing a Master bedroom with ensuite

Bubble rating
5 out of 5 bubbles

Thermae Bath Spa

Bath, Somerset

A very popular, very affordable spa, built around the natural hot springs in Bath. You can't beat the heritage of the site, the wonderful natural spring waters and the dramatic modern spa building that now houses the thermal springs.

Spa type
Day spa

Where?
The Hetling Pump Room
Hot Bath Street
Bath, Somerset BA1 1SJ
01225 331234

Signature treatment
Watsu: water-based massage and floatation

Brands
Moor, Pevonia

Expect to pay
Treatments:
£55 for 55 minutes
Bathing: £24 for two hours in New Royal Bath; £34 for four hours; £13 for one-and-a-half hours in the Cross Bath

Bubble rating
4 out of 5 bubbles

What's on offer

Spa bathing in two separate buildings; the small Cross Bath pool is where the Bath natural spring rises to the surface. The hot water flows out of the ground in a circular fountain held in a polished metal bowl. In the New Royal Bath, the Minerva pool has massage jets and grand columns but, for many, the star of the show is the open air rooftop pool. Or perhaps the circular glass steam rooms.

Many treatments make use of the natural thermal waters, including Vichy Showers.

We loved

The Watsu treatment: the relaxing combination of warm water, being gently held and moved, and the sun and shadow on your face is extraordinary. We also loved lounging in the rooftop pool.

Competitive treatment prices. There's a very mixed clientèle at Thermae. It's a real people's spa.

We didn't love

The small, dark changing area, plus the spa can get very busy. Choose the day and time of your visit carefully.

Food file

The Springs Café offers paninis, a salad bar and smoothies. Most produce is locally sourced.

Who would like it

People wanting a great spa experience at a rock-bottom price.

Don't miss

The dramatic rooftop pool; swim while looking out across the city to the hills.

Thoresby Hall Hotel & Spa

Newark, Nottinghamshire

Good value spa-ing at sensible prices, in a dramatic Victorian hall in acres of parkland. You'll be bewitched by the enchanting views from the pool, the space-age treatments and the spectacular suppers.

What's on offer

Despite its grand exterior, Thoresby Hall is a budget hotel with a spa. There's an 18-metre pool with glass roof, and a warm, bubbly hydrotherapy pool, a sauna, very hot steam room, ice cave, small aroma-cave, experience shower, sanarium, rasul mud therapy room and impressive relaxation room with flagstone floor and glass roof and wall. Spa hostesses help you with the (very confusing) layout.

Treatments include ESPA massages, facials and envelopments, Jessica manis and pedis, beauty treatments, St Tropez tanning and men's spa treatments.

We loved

The Rejuvenate Me ESPA holistic back, face and scalp treatment. Our therapist was perceptive and interested, our back massage good and our facial excellent.

We didn't love

That the spa was crowded in the afternoon, with people waiting to use the hydrotherapy pool and some queues at the reception area.

Food file

The bistro, with its wonderful brick vaulted ceilings, serves simple but adequate hot and cold food.

Who would like it

Warners, who own Thoresby, often appeal to older couples, and they offer very good value breaks. Probably not ideal for single spa goers.

Don't miss

If Hogwarts had a swimming pool, it would have this view.

Spa type
Hotel spa

Where?
Thoresby Hall Hotel & Spa,
Thoresby Park
Near Ollerton, Newark
Nottinghamshire NG22 9WH
01623 821000

Signature treatment
Total body care with
hot stones

Brands
ESPA, Jessica, St Tropez

Expect to pay
Treatments:
£48 for 55 minutes
Stay: from £200 per night
in a standard Ambassador
room

Bubble rating
4 out of 5 bubbles

Thornton Hall

Thornton Hough, Wirral

The main hotel is traditional and imposing, but has an unlovely modern wing and car park that dominate your first impressions. There's a large health club with a great pool and heat areas, while the newly opened separate Lodge offers a quieter and more private setting for individual and clinical treatments.

Spa type
Hotel spa

Where?
Thornton Hall Hotel and Spa
Neston Road
Thornton Hough, Wirral
Merseyside CH63 1JF
0151 336 3938

Signature treatment
ESPA Total Holistic body care with hot stones

Brands
CACI, Clarins, Elemis, ESPA, MD Formulations

Expect to pay
Treatments:
£50 for 60 minutes
Stay: from £69 per room for a Club double for one night

Bubble rating
4 out of 5 bubbles

What's on offer

In the health club, a 20-metre pool, a nicely hot sauna and steam room, two outdoor hot tubs, loungers around the pool and, on sunny days, in the garden. There's a large gym, too.

Treatments on offer include a good range of massages and facials, as well as manis and pedis, tanning treatments, waxing, tinting, and electrolysis. In the Lodge, you can have more clinical treatments, such as hair or red vein removal, and colonic hydrotherapy, as well as several Elemis treatments and non-surgical facelifts.

The changing rooms are designed with beauty in mind, with hairdryers and large illuminated mirrors.

We loved

The pool is a good size for a swim and there were many groups obviously having a good time. We also loved our Elemis Visible Brilliance facial in the Lodge, and the range of treatments on offer.

We didn't love

Inside the Lodge, there's only a small and rather intimate waiting area.

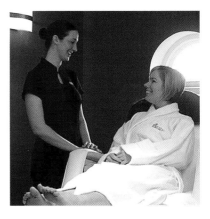

Food file

A café in the health club serving salads, snacks and pasta dishes; more formal dining in the evening in the 2AA rosette oak-panelled Italian Room restaurant.

Who would like it

Spa-goers with an eye for value for money, and those who want their spa treatments in privacy.

Don't miss

The two outdoor hot tubs.

Titanic Spa

Linthwaite, West Yorkshire

Once home to the Titanic textile mill, this huge industrial building is now a revitalised spa and apartments that share the same name. The UK's first eco-spa earns full marks for green-ness and excellent treatments, although there's a sometimes uncomfortable split between the spa and the health club.

What's on offer

The atmosphere is one of space, with cool greens and browns. The entrance hallway is beautifully done in stone.

Facilities include a 15-metre pool with soft salt-regulated water; a large steam room and sauna; and an ice room and aromatherapy room. For the adventurous: an underwater anti-stress massage, or a session in the organic mud chamber. For the fit: a small gym. For afterwards: snuggling down on bean-bags in a sunken pit.

There is a wide range of treatments by Decléor and Elemis, plus manicures and pedicures, and there is a hair salon.

We loved

The way they've reclaimed the building, giving something that was decaying a new lease of life. Our hammam treatment was great; the room was steamy and warm, with a black marble plinth.

We didn't love

The split between the spa and the health-club part of Titanic. You have to walk through the public reception area.

Food file

The food menu is a little light on salads – more paninis than poached pears – but it's fresh and tasty. On sunny days, you can sit outside on the terrace and listen to the river running below.

Who would like it

Everyone within a 100-mile radius.

Don't miss

Swimming in the gorgeously soft, salt-regulated pool.

Spa type
Day spa

Where?
Titanic Spa
Low Westwood Lane
Linthwaite
Huddersfield
West Yorkshire HD7 5UN
01484 843 544

Signature treatment
Decléor Fruit Herbal Velvet Sensation

Brands
Carita
Decléor
Elemis

Expect to pay
Treatments:
£65 for 55 minutes
Stay: from £69 per night in a double room

Bubble rating
4 out of 5 bubbles

The Treatment Rooms

Brighton, East Sussex

If muted, soft atmospheres, woody fragrances, and slow, deep, soothing massages are your cup of tea, then this is next door to heaven. You'll be very reluctant to leave the fluffy cloud of bliss at these top-notch Brighton treatment rooms.

What's on offer

Inside a modest-looking Brighton townhouse, you'll find ten calming treatment rooms. There are no pools or heat facilities here, but you will find a relaxing atmosphere as well as effective treatments for beauty and well-being, including a wide array of facials; choose from aromatherapy, specialist for delicate skin, or a booster for a pick-me-up. The sebo-control facial offers a way to beat shiny oily skin. Oxygen therapy, microdermabrasion and Restylane are available, too.

We loved

The bright and spacious shop, with tempting products from Aromatherapy Associates, Dibi, Refinery, Eve Lom and other sophisticated brands that focus on natural ingredients.

Our comforting Aromatherapy Associates Enrich body wrap: a deeply soothing and nurturing treatment recommended for anyone with a spare £85 who feels a little bruised by the big bad world. We also loved the exotic full body scrub, which uses ground coffee beans in macadamia and coconut oil to exfoliate and prepare your skin for the treatment.

Our therapist's sense of timing and handling of personal space: it was exquisite: we had all the space and time we needed to let our senses expand.

The beautifully lit and fragrant relaxation room; the furnishing is inspired by South East Asia, and the low (but dramatic) lighting is cleverly created by using drapes with hidden lights.

We didn't love

Hearing the sound of footsteps up and down the long corridor outside the treatment room; our Spy spent part of her wrap pondering how people could be persuaded to hush...

Food file

Herbal tea, fruit and water.

Who would like it

Anyone with a vaguely hedonistic streak, regardless of age, shape, denomination or gender: all can feel equally at home here.

Don't miss

The Eve Lom facial. You'll feel like the clichéd million dollars.

Spa type
Treatment rooms

Where?
The Treatment Rooms
21 New Road
Brighton
East Sussex BN1 1UF
01273 818444

Signature treatment
The Treatment Rooms ritual: exfoliation, hot stone massage and facial

Brands
Aromatherapy Associates, Dibi, Eve Lom, Refinery

Expect to pay
Treatments:
£52 for 55 minutes

Bubble rating
5 out of 5 bubbles

Utopia Spa at Rowhill Grange

Rowhill Grange Hotel, Wilmington, Kent

The country-house hotel and the modern spa make a pleasing blend of the traditional and the contemporary. Rowhill Grange is an ideal environment for a spa day or stay for revitalising and pampering.

Spa type
Hotel spa

Where?
Rowhill Grange Hotel
and Utopia Spa
Wilmington
Kent DA2 7QH
01322 612718

Signature treatment
My Kinda Skin
Prescriptive Facial

Brands
Temple Spa

Expect to pay
Treatments:
£68 for 55 minutes
Stay: from £210 for a
standard double room

Bubble rating
4 out of 5 bubbles

What's on offer

An English country manor house, dating back to 1870, set in acres of Kent countryside, with a stylish, spacious and contemporary spa.

The pool area looks like a Roman bathhouse, with stone columns. There are two pools and over forty treatments to choose from, including facials, scrubs, wraps, massages (including lymphatic drainage) and relaxing body treatments. The gym has a complete range of exercise and weight-training equipment, and a fitness studio offers a regular timetable of classes.

We loved

The courteous staff. The My Kinda Skin Prescriptive Facial. The Breakfast Smoothie. The award-winning gardens with manicured lawns, a small lake, and black swans.

We didn't love

It was a little unnerving to have other guests (with children) staring at us in our bathrobes as we lunched.

Food file

Rowhill Grange has two restaurants, the 3AA award-winning restaurant Truffles, and the more relaxed Elements where we enjoyed buffalo mozzarella, plum tomatoes and basil pesto, followed by pumpkin and pecorino romano ravioli with wilted spinach, pine nut and rocket.

Who would like it

Anyone with any excuse to celebrate.

Don't miss

The stainless-steel Jacuzzi.

Vale Hotel, Golf and Spa Resort

Hensol, Cardiff

With 19 treatment rooms, this is Wales's largest health spa, and it offers a wide range of treatments, too. Adjoining a modern hotel, in the middle of a golf course, the pool and heat facilities are accessible to hotel guests and health-club members, while the spa is an oasis of calm upstairs.

What's on offer

The 4-star luxury hotel is set in 650 acres of parkland with two championship golf courses. The health club and spa are in an adjoining building. Facilities shared with health club members include the swimming pool, where you can also find two rather functional steam rooms (think white plastic seats rather than twinkly tiles), a sauna and a whirlpool bath. There is a large and busy gym.

You have a huge range of treatments to choose from; as well as massages, facials, scrubs, wraps, manis and pedis, you can have tanning treatments, waxing, tinting,

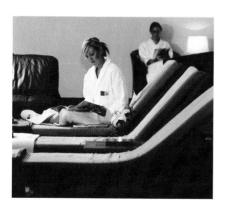

electrolysis and sunbeds. If you're more holistically inclined, you can try shirodara, reiki and reflexology.

We loved

The wide range of treatments on offer, and also the interactive way our therapist climbed onto the couch to give a proper bamboo massage; the friendliness and helpfulness of the spa staff.

We didn't love

The rather tired changing rooms; we do love the fact that these are not shared with the health club, though!

Food file

Herbal teas and coffees in the relaxation lounge; in the evening, grander food in the hotel.

Who would like it

Anyone who wants to combine a country-side or golf break with a little light spa-ing.

Don't miss

The interactive bamboo massage.

Spa type
Hotel spa

Where?
Vale Hotel, Golf
and Spa Resort
Hensol Park, Hensol
Cardiff CF72 8JY
01443 667800

Signature treatment
Vale Spa Indulgence facial

Brands
Clarins, Gerard's

Expect to pay
Treatments:
£50 for 55 minutes
Stay: from £70 for bed and breakfast in a standard double room

Bubble rating
4 out of 5 bubbles

Verbena Spa

The Feversham Arms, Helmsley, North Yorkshire

A relaxed, informal spa in a hotel on the edge of the North Yorkshire Moors. This spa has a country feel with a supremely peaceful atmosphere.

What's on offer?

Some great heat experiences: saunarium, aromatherapy and salt vapour rooms, monsoon shower, ice cave, rasul, outdoor hot tub and outdoor heated swimming pool. The outdoor pool and hot tub are in the spa garden, where a little oasis retreat has been designed around the pool.

Seven treatment rooms, including one double. A manicure and pedicure area. A wide range of Elemis and Anne Sémonin treatments, including wraps, massages, facials and rituals, with treatments for couples, mums-to-be and teens. There are also some suitably sturdy 'Man Spa' treatments. You can book beauty treatments and waxing, too.

The relaxation room is not your usual silent, dimly lit version. This is a large room filled with large comfortable sofas that swallow you up, and a vast selection of magazines on offer.

We loved

The changing rooms with bright red lockers. The treatment rooms: lots of natural materials and natural light. Delightful treatment beds.

The Royal Miracle Ice Facial: it has all the stages you would expect to find in a normal facial, but incorporates the neuro-cosmetics Express Radiance Ice Cubes.

The lemon tea on arrival and the blackberry sorbet at the end of our treatment.

We didn't love

The hot tub closed once it got dark.

Food file

The Juice Bar offers a selection of drinks, home-made smoothies and pastries throughout the day. There is a vast selection of teas and infusions, coffees and other hot drinks, wines and champagnes. The lunch menu provides a perfect selection of spa foods; soups, pasta, salmon and grilled chicken.

Who would like it?

Anyone who is fed up with run-of-the mill, clinical, minimalist, scientific or Thai environments.

Don't miss

The outdoor hot tub!

Spa type
Hotel spa

Where?
Verbena Spa
The Feversham Arms
Helmsley
North Yorkshire YO62 5AG
01439 770 766

Signature treatment
Royal Miracle Ice facial

Brands
Anne Sémonin
Elemis

Expect to pay
Treatments:
£65 for 60 minutes
Stay: from £210 per night in a petit double including dinner, bed and breakfast

Bubble rating
5 out of 5 bubbles

The Vineyard Spa

The Vineyard at Stockcross, Newbury, Berkshire

This luxury hotel has a compact and elegant spa that delivers relaxation on a poolside tray – along with a gourmet chocolate, of course. Tear yourself away from the pool for long enough, and you'll discover unusual, well-delivered spa treatments, and an indulgent Michelin-starred restaurant.

What's on offer

There is a small, circular pool housed in a high, glass dome with glass walls, so you almost feel as if you are outside. There's a snail shower, large Jacuzzi, and sauna and steam rooms. The entire pool area is for relaxing in – there's no separate relaxation room.

The Vineyard is not for you if you want exercise classes or a good workout (you won't find a gym here). It's a spa where you slow down and relax; the aim of the day is to pamper and unwind.

The treatments on offer include a variety of massages, ESPA, Darphin and Ishi facial and body treatments, all sorts of treats for two, specific therapies for men and for mums-to-be.

The Vineyard also offers a variety of spa stays and spa days; you can also chill out after work with a very affordable spa evening, alone or with a friend.

We loved

The diligent, low-key service: plenty of fresh towels delivered to your poolside seat, and a general sense of being looked after. And the robes are among the best you'll ever be asked to wear at a spa: soft, fluffy, and a rich cream colour.

We didn't love

You have to walk through the hotel in your robe to get to the treatment area. You go past the kitchen. We are nosy enough to find this interesting.

Food file

Light and healthy Bento-box lunches, followed by a wonderfully good two-Michelin-starred restaurant for a dinnertime trip to heaven.

Who would like it

Anyone keen on good food who wants to try a top quality treatment, too.

Don't miss

Relaxing by the pool; allow yourself enough time to let the Vineyard's serenity soothe your stresses.

Spa type
Hotel spa

Where?
The Vineyard at Stockcross
Stockcross, Newbury
Berkshire RG20 8JU
01635 528770

Signature treatment
Balinese Journey: body brushing, hot mitts, and Balinese massage

Brands
Darphin, ESPA, Ishi

Expect to pay
Treatments:
£71.55 for 55 minutes
Stay: £399 per night in a Luxury Double room with dinner, breakfast and a 25-minute treatment

Bubble rating
5 out of 5 bubbles

Vitality Detox Retreat

West Wittering, West Sussex

Not a hotel or true spa, but a detox retreat in an inviting, tastefully decorated, spacious house near a beach on the outskirts of the charming village of West Wittering near Chichester. When only complete withdrawal from the world will do, Vitality Detox will transport you to another planet of calm and self-healing.

Spa type

Spa retreat

Where?

Vitality Detox Retreat
Brook House
Pound Road
West Wittering
West Sussex PO20 8AJ
01243 514995

Expect to pay

Treatments:
£40 for 50 minutes
Stay: 7-day retreat; single rooms start from £1,000

Bubble rating

4 out of 5 bubbles

What's on offer

Vitality Detox is run by Mandy Elliott, a trained homeopath and colonic hydrotherapist, and Jem Friar, a naturopath, yoga teacher and bodyworker. They offer an intimate and friendly atmosphere, lots of personal attention and an amazingly calm and kind zeitgeist. The kitchen, with its large central table, is the gathering area, and there's a large 'common'/yoga room.

We booked in for a detox package with juice fasting, colonics, therapies and nutritional talks. Yoga, Chi Gung, meditation, lots of massage, colonic hydrotherapy, structural rebalancing, sports massage, reiki, homeopathy, life counselling, dietary advice and aqua detox. We left full of a new positive energy.

We loved

The way we felt after each excellent, therapeutic treatment: the remedial and relaxation massage left us feeling inches taller, and bright and cheerful.

We didn't love

The pre-fast 'fast' – but it was worth it.

Food file

Delicious juice, mostly. Then – oh joy! – broth in the evening, a wonderfully hot and filling extraction of vegetables.

Who would like it

People with busy lives. Some people are quite ill or in recovery, others want to give up smoking or drinking, and others just need a real break. (There is a sprinkling of local celebrities, who have been known to detox. We'll say no more.)

Don't miss

Emmy, the dog, is a delightful companion on the beautiful beach.

Good Spa Guide **gift vouchers**

The **perfect** present!

Redeemable at over 150 UK spas, our spa gift vouchers are the ideal gift for anyone who needs a little me-time.

A massage in Manchester? A pedicure in Peebles? A facial in Fulham? The lucky recipient can choose the treat, time and place to suit themselves. **You can see the full list of spas that accept our vouchers at www.goodspaguide.co.uk/gifts** – and you can see that we've got the country covered.

Our gift vouchers are available in units of £25, £50 or £100, so you can choose exactly how much to lavish on your lucky recipient. And our vouchers are valid for a full year, so there's plenty of time to choose which spa, which treatment, and which date.

We send out your vouchers in a stylish envelope with our FREE 'How to spa' booklet, so they feel like a real gift.

To purchase your gift vouchers, just call our FREE voucher hotline on: 0800 321 3132. You can pay instantly by debit or credit card.

You can also send a cheque to *The Good Spa Guide Ltd*, and we'll despatch your vouchers by first-class post. Send to: The Good Spa Guide, Unit 6, Hove Business Centre, Hove Park Villas, Hove BN3 6HA

Don't forget to include your name and address so we know where to send your vouchers!

If you order your vouchers by 4pm, Monday to Friday, then we can post your spa gift out first class. We can also organise special delivery. Just give us a call.

Waterfall Spa

Leeds, Yorkshire

This plush, professional spa, in the heart of Leeds city centre, offers great treatments and facilities. Waterfall is a women-only spa. It feels like a place to pamper and indulge, gossip and have fun.

Spa type
Day spa

Where?
Waterfall Spa
3 Brewery Wharf
Dock Street
Leeds
Yorkshire LS10 1JF
0845 634 1399

Signature treatment
Rasul Deluxe

Brands
Waterfall

Expect to pay
Treatments:
£75 for 65 minutes

Bubble rating
4 out of 5 bubbles

What's on offer

A small, well designed spa; the main spa area has a good sized Jacuzzi, an experience shower, a sauna and steam room, plus a relaxation room. No pool or exercise equipment.

The treatments use Waterfall's own range of spa products. They obviously like mums at Waterfall; they have six treats for mums-to-be, including something called a '100-pillows massage'.

They offer a Javanese Lular Ritual – a traditional pre-wedding pamper – that looks great and is unusual. There's also a rasul mud chamber, a range of wraps and exfoliations, the usual pedicures and manicures.

We loved

You may love the fact that it's girls only, but without being too girly.

We didn't love

It's small – there's not enough to fill a whole day – and the customer service is patchy, customers report. As is the chocolate fountain.

Food file

Light bites of sandwiches, snacks, salads, and cakes, as well as more substantial meals (book ahead).

Who would like it

Busy, hard working, women who need some me-time away from work or family responsibilities.

Don't miss

A Rose, Raspberry and Cocoa facial after relaxing in the hydrotherapy pool, tropicarium and steam room.

Whittlebury Hall

Towcester, Northamptonshire

If fun is what you're looking for in your spa day, you'll find it at Whittlebury Hall. The spa primarily provides a relaxing, sharing experience for friends, with some professional treatments as the icing on the cake.

What's on offer

A dedicated spa building attached to the main hotel has at its heart a heat-and-ice experience with a hydrotherapy pool and ceramic heated loungers. There's also an aromatherapy crystal steam room and a salt steam room, a caldarium, the milder heat of a sanarium and tepidarium, foot spas, a traditional sauna and a super-cool ice cave. There's a pool, large enough for lap swimming, a gym with windows overlooking the golf course, and a varied schedule of classes in the exercise studio.

We loved

Our ESPA detoxifying algae wrap was professionally and thoughtfully done. Your therapist will take care to make you feel comfortable at all times, which is no mean feat when she's asking you to wear paper knickers, smearing you with algae and wrapping you up like a chicken.

We didn't love

The number of people there: we had to queue perhaps once too often, whether it was for lunch, or a space in the pool.

Food file

You are given a timed slot to go to the Terrace Café for your lunch. Be on your marks, at the appointed hour, as a queue soon builds up.

Who would like it

If you're looking for a group spa day with good value, you'll find it here.

Don't miss

The class schedule is published in the morning. Sign up early for any that appeal as numbers are limited.

Spa type

Hotel spa

Where?

Whittlebury Hall
Towcester
Northamptonshire
NN12 8QH
0845 400 0002

Signature treatment

The day spa mud wrap floatation

Brands

ESPA, Elemis

Expect to pay

Treatments:
£55 for 50 minutes
Stay: from £215 for bed and breakfast in a standard double room

Bubble rating

4 out of 5 bubbles

Zen Lifestyle Teviot Place

Edinburgh, Scotland

Deservedly popular for their high quality treatments, these smart treatment rooms are dedicated to beauty rather than spa. Come here to be plucked, pampered and polished from top to toe.

Spa type
Treatment rooms

Where?
Zen Lifestyle Teviot Place
2–3 Teviot Place
Edinburgh EH1 2QZ
0131 226 6777

Signature treatment
Zen custom facial

Brands
Elemis
MD Formulations
Murad
Priori

Expect to pay
Treatments:
£85 for 90 minutes

Bubble rating
4 out of 5 bubbles

What's on offer

The shop front on Teviot Place makes a purple statement. Inside, all is spick, span, light and bright, with wooden shelves laden with gleaming products. It feels much more beauty salon than spa, so don't expect to come here and waft around in a robe.

For a small salon, Zen Lifestyle offers a wide range of treatments, including facials and massages, from brands including Elemis, Murad, and Jane Iredale mineral make-up. They offer hot bikini waxing and non-surgical cosmetic treatments.

We loved

The very good, if busy, Three Week pedicure, which uses a bio-gel that bonds to your nails rather than nail polish, so you can expect no chips, flakes or scratches for at least three weeks.

We didn't love

We would have preferred our pedicure to take place in a chair instead of on a treatment bed – your bum gets very numb.

Food file

Herbal teas, organic wine, complimentary chocolate. They'll order food from a local café from a menu of healthy options.

Who would like it

Busy Edinburgh glamour-pusses – Zen Lifestyle, and its sister salon in Bruntsfield Place, are open seven days a week, and offer early-morning and late-evening appointments to fit in around busy lives.

Don't miss

Trying out these tempting treatments – we'd have stayed longer if we could have.

Gleneagles,
see page 115

The A–Z
of spa treatments

The A–Z of spa treatments

a IS FOR...

Abhyanga

See **Massage**

Acupressure

Acupuncture without the needles. This ancient Chinese holistic medical practice identifies 'meridians' or energy paths that form an invisible map across your body. Your Qi (say 'chee') or life energy flows along these meridians. Acupressure applies finger-tip pressure at strategic points along your meridians to remove blockages and improve the flow of energy around your body. When your Qi flows free, the happier and healthier you will be.

Good for   A huge range of physical and emotional health problems, including migraine and problems with vision; muscular and joint pain; treating addictions; and helping you to lose weight.

See also   **Shiatsu**; **Reflexology**; **Reiki**; **Qi**; **Meridians**; **Thai massage**; **Tui Na**

Affusion shower

See **Vichy shower**

Ai Chi

A combination of tai chi, shiatsu and a pool.

Good for   Improving balance and posture, muscular strength and tone; general health and wellbeing.

See also   **Tai Chi**; **Shiatsu**; **Pilates**; **Watsu**; **Yoga**

Algae

In wraps or masks, marine algae nourishes your skin.

Algotherapy

This is a blanket term for any spa treatment that involves algae, seaweed or other marine ingredients. These can be slathered onto or around your face or body, or added to a bath or pool. Doesn't necessarily smell all that great.

Good for   Helping your body to sweat out toxins; improving the tone and radiance of your skin; refreshing and relaxing you generally.

See also   **Wraps**

Loch Lomond Golf Club,
see page 141

| American facial | Facials in the United States are a bit different from ours (they call ours 'European facials'). We go for a facial as much for the luxurious comfort of having creams, lotions and oils smoothed and massaged into our skin, as for the potential results. An American facial is results-focused and usually features 'manual extraction' where blackheads and other impurities are removed by hand or 'implement'. At best, this is uncomfortable; at worst, painful. The American facial can feel more like a procedure than a treat(ment). But the results can be quite dramatic. |

| | Good for | Really clearing out your pores and ensuring you leave with healthier skin. |

| | See also | **Facial**; **European facial** |

| Anthotherapy | Spa treatments in caves! A bit like having a treatment in a steam room or sauna, as some caves are hot and wet, others hot and dry. The caves are heated by a nearby hot spring or volcanic rock, and vary in temperature. You may find a whole range of thermal caves but, if you do, it means you're not in the UK any more. |

| | Good for | Relaxing; easing sore muscles and tired minds; having something unusual to talk about at parties. |

| | See also | **Heat treatment**; **Thermotherapy** |

| Arctic shower | As it sounds – a shower cold enough to turn you blue. |

| | Good for | Refreshing you after a heat treatment. |

| | See also | **Ice fountain**; **Heat treatment**; **Hydrotherapy**; **Thalassotherapy** |

| Aroma bath | See **Baths** |

| Aroma room | Usually a feature of a thermal suite of steam rooms, saunas and other heat facilities, an aroma room or aroma grotto is a warm, tiled or rock-lined room with seating for a few people. Aromatic steam from essential oils is wafted into the room. |

| | Good for | It depends on the oil used: with eucalyptus, this can be a great way to treat a cold and clear your sinuses; lavender will make you feel snoozy and calm. |

| | See also | **Aromatherapy**; **Aroma bath**; **Phytotherapy** |

Aromatherapy	Aromatherapy uses warm essential oils to activate your sense of smell and increase your sense of wellbeing. The oils are massaged into your skin, dropped into water for you to bathe in, or blended with other oils or steam for you to inhale. The powerful oils used in aromatherapy are extracted from plants, shrubs, flowers, bark, peel, resin, grasses, fruits, roots, trees, petals, stems or seeds. Our sense of smell is very powerful and triggers memories and emotions. The therapist uses this fact to bring you a very particular experience, from making you feel relaxed to energising you.

Good for	Can be used to relieve stress, anxiety, sleeplessness and bad temper, and can also energise you.

See also	**Baths**; **Massage**; **Phytotherapy**

Ayurveda	An ancient Hindu medical practice based on the idea that the body, mind and spirit must be treated together. The treatment starts with an assessment of your health and lifestyle, to personalise it to suit your 'dosha'. Ayurvedic therapists are trained to focus on the 'marma points' – similar to the pressure points in reflexology, acupuncture and acupressure. A favourite among celebrities, Ayurveda is a lifestyle, not just a treatment.

Good for	Detoxing; cleansing; boosting your immune system; improving whole-body health and wellbeing; making changes to your lifestyle so that you can be happier and healthier.

See also	**Ayurvedic massage**; **Dosha**; **Indian head massage**; **Shirodhara**

Ayurvedic massage	See **Massage**

 IS FOR…

Balinese Boreh	This invigorating spa ritual traditionally begins with a foot bath and massage, followed by a relaxing face and head massage. A warming Boreh Wrap envelops you in spices – sandalwood, ginger, cinnamon and ground rice. Once you're unwrapped, the herbal paste is rubbed into your body to polish the skin. Finally, moisturising oils are rubbed into your skin.

Good for	Deep relaxation, loose muscles and nurtured, soft skin.

See also	**Balinese massage**; **Indonesian massage**; **Wraps**

Balinese massage	See **Massage**

Hand Picked Hotels, see pages 48, 156, 177

Balneotherapy	See **Baths**
Baths	See pages 250–252
Bleaching	A technique to blanch the hairs on your face or body; it carries the same risks of mild skin-burning as depilatory creams, without removing the hair.
	Good for What it says – rendering your body hair translucent.
	See also **Hair removal**
Body polish	See **Scrub**
Body treatment	A blanket term for a whole range of holistic procedures aimed at helping you achieve something specific for your body. You might be:

- massaged or scrubbed with something – a specific oil, cream or mineral
- wrapped or enveloped in something – mud, seaweed or even plastic
- immersed or soaked in something – from water to algae
- stroked, treated with or exposed to something – such as brushes, magnets, or electric current or lights.

Good for   Anything from soothing muscles, and relieving stress, to detoxing after over-indulging on holiday.

See also   **Wraps**; **Scrub**; **Heat treatment**

Botox	Botox is an artificial substance, and a brand name for a laboratory-produced chemical called botulinum toxin. It relaxes and 'freezes' facial and other muscles. Botox is used to get rid of lines and wrinkles. Its effects last a few months and develop slowly over a week or so after it is first injected.

Good for   Ironing out existing lines and wrinkles around your eyes, mouth, nose and forehead; 'training' your muscles not to crease – but watch out! Remember: your face should still move.

See also   **Collagen**; **Facial filler**

Bowen technique	See **Massage**
Brine bath	See **Baths**
Brossage	A body polish that is carried out with lots of small, soft-bristled brushes. These soft brushes are also sometimes used in facials.
	Good for Boosting exfoliation and circulation.
	See also **Scrub**

baths

Roman baths, Turkish baths, hot springs, babbling brooks – water is the essence of a traditional spa. You can have a spa bath as part of a package or as a treatment on its own. In a spa, your bath will probably be bigger than at home and will certainly feel more luxurious. You'll enjoy it in a room that is specially lit, scented and heated just for you. Submersion in water is a treat in itself. But, while just being in warm or hot water cleanses and relaxes you, it's what you add to the water, and the ritual and time you take over it, that really distinguishes these baths.

Different types of bath

Aroma

A bath containing water infused with herbs and essential oils. It smells nice, hence the title! Great for relaxing, cleansing or refreshing.

Aromatherapy

A hot bath infused with sensual essential oils will soothe and relax, or invigorate you, depending on which aromatherapy oils are added to it. Eucalyptus is particularly good if you have a cold or blocked sinuses. Lavender will soothe and relax you.

Balinese multi-steam

A gentle, sensual and very relaxing experience in which a steam bath is infused with subtle aromas of jasmine oil, believed to soothe the spirit.

Balneotherapy

A fancy term for a warm mineral bath. Your body is massaged by strong jets of water, which may alternate between hot and cooler temperatures. Good for boosting circulation, cleansing your skin, and soothing tired limbs.

Brine

Salt or salts are added to the water to relieve aches and pains.

Flower	Flower petals and essence are added to the water. There are many variations, including **Japanese flower** and **Indian blossom** baths, and each promises a slightly different experience. Take your pick!
Foot	A favourite pre- and sometimes post-ritual treatment. The therapist will begin by placing your feet into a shallow bowl/bath of water that has been treated with herbal or plant oils. The water will probably be warm. This kind of footbath feels very luxurious and pampering, and is a pretty good bet for a therapist worried about whiffy feet.
Herbal	A full-sized or foot bath containing herbs and possibly essential oils. As you bathe in hot or tepid water, you breathe in the aromas of whatever has been added.
Hot tub	Similar to a Jacuzzi except it is usually made of wood and is more for soaking than luxuriating. Strictly speaking, not very bubbly.
Jacuzzi	A (usually) circular bath, large enough for several people, with a seat-level inside. The water is warm, and bubbles vigorously. Jets of water provide gentle massage and a bubbling water surface for a bath that is more invigorating and luxurious. An outdoor Jacuzzi is a real treat – watch the bubbles leak steam into the cold air while you snuggle down in your hydro-blanket. Think James Bond and champagne. Good for relaxing and restoring your spirit at the end of a hard day, and it'll soothe tired muscles too.
Japanese enzyme	Japanese spa-ing is all about purity and simplicity. And this bath is a really refreshing, cleansing and exotic treat. You sit in a wooden tub or deep barrel, which is filled with an aromatic blend of Japanese plant enzymes. You get a cup of hot enzyme tea while you're in there. The enzyme-infused water is thought to boost circulation. It's unusual and fun.
Japanese salt-steam	Gently-heated mineral water infused with herbs and plants. The gentle heating of this salty water produces a really bracing, salty, aromatic mist. One of these baths will clear your sinuses, relieve stress and anxiety and boost energy – all at the same time.
Kneipp	Father Sebastian Kneipp devised these herbal and mineral baths of different temperatures, from which various health benefits are derived. The Kneipp system combines these with purifying diet, exercise and spiritual practices to improve general health and fitness, both emotionally and physically.

Mineral	Minerals – salts, muds, and water containing them – have been renowned for their health-benefits for centuries; the Dead Sea, the salt flats of Turkey and the Blue Lagoon in Iceland are three of the most famous. People still travel to find them in order to have their minds, bodies and souls refreshed, cleansed and renewed, and to treat specific conditions from psoriasis to osteoarthritis.
Mud and algae	There are various kinds of mud and algae baths. You might have a mineral-style bath whose ingredients are mud- or algae-based. Alternatively, this treatment is as it sounds: you immerse yourself in mud or algae. Both are actually surprisingly warming and relaxing. Once you've got over the initial oddness of getting into a bath full of goo... You will usually be in there for between 10 and 20 minutes. The aim is to detoxify and deeply relax your muscles and leave your skin feeling soft and hydrated.
Oil/cream	Essential oils and creams are dissolved in the water or rubbed into your skin before you get into the bath. The water activates the oils and makes their effects more intense, so you feel truly relaxed – a real aromatic treat.
Ozonized	This hot bath bubbles clean, oxygenated water around you. Feels great.
Peat	Back to nature, anyone? We know it doesn't sound promising but the peat is full of proteins and minerals that are great for your skin and actually smell pleasantly musty and earthy. There are different ways of 'doing' this. Sometimes, spas will mix the peat with other ingredients to make a sweeter smelling herbal paste which is rubbed into your skin by you or a therapist, before or during your bath. Alternatively, it may be added to the water.
Whirlpool	Similar in some ways to a Jacuzzi, a whirlpool features warm water, under-water jets to massage your body, and constantly moving water. A relaxing and fun way to improve circulation.

Good for	Different kinds of baths will propose different health and relaxation benefits – bathe in the choice of possibilities!
See also	**Heat treatment**; **Hydrotherapy**; **Indian blossom steam room**; **Pools**

C IS FOR...

Caldarium

A warm room into which steam is piped – similar to an aroma room.

Good for   Depends on the aroma, of course, but generally relaxing and calming.

See also   **Aroma room**; **Aromatherapy**; **Laconium**

Cathiodermie

A skin treatment that uses a very low electrical current to help boost circulation and cleanse your pores deep down.

Good for   Deep cleansing.

See also   **Ionithermie**

Chakra

A Sanskrit word referring to the energy system in our bodies. Many holistic health approaches and forms of massage focus on the chakras – by applying pressure to the chakra points, it is believed that our tension can be unlocked and released, soothing and bringing emotional and physical relief.

See also   **Acupressure**; **Qi**

Champissage

Another term for Indian head massage (see **Massage**).

Collagen

This naturally-occurring substance makes up about a quarter of the protein in your body. It is the main support of skin, tendon, bone, cartilage and connective tissue. It is used in creams and can also be injected to plump out your skin, reduce the appearance of fine lines and enhance your lips and cheekbones.

Good for   Ironing out fine lines and wrinkles and making you look brighter and younger.

See also   **Botox**; **Facial filler**

Colonic irrigation

There is no polite way to say this, so let's be clear. In colonic irrigation, a tube is inserted up your bottom and water is pumped gradually through your colon. As the water comes back out, it brings all the horrible sludge that you've been storing out with it.

Good for   A really meaningful detox, it literally flushes out your system; temporary weight loss.

See also   **Wraps**

Colour analysis	Usually part of a beauty and style consultation or 'makeover'. A therapist makes an analysis of which colours will suit you best.
	Good for Enhancing your body image; making sure you look your best.
	See also **Makeover**
Cranio-sacral therapy	See **Massage**
Cross-fibre friction	See **Massage**
Crystal massage	See **Massage**
Crystal therapy	A healing practice dating back to ancient civilisations such as the Incas and Mayans. Quartz crystals and other stones are placed on strategic points on your body to stimulate vibrations and release energy blockages.
	Good for Releasing tension; facilitating healing.
	See also **Acupressure**; **Massage**
Cupping	This traditional Chinese medical practice temporarily leaves raised, red 'wheals' on your skin, as nobly exhibited by Gwyneth Paltrow in a backless dress. A heated cup is placed on your body and a vacuum created, sucking up your skin. The immediate effects are a bit alarming (see Gwyneth) but it is a deeply relaxing treatment.
	Good for The suction drains excess fluids and toxins from the muscle tissue, stimulates the nervous system and brings blood flow to your muscles and skin.

d IS FOR...

Dead Sea mud	See **Mud**
Deep sea minerals	Rich in chlorophyll and detoxifying minerals, sea algae, seaweed, sea water and mud are applied in treatments to your skin. Often used in wraps.
	Good for Detoxifying the skin, energising by stimulating circulation of oxygen in blood around the body; improving skin tone and texture; discouraging cellulite.
	See also **Baths**; **Wraps**

Deep tissue massage	See **Massage**

Dosha

The central element of the ayurvedic system of healthcare, a dosha is a unique mix of energies:

- 'vata' – blood, circulation and healing
- 'pitta' – heat and metabolism
- 'kapha' – your spiritual and philosophical make-up.

Every human being has a different blend of these energies and therefore a different dosha. A person's dosha determines the most balancing and healthy lifestyle for them, including the best food and exercise.

See also   **Ayurveda**

 IS FOR...

Esalen massage   See **Massage**

European facial

The 'common-or-garden' facial on this side of the Atlantic, this is a soothing facial that includes techniques to improve our skin while making us feel pampered and relaxed. It usually involves cleansing, exfoliating and a mask, and may include massage while you're waiting for the mask to work its wonders.

Good for   Working different magics for your skin, while relaxing and refreshing you.

See also   **American facial**; **Exfoliation**; **Indian head massage**

Exfoliation

The removal of the top layer of dead or tired skin cells to reveal your lovely fresh peachy layer underneath.

Good for   Instantly improving your skin tone and texture; improving circulation of oxygen to the surface of your skin to make it look brighter and fresher.

See also   **Brossage**

**Bedruthan
Steps**, see
page 40

Eye treatment

You can choose from a huge range of non-surgical eye treatments, all aimed at making you look even younger and more beautiful. Available in the high street as well as spas, and many are cheap and quick. They can help firm your skin, brighten your outlook and shape your brows.

There are four main sorts of eye treatment:

- Grooming: plucking, shaping and tinting
- Lotions and potions to reduce puffiness, dark circles and light wrinkles
- Non-surgical procedures, such as Botox injections, to iron out deep lines and retrain your facial muscles
- Massage and electrotherapy to stimulate lymph and oxygen flow around the eyes, to revitalise and refresh.

Good for   Making you look fresher and younger, and making sure the attention is on your eyes – not the bags underneath them.

See also   **Botox**; **Collagen**

f IS FOR…

Face mask

A blend of ingredients applied generously to your skin, left (usually) for around 10–15 minutes and then removed. There is an abundant variety, based on clay, oils, algae, seaweed or creams. Each will bestow different benefits on your skin. Some harden as you're wearing them, others soak into your skin. In a spa treatment, a face mask often signals 15 minutes of something else – while it's working its magic on your face, your therapist might massage your hands, feet, head or some other deserving limb.

Good for   All sorts of things, depending on the mask, from cleansing, firming and drawing out skin impurities to deep moisturising.

See also   **Facials**; **Exfoliation**; **Gommage**

Facial

A beauty treatment for your face. The facials on offer at spas are many and diverse, and might feature massage, mud, hot stones, aromatherapy, electrical currents, microdermabrasion, peels…

Good for   This depends largely on the type of facial that you have. Its title should give you an idea of its general intention. Pretty much all facials will cleanse, exfoliate, tone and moisturise your skin.

See also   **American facial**; **Cathiodermie**; **European facial**; **Microdermabrasion**

| Facial filler | This refers to cosmetic or spa treatments and beauty products that literally fill in the wrinkles and lines in your skin. The term covers creams and injections, all of which are referred to as 'non-surgical procedures'... although injecting chemicals into your skin sounds pretty borderline surgical to us. But the results of facial fillers – both creams and injections – can be quite stunning and take years off you in a single stroke. Hurray! |

Different types of facial filler

Filler creams These are not necessarily the same as age-defying or anti-wrinkle moisturisers, in that they may not offer preventative treatment. Many act as a kind of Polyfilla, resurfacing your skin and offering immediate but temporary results. Collagen is often included in these creams.

Injected fillers Injected fillers, such as Collagen and Perlane, can be used to plump up and reshape areas of your face, such as lips, cheeks and nose, and fill in scars. The effects of injected fillers can last for up to nine months.

Good for   This depends partly on which you go for, your skin type, and your skin's receptiveness to the product. But there's no denying that fillers can visibly and often immediately reduce the appearance of wrinkles and sometimes even quite deep lines.

See also   **Botox; Collagen**; **Facial**; **Non-surgical facelift**

| Fangotherapy | See **Mud** |

| Floatation | Floatation is a deeply relaxing body treatment that allows you to experience total weightlessness. It's like... physical dreaming. Unlike floating in the ocean or a pool, where you need to contribute physically to staying afloat, this spa treatment allows you complete effortless relaxation. Some floatation treatments indulge your other senses as well, with lights, sounds and variations in temperature all helping to make it a whole-body experience that should ooze into your whole consciousness. Floatation tanks allow privacy and quiet, which is why this treatment is often described as returning you to a womb-like state. |

Different types of floatation

Wet floatation Salts are added to pure, clean water to allow it to take your full body weight. You might have a Dead Sea, mineral, aromatherapy or herbal floatation, which simply describes the kind of salt that has been added to the water to make you float. Each mineral will do different things for you and your skin – they might be detoxing, softening or sensuous.

Dry floatation This can be combined with other treatments, and you don't have to get wet. You are cocooned in a kind of plastic blanket, which is full of water. You can have a cream/mud/ aromatherapy body treatment that includes dry floatation – the warm water surrounding you helps your skin absorb the oils and lotions more effectively.

Meditation floatation Likely to include special lights and gentle music to help you relax deeply.

Good for   Really deep relaxation; relieving stress on joints and muscles; encouraging easier and deeper sleep; causing your body to release endorphins, which relieves pain and may lower blood pressure, and makes you feel brighter and happier!

See also   **Relaxation massage**; **Shirodhara**

Flower bath	See **Baths**
Footbath	See **Baths**
Frigi-thalgo	A cold wrap designed to eliminate excess water from body tissues.

g IS FOR…

Geothermal   Describes naturally occurring hot springs. Often found in volcanic areas.

Good for   A mineral burst of soothing waters, relaxation and fun.

See also   **Heat treatment**; **Pools**

Gommage   An unusual spa treatment that uses a mixture of clay, oils and herbs to exfoliate your body. Smoothed onto your skin in long, stroking movements, it is a kind of mask applied to your body like a massage.

Good for   Depending on the ingredients of the gommage, this can be used to exfoliate, hydrate or draw out toxins; very relaxing.

See also   **Exfoliation**; **Wraps**

Green tea   The favourite drink offered to health spa-goers and generally drunk by anyone with good intentions. A light but distinctively flavoured hot beverage.

Good for   Believed to flush out toxins and rehydrate you.

See also   **Phytotherapy**

h IS FOR...

Hair removal   See page 262

Hammam   A hammam can be either a single, tiled steam room or a suite of steam rooms and pools for communal use. In UK spa-terms, 'hammam' usually describes a single room with central water taps and recessed bench-seats. They are often referred to as 'chambers' (serail mud chamber, for example) but don't be alarmed – they are more like exotic luxurious grottos.

In a more traditional Turkish hammam, you will find many different rooms and chambers, each offering different water-based benefits. There is often a suggested order for using the facilities to gain maximum benefit. Your visit may include a luxurious, rigorous soap-wash and a short massage with essential oils.

Good for   Getting really clean and chilling out in a deeply sensuous environment.

See also   **Heat treatment**; **Rasul**; **Saunas**; **Serail**; **Steam rooms**

Le Kalon,
see page 137

| Heat treatment | A heat treatment uses wet or dry heat to cleanse you, relax you and relieve your body of aches and pains. In a steam room, hot, wet air is pumped into the room. In a sauna, the heat is dry and is pumped into the room using vents or generated by stones being heated in the room. |

Heat treatments can:

- cleanse your skin by opening up the pores and drawing out dirt and toxins
- stimulate your circulation, boosting your immune system and encouraging your body to heal itself of infections and scarring
- remove calcium deposits from the blood vessels and so break down scar tissue
- help shift a cold, opening your airways and helping you breathe more easily, and relieving headaches and sinus problems
- ease rheumatic and muscular pain, as the heat warms and soothes the muscles and encourages better mobility in your joints
- relax you, as stress and tension melt away.

Good for — Strangely, a good way to think about a heat treatment is to compare it with having a fever. A fever is one of your body's natural tools for healing itself. In many ways, heat treatments recreate your body's own natural state of fever, and offer the same benefits. The difference, of course, is that steam rooms and saunas are a pleasant experience!

See also — **Fangotherapy**; **Rasul**; **Sauna**; **Steam room**; **Serail**; **Wraps**

Hellerwork — A series of different spa treatments, each lasting about an hour and a half. Developed by Joseph Heller (hence the name), Hellerwork takes a holistic approach to your health, featuring discussions about your lifestyle, diet and general health, as well as deep tissue massage and body work.

Good for — Preventing injury; posture; general health.

See also — **Ayurveda**; **Meditation**; **Pilates**; **Yoga**

Herbal bath — See **Baths**

hair removal

There is an assortment of ways to remove any hair you don't want, occupying a spectrum that features: discomfort > inconvenience > mess > pain.

All the options for hair removal are vastly-improved experiences when carried out by a third party in a professional establishment, particularly if you can follow the hair removal with a soothing body treatment, massage or water therapy.

Depilatory creams and foams The coward's first port of call, as it seems like the gentlest option. But beware...

- leave it on for too short a time and you'll have almost as much hair as you started with
- leave it on for the right amount of time (which, incidentally, depends on your skin and the type of hair you have as much as the producer's recommendations) and you may still have some stragglers that you have to pluck
- leave it on too long and you may get minor burns.

Electrolysis Removes hair and discourages it from growing back. But it does involve mild electricity, a lot of patience and accuracy. Electrolysis is effective but very time-consuming and potentially expensive.

Plucking In the category of 'mild discomfort', plucking is usually only feasible for eyebrows and stragglers, as it's time-consuming and a bit tricky.

Shaving An effective but short-term solution. For women, shaving should only be carried out on legs and underarms, never on the face. For men, the opposite is true. Only ever to be carried out with care, cream and a high-quality razor.

Waxing The most effective means of removing hair, this is also (in what we'll describe simply as 'some areas') the most painful. It is many people's chosen method of holiday hair-removal as you can depend on it lasting for a few weeks without embarrassing regrowth. You have a choice of hot and cold, molten and glue-like strips and, probably, spatulas: some to apply the wax and another to bite down on hard during the procedure to prevent you from crying out.

Many spas can also offer you other hair removal treatments. These include:

Light/laser therapy The most hi-tech option, this procedure definitely falls into the pseudo-medical category, as it involves a full consultation, a doctor on site and, in many cases, the wearing of goggles by you and the person carrying out the treatment. It isn't cheap and is very time-consuming but should give you permanent hair removal.

Sugaring This sweet-sounding option is similar to waxing but the sugar applied is cooler and sticks to your hair more than your skin, so is more comfortable. Some say it is ultimately less effective than waxing, but a good 'sugarer' will do as good a job with less pain.

| Holistic | A holistic treatment is one that aims to do you good through and through! It will include healing therapies that usually take into account your lifestyle, health, diet and exercise routine, and tailor the treatments to you. Many different treatments can therefore come under the banner of 'holistic'. Some spas offer holistic health services; this means you may have a health and lifestyle assessment, and receive advice on how to change various aspects of your life to make you feel and look better. |

Good for   Launching into a new, healthier, happier you!

See also   **Acupressure**; **Ayurveda**; **Jin shin jyutsu**; **Lomi lomi**; **Reflexology**; **Shiatsu**

| Hot poultice | A tightly-packed mixture of herbs, covered with muslin, which is heated and used to massage along pulse points on your body during a treatment. It feels similar to stones, as it is pressed and rolled along your skin. This is a deeply relaxing and unusual treatment that smells soothing and feels very comforting, particularly when padded onto the soles of your feet and the palms of your hands. |

Good for   Relaxation; aromatherapeutic blast.

See also   **Aromatherapy**; **Phytotherapy**; **Pressure point**; **Relaxation massage**

| Hot stone massage | See **Massage** |

| Hot tub | See **Baths** |

| Hydrotherapy | Therapeutic whole-body treatments that involve moving and exercising in water – physiotherapy in a pool. Hydrotherapy pools are different from ordinary pools, as the temperature, pressure and movement of the water is changed according to who's using the pool, and why. You can have hydrotherapy in any pool, however, as it is largely to do with movement. |

Some spas have a series of hydrotherapy pools, each of which is differently powered, heated and treated to allow you to have fun, be invigorated or be soothed, depending on what's in the pool and how the water is moving.

⬤

Scarlet Spa,
see page 189

Different types of hydrotherapy

Hydro-massage Powerful jets of water massage you while you are in the pool. The jets are usually placed at different heights so you can use them on specific parts of your body. The water is usually warm, and may also contain minerals or essential oils to introduce another dimension to the massage.

Colonic hydrotherapy Your basic enema, colon hydrotherapy is carried out with water to really sluice you out and rid you of your toxins.

Marine hydrotherapy A form of thalassotherapy, where jets of salt water are used to massage the body.

Scotch hose/Jet blitz As it sounds, really! Like the tactic used for crowd dispersal, you pay someone to spray you with hot, cold and tepid water from a high-pressure hose. It's supposed to relieve tension.

Good for   Being immersed, buoyant or massaged in water can relieve our bodies in a variety of different ways. Hydrotherapy can help with many physical and emotional complaints, including back pain, rheumatic pain and arthritis, anxiety and stress, poor circulation, muscle and joint pain, headaches and even neurological conditions such as strokes or brain injuries.

See also   **Floatation**; **Pools**; **Thalassotherapy**

I IS FOR...

Ice fountain

This is a fairly grand name for what is essentially an open ice-making machine. Crushed ice is provided in basins in the spa, so that you can rub handfuls of the stuff over your body to cool you down between heat treatments. Can be very refreshing rather than frightening, when you're hot, hot, hot.

Good for   Giving your circulation a good workout; making you really appreciate a hot shower.

See also   **Arctic shower; Hydrotherapy; Sauna**

Indian blossom steam room

Steam infused with eucalyptus or menthol is released around you as you sit in a tiled or wooden-benched room. Jasmine may be blended with the other aromas. Versions of this treatment include 'aroma rooms' or 'aroma grottos' in some spas. A **tropicarium** is also a version of this, as it wafts similar essential oils to clear out your respiratory system.

Good for   Clearing out your sinuses and energising or soothing you, depending on what's in the steam.

See also   **Aroma room; Heat treatment; Hydrotherapy**

Indian head massage

Also called **Champissage**. See **Massage**

Indonesian massage See **Massage**

Ionithermie

A spa treatment that uses mild electrical currents to stimulate the nerves in your body. Using pen-like instruments, the therapist applies very short bursts of current, which tingle a little when applied. It's odd, but not painful. Often a feature in slimming, detoxing and shaping spa treatments.

Good for   Stimulating the lymphatic system to work harder to clean out your toxins. It can also help tighten up the muscles in your 'problem areas'. It's weird, true, but it can be effective at improving the tone of localised muscle.

Iridology

A way of assessing your holistic health by analysing the iris of your eye.

See also   **Ayurveda; Hellerwork**

j IS FOR...

Jacuzzi   See **Baths**

Japanese bath   See **Baths**

Jet blitz   Also known as **Scotch hose**. See **Hydrotherapy**

Jin shin jyutsu   A holistic, healing treatment, which uses gentle touch to balance your body, mind and spirit. Jin shin jyutsu is a bit like acupuncture, in that it is based on the idea that our bodies are mapped by paths which carry 'Qi' or energy; when the energy flows freely, you are balanced and healthy. When the flow of energy is blocked, you experience pain and discomfort. Jin shin jyutsu helps unblock and keep your energy flowing by tapping into your energy paths via points on your body similar to acupoints in acupuncture.

Good for   Relieving muscle or joint pain; helping with breathing problems, sleeping and eating disorders, anxiety, stress and depression.

See also   **Acupressure**; **Reiki**; **Meridian**; **Shiatsu**

Brandshatch Place, see page 48

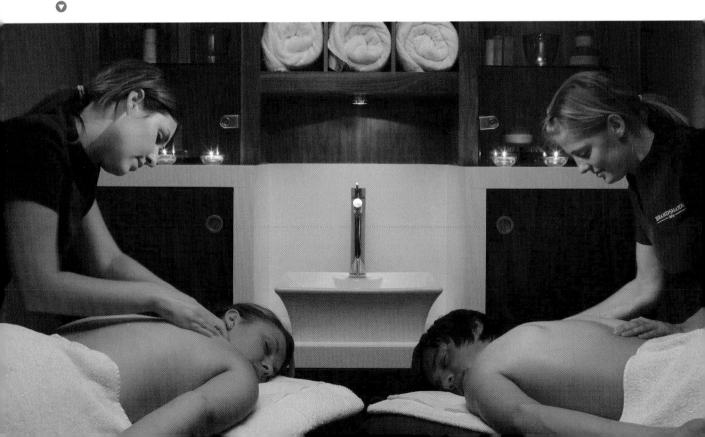

K IS FOR...

Kneipp system   See **Baths**

Ko bi do   A Japanese facial massage using acupressure along the facial meridians with the aim of preventing wrinkles.

l IS FOR...

Laconium   See **Sauna**

Lomi lomi   See **Massage**

Lymph   The clear, yellowish fluid that flows around your body, carrying white blood cells and antibodies to your tissues and organs. These are essential to your immune system and help you fight infection. Day after day, we dump toxins into our bodies: we eat badly, live in dirty cities full of pollution, drink too much alcohol and eat too much sugar, and our lifestyles are unforgiving and unhealthy. Your lymphatic system's job is to flush all the toxins away, and keep you healthy.

Good for   Getting your lymph moving smoothly around your body will help your immune system to work efficiently to remove and prevent infection.

See also   **Deep tissue massage**; **Lymphatic drainage massage**

Lymphatic drainage massage   See **Massage**

IS FOR...

Makeover   A makeover aims to renew you and refresh your whole look by transforming your beauty and shopping habits. It usually includes an assessment of the colours of clothes and make-up that suit you best, a haircut, a full make-up, and some information and inspiration on how to combine colours and clothes to suit your body shape and skin tone.

Good for   Making you look better and feel more confident.

See also   **Colour analysis**; **Manicure**; **Pedicure**

Manicure	A beauty treatment for your hands and nails. A manicurist uses a variety of tools, creams, oils, waxes and massage techniques to clean and shape your nails, care for your cuticles and generally improve the look and feel of your hands. Different kinds of manicure include different things – a different shaping of the nail, different oils and cream, or even electro-pulse or hot stone massage.

Different types of manicure

American A very natural-looking manicure that shapes the nails to your finger tip.

French This classic manicure uses clear or ivory-coloured polish on the body of the nail, and whitens the tip. The nail is cut more or less square.

Hot stone manicure Features a hand massage and uses hot stone therapy to soothe and relax your hand.

Intensive paraffin wax Warm wax is rubbed into your nails, hands and wrists to moisturise and soften.

Luxury This whole-hand treatment will include a hand massage, softening paraffin wax and heated mittens, or a wrap that warms and soothes your hands, and softens and hydrates your nails.

Good for   Improving the texture and health of your nails and skin, as well as leaving the nails looking polished and perfect.

See also   **Pedicure**

Marine treatments	From hydrotherapy using sea water to algae wraps and mineral mud masks, marine treatments use nutrients from the oceans to rehydrate and remineralise.

See also   **Algae**; **Deep sea minerals**; **Thalassotherapy**

Marma	Part of ayurvedic medical practice, marma points are similar to pressure points in acupressure, acupuncture and Shiatsu. They are points along the energy paths that map your body, which, when pressed, release tension and unlock pain.

See also   **Acupressure**; **Chakra**; **Meridian**; **Qi**; **Reflexology**

massage

There are many different kinds of massage, each springing from broadly different origins and aims, but all involve the stroking, kneading, warming, rolling and pressing of skin and muscles. Massage encourages blood flow, which increases the amount of oxygen and nutrients that reach your organs and tissues.

Different types of massage

Abhyanga
One of the massage techniques that makes up the Indian holistic medical practice, Ayurveda. Herbal oils are especially chosen to suit you to make sure you have a unique, relaxing, muscle-soothing massage.

Aromatherapy
The aroma of essential oils can affect how you feel. During an aromatherapy massage, your skin absorbs the warmed essential oils, which can improve the effectiveness of the massage. Depending on the oils used, aromatherapy massage can relieve stress and anxiety, help you relax and sleep better, soothe pain, including tired or aching muscles, improve flexibility, improve skin tone, aid concentration and calm your temper.

Ayurvedic
A general term, and generalised massage, covering a variety of ancient Indian techniques. A typical ayurvedic massage will be tailored to your needs, using essential oils chosen especially for you, after an initial lifestyle and health assessment. It will involve a variety of strokes and movements, again, designed according to your needs. It may focus on a particular area of your body, such as your head or shoulders.

Balinese
Related to Ayurveda and its techniques, Balinese massage uses a combination of gentle stretches, acupressure and aromatherapy oils to stimulate the flow of blood, oxygen and 'Qi' around your body, relax and soothe you. Helps to soothe damaged tissue, relieve strained muscles and joint pain, boost circulation, and good for sleep problems, stress and anxiety.

Bowen technique
Named after its Australian founder, Tom Bowen, this is a gentle massage-and-release technique that intermittently uses light, rolling pressure and then rest. It aims to give your muscles room to breathe and adjust. No oils are used and you wear loose-fitting clothing. It can improve circulation and posture, is often used with people recovering from injury and is popular with older people, disabled people and children.

Champissage	Another term for **Indian head massage**.
Cranio-sacral therapy	This head massage helps to release tension, reduce the pain and regularity of headaches and migraines, and improve vision and concentration. It can be quite uncomfortable if you are storing a lot of tension in your scalp, as the therapist will have to work harder to release it.
Cross-fibre friction	A specialist massage technique that is a feature of deep tissue and sports massage. The therapist applies pressure across the muscle, at right angles to the fibres, instead of rubbing along it. Used for improving circulation, stimulating lymph and blood flow, unlocking pain and tension in the muscles.
Crystal	Massage using warmed crystals and/or a crystal wand. Similar in practice to hot stone therapy, but therapists who use crystals believe them to promote self-healing, balance and peace.
Deep tissue	Does 'what it says on the tin', working on the deeper layers of muscle tissue. Similar to Swedish massage, deep tissue massage uses slower, firmer strokes and pressure than other treatments. It also uses deep finger pressure that concentrates on particular areas, and follows or goes across the fibres of muscles and tendons. It's good for unknotting and loosening muscles, refreshing and relaxing, increasing blood flow (and therefore the oxygen flow around your body), and getting rid of toxins in very sore and strained muscles, which helps them to strengthen and heal. It's often used to treat people who are recovering from accidents, and for sports injuries.
Esalen	A deeply relaxing combination of Swedish massage and sensory relaxation techniques, Esalen is a very comforting massage that uses long, stroking movements and gentle stretching. It can be quite a hypnotic technique and leaves you feeling serene.
Hot stone	Also known as **thermotherapy**, hot stone massage uses heated basalt stones laid or rolled on strategic parts of your body. The direct heat relaxes the muscles, making for a more effective and intense massage. The stones are often coated in fragrant oil to increase your sense of relaxation and calm. Hot stones expand the blood vessels and sedate the nervous system; cooler ones constrict the blood vessels and gently wake the nervous system up. The combination of relaxing warmth and refreshing coolness is thought to encourage the body to detox and heal, increasing lymph flow and helping to flush out waste.
	Note: LaStone Therapy is a brand name for this treatment.

Indian head	Also known as **champissage** and **shiroabhyanga**, this ancient treatment has been practised in India for thousands of years, and is incredibly relaxing. Part of the Hindu practice of Ayurveda, Indian head massage focuses on your head, neck and shoulders, combining chakra-cleansing massage with the aromatic power of essential oils. It uses a variety of techniques to tap into your seven chakras (meridians/paths of energy) and encourage healing and balance in your whole body. These massages can relieve aches, pains and tension in your neck, back and shoulders; improve the texture of your hair; stimulate the flow of blood, lymph and oxygen in your upper body; clear your sinuses; relieve stress; and help you sleep better.
Indonesian	A combination massage that uses deep tissue massage, acupressure, Ayurveda and aromatherapy, as well as some gentle rocking. Some of the massage is given through cloth, then oils are smoothed and rubbed into your body to relax and revive you.
Lomi lomi	Also known as the 'loving hands' or Hawaiian massage, 'lomi lomi' translates to 'rub rub' in Hawaiian, and reflects the broad, flowing strokes made with the therapist's fingers, thumbs, palms, arms and elbows. Macadamia, palm and coconut oils are usually used to keep the strokes smooth, and moisturise and nourish the skin. Lomi lomi is based on the belief that memories are not just stored in the brain and mind, but also in every cell of the body. The long, continuous strokes of the massage are designed to help the body let go of its old patterns and behaviours, which can cause stresses and strains in the muscles. It's a nurturing massage that is good for releasing muscular and emotional tension.
Lymphatic drainage	A therapeutic treatment that uses pulsing motions to boost the flow of lymph around your body, refreshing your immune system and flushing out toxins. It can help your body fight infection or speed up healing and recovery from illness, and is also a popular and effective treatment for cellulite, reducing water retention and boosting weight loss.
Oleation	Also known as **snehana**, oleation is part of the ancient Hindu medical practice of Ayurveda. It is a kind of lymphatic drainage massage using essential oils, designed to increase the flow of lymph around the body.
Pinda Swedna	A relaxing, cleansing massage in which the therapist applies rice boiled in milk, and herbs.
Pizzichili	An unusual treatment in which two therapists massage you together, as they pour warm oil all over your body. Deeply relaxing.

Polarity

This deep tissue massage works along your meridians using rocking, holding and assisted stretches to balance your electromagnetic energy. Usually, you'll be wearing loose-fitting clothing. Good for unlocking knots in the muscles, this treatment is soothing and comforting.

Reiki

Meaning 'universal life-force/spiritual energy', reiki is a gentle, holistic form of healing massage therapy based on the idea of balance and 'Qi'. It aims to ensure your energy flows freely, encouraging healing and increasing your sense of well-being. It is done in normal clothing and is far less physical than other treatments, the practitioner channeling their own reiki into your body by laying their hands on or near you. It can be a very powerful experience. Reiki affects each person differently. It is generally relaxing, can help with physical problems and can help to relieve muscular aches and pains. There is some scepticism about the benefits of reiki but it is generally thought to be helpful for stress and depression, and to promote healing.

Relaxation

Most massage treatments will relax you, whatever else they do. Relaxing you is the only aim of this massage, so it's one of the most indulgent you can have. It is usually a full-body treatment involving soft music, subtle lighting and aromatherapy oils. You will have a long, luxurious massage using all kinds of techniques, including long strokes, gentle kneading and rolling of skin and muscle, and perhaps some rhythmic rocking from side to side.

Shiatsu

Shiatsu means 'finger pressure' and this healing practice is sometimes described as 'acupuncture without needles'. Sometimes known as **Zen Shiatsu**, it is a feature of many Japanese spas. It's a whole-body, holistic treatment that combines massage, acupressure and stretching. It will leave you feeling soothed and calm, and is good for improving circulation, releasing toxins, and relieving pain and stiffness.

Shiroabhyanga

Another term for **Indian head massage**.

Shirodhara

A ritual massage that is part of Ayurveda medical practice, shirodhara is a deep and soothing massage in which warmed oil is poured slowly onto your forehead – onto your 'third eye' – to help you focus and relax.

Sports

Because each sport uses the muscle groups in different ways, a qualified sports massage therapist will have a sound knowledge of the muscular and skeletal systems, and tailor the treatment for each individual athlete. A good sports massage will relax your muscles, help you fight fatigue, relieving any swelling around your joints, and boost your circulation and immune system.

Swedish	The five main techniques used in Swedish massage – stroking/gliding, kneading, rubbing, tapping/'pounding' and vibration – are probably what spring to mind when you think about a 'typical' massage. They're not designed to punish you! Just to improve your circulation, soothe your muscles and make you relaxed.
Thai	Combining acupressure, Shiatsu and yogic stretches with regular massage techniques, Thai massage earned its nickname 'yoga for the lazy' through its gentle techniques and passive stretches. Starting at the feet and moving up to the head, the body is carefully moved, loosened, stretched, rubbed and pressured. Although Thai massage works on the body, the belief system behind it is aims to connect and balance body and mind.
Thai herbal heat treatment	This relaxing and aromatic treatment features a massage using essential oils and hot poultices of sweet-smelling herbs placed on pressure points around the body. This is a full-body relaxation massage that will leave you feeling really special and relaxed – a real zone-out treatment.
Traeger	Characterised by rhythmic rocking to loosen muscles and release tension in your joints. Named after its creator, Traeger massage involves no oils, pressure or rubbing, and you wear loose clothing to receive it. A very gentle, nurturing treatment, it is particularly good for people who aren't keen on more conventional massage techniques, or have fragile, broken or very sensitive skin.
Tui Na	Chinese medical massage. It aims to exchange energies between the client and therapist, bringing balance and wellbeing, realigning your body, improving the flow of blood and calming your spirit. Tui Na means 'push pull' and the therapist uses a combination of massage techniques, including acupressure, manipulation and assisted stretches. You receive Tui Na wearing loose clothes.
Vichy shower	A relaxing massage carried out under a Vichy shower. The temperature is altered during the massage and this, combined with the massage, makes for a very unusual and refreshing treatment.
Watsu	Shiatsu in warm water. The massage uses deep acupressure techniques and long slow rhythmic strokes, and the therapist will also work on some stretches with you. A relaxing massage that is often used in rehabilitation with people who have had injuries, or have arthritis.

mud

Mud is rich in minerals, which is why it's such a sumptuous treat for your skin. Much nicer than it sounds. Honestly.

Dead Sea mud

You can have it slathered in thick layers onto your body and face and left to dry, before being removed with warm water. Or you can actually bathe in the mud. Good for alleviating pain from arthritis and rheumatism and general muscle tension, and drawing out toxins. Great for moisturising your skin – it will leave it feeling impressively soothed and smoothed.

Fangotherapy

'Fango' is Italian for 'mud' and fangotherapy is a common treatment in Italy – it's often used in conjunction with balneotherapy (see **Baths**). Used in baths or heat packs, the mud is rich and thick, sometimes mixed with other minerals and essential oils. It's slathered on and left for 10 or 15 minutes. Then you're hosed down and usually led to a mineral bath. Leaves your skin soft and muscles soothed.

Parafango

A combination of paraffin and mud, usually applied as a warming body mask or wrap.

Rasul

A traditional Arabian body treatment involving steam and mud. Slathered in mineral-rich muds of various colours, you sit in a tiled steam room for around 15 minutes. Afterwards, the mud is washed off with cool water. This is an unusual, deeply sensual treatment. It really warms and soothes the muscles, softening the skin, sweating out toxins and leaving you feeling both relaxed and wide awake.

Serail

A serail is a small, tiled, Arabian-style steam room, often used for mud treatments. Different kinds of cleansing mud are applied, one each to your body, face and scalp. Covered in mud, you then take a seat in the serail/steam room and the combination of heat and mud deep-cleanses your skin and soothes your deepest muscles. After about 15 minutes, just as the mud starts to slip and melt over your body, you have a cool shower to rinse it away. This is a sensual experience, and deeply relaxing.

Thalassotherapy

From the Greek word for 'sea', thalassotherapy refers to a variety of treatments that use seawater, seaweed and other marine derivatives. Mud baths, underwater showers, hydro-massage, aromatherapy, and seaweed, mud and algae wraps all aim to help restore your body to a state of serenity fit for a mermaid. It's good for toning your muscles, cleansing your skin and reducing the appearance of cellulite, too!

Meditation	A method of achieving free-flowing, deep thought and mental release based on focused breathing. It requires discipline and practice.
	Good for Working through emotional problems or processing past difficulties and experiences. Meditation is not always relaxing, and can be very difficult, but practised regularly it can bring balance and a sense of calm and peace.
	See also **Ai Chi**; **Tai Chi**; **Yoga**
Meridians	Energy paths that map your body. Acupressure, Shiatsu and reflexology are just three of the treatments that use these paths.
	See also **Ayurveda**; **Acupressure**; **Chakra**; **Reflexology**; **Shiatsu**
Micro-dermabrasion	A form of exfoliation using a device that blasts fine crystals onto the skin and vacuums them up, together with any dead skin and dirt. Microdermabrasion is often a feature of an exfoliating or radiance facial.
	Good for Really fresh, radiant skin in a short amount of time.
	See also **Exfoliation**; **Facial**
Mud	See opposite
Myofascial release	Fascia is a tough tissue that surrounds every muscle, bone, organ, nerve, and blood vessel in your body. Myofascial release is a stretching technique that releases tension, and therefore pain, deep in the body. It is used by physiotherapists to treat patients with some soft tissue problems. It is also called 'connective tissue massage'.
	Good for Recovery from injury or deep muscle pain.
	See also **Deep tissue massage**; **Rolfing**; **Thai massage**

n IS FOR...

Non-surgical facelift	A facial treatment that improves the quality and tone of your skin without surgery. This could involve anything from regular facials to facial exercises and stretching. It also covers medical-style procedures such as injections of facial fillers, and Botox.
	Good for Making skin appear brighter and younger; reducing lines and wrinkles; improving tone and texture of skin.
	See also **Botox**; **Collagen**; **Facial**

Bishopstrow
House, see
page 42

O IS FOR...

Oleation   See **Massage**

**Oxygenated/
ozone-treated pools**   See **Pools**

P IS FOR...

Panthermal

A very unusual treatment and, as yet, we haven't found it available in the UK. You have to lie in a metal tube while hot air is piped around you, after which warm water is jetted onto you from different taps along the tube.

Good for   Treating cellulite, apparently.

See also   **Heat treatments**; **Hydrotherapy**

Parafango   See **Mud**

Pedicure

A beauty treatment for your feet. Using different instruments, potions, waxes and polish, a pedicurist removes dead skin, softens hard skin and shapes and treats toe-nails. It can be combined with massage, hot stones, a herbal or aromatic rub or a soak in scented oils.

A pedicurist is not a chiropodist; a pedicure is not a medical procedure, although a regular pedicure can support the work you're having done by a chiropodist, and, in fact, prevent you from needing further treatment.

Good for   Leaving your toes looking filmstar-tastic.

See also   The different types of pedicure are in line with the different kinds of manicure. See pages 197–198.

Perlane   See **Facial filler**

Phytotherapy

Meaning 'plant' therapy, this is a blanket term for healing treatments using botanical products such as plants, herbs, seaweeds and essential oils, taken in baths, massage, wraps, inhalation and even tea.

Good for   General health, soothing and detoxifying the skin.

See also   **Ayurveda**; **Green tea**; **Heat treatment**

Pilates	A deep body-conditioning technique that strengthens muscles and improves balance and posture. A series of poses and stretches help tone and strengthen your muscles; in this way, it's similar to yoga. However, Pilates does not usually involve meditation and is not an aerobic exercise. Devised by Joseph Pilates in the 1920s, Pilates aims to teach you how to use your muscles properly to protect and support you, preventing injury and strain. For this reason, Pilates is increasingly popular with people whose work is very physically demanding, from ballerinas to prop forwards to builders.

Note: Pilates is particularly good for pregnant women as it can help improve posture and weight-bearing, reducing the risk of injury and pain.

Good for	Flexibility; muscle strengthening; famously good for backs; preventing injury or muscle strain ; improving posture; reducing stress; improving co-ordination.
See also	**Deep tissue massage**; **Thai massage**; **Traegar massage**; **Yoga**
Pinda Swedna	See **Massage**
Pizzichili	See **Massage**
Polarity	See **Massage**
Polish	See **Scrub**
Pools	Spas often have a range of pools and baths for you to try out.

Hot/thermal pools and springs Outdoor, naturally occurring pools, usually rich in minerals. There are many well-known hot springs or 'geysers' across the world, from New Zealand to Iceland. These can be extraordinary, but they often also smell of sulphur. Bathing in something that smells like bad eggs isn't always the spiritual experience you'd imagined.

Oxygenated/ozone-treated pools Swimming in an oxygenated or ozone-treated pool really is a treat compared with the average public pool. The water is less chlorinated, which means your eyes don't get so sore and it's less drying for your skin. Your hair won't suffer so much, either. It also seems to make it easier to swim for longer, with the added advantage that you don't smell strongly of chlorine when you come out.

Plunge pool After a sauna, Swedes are encouraged to run outside and roll around in the snow. A plunge pool is designed to work on the same principle, boosting your circulation after a heat treatment with a quick, deep, cold splash.

Good for   Cleansing, relaxing, exercise and fun.

See also   **Baths**; **Hydrotherapy**; **Thermotherapy**

Pressure point

If you think of your body as being mapped by 'ley lines' of Qi, pressure points are key stations along those lines where the therapist stops, applies pressure and moves on – a bit like joining-the-dots of your body's energy paths.

Good for   These are 'massage-keys' to unlock pain and knots in the muscles, and tension in the spirit!

See also   **Acupressure**; **Reflexology**; **Shiatsu**; **Thai massage**

Q IS FOR...

Qi

Qi (say '**chee**') is your energy force, which flows along the meridians that map your body. When your Qi is flowing properly, you are balanced, well and healthy in mind, body and spirit. Get a blockage and you'll feel unbalanced, emotionally and physically. The flow of your Qi, and blockages in it, correspond to physical and emotional health problems.

Good for   The free flow of Qi ensures better mental and physical health.

See also   **Acupressure**; **Reflexology**; **Shiatsu**; **Thai massage**

Qi Gong

Say '**chee gung**'. Similar to yoga, Qi Gong is a physical practice that features postures, slow flowing movement and controlled breathing, intended to bring your body and mind into balance.

Good for   Muscular strength and tone; balance; relaxation.

See also   **Ai Chi**; **Tai Chi**; **Pilates**; **Yoga**

r IS FOR...

Rasul   See **Mud**

Reflexology   This therapy works on the principle that there are pressure points on your feet that correspond to all the organs, glands, tissues and muscles in the rest of your body. By applying informed pressure to points on your feet (and hands), you can treat and heal problems elsewhere in the body.

Good for	Relieving back and muscle strain; sports injuries; stress; anxiety and depression; sleep and eating disorders; poor circulation; irritable bowel syndrome; migraine; pre-menstrual tension; symptoms of the menopause; breathing difficulties such as asthma.
See also	**Acupressure**; **Qi**; **Reiki**; **Shiatsu**; **Thai massage**

Reiki   See **Massage**

Relaxation massage   See **Massage**

Rolfing   Named after its creator, Ida Rolf, this bodywork technique aims to improve balance and flexibility. Through assisted stretches and other manipulations, the therapist helps to improve the flow of energy through your body.

Good for	Balance and posture, therefore reducing muscular spasms, aches, pains and tension, and improving your sense of well-being and general health.
See also	**Deep tissue massage**; **Hellerwork**; **Traegar massage**

S IS FOR...

Salt glow   See **Scrub**

Sauna   Essentially a small heated room, the sauna is generally associated with mountainous regions – we tend to think of a small wooden cabin in the snow. Saunas give a fairly extreme, dry heat, which usually comes from very hot rocks. You can usually regulate the temperature by pouring water over the hot rocks with a ladle. Traditionally, you would complete your sauna experience by running outside and rolling in the snow. But there's really no need for that when there are perfectly good showers and pools available in a spa.

Different types of sauna

Finnish/Swedish sauna These are similar to each other, except Finnish saunas have an automatic water spray onto the heated coals. Scandinavians advise you to follow this hot sauna with a quick plunge into a cold pool or the snow. This stimulates your circulation, energises your spirit and brings down your body temperature all in one go... you can imagine it would. It is quite common for a Scandinavian household to have its own sauna for use with family and friends.

Rock sauna A type of Finnish sauna that has walls of rock rather than wood; this varies the type of heat you experience.

Tyrolean sauna From the Tyrol region of Austria, these saunas are in wood-lined cabins. You are advised to follow the heat treatment with an ice shower.

Bio sauna A cross between a regular sauna, a tepidarium and a multi-sensory room. Wet and dry heat distribute herbal aromas to the sauna, and the whole experience is made even more relaxing by gently-changing coloured fibreoptic-lights.

Laconium A laconium gives a gentler heat than most saunas and is designed to raise your body temperature gradually. It's a good one to start with as it's very mild and gets you 'into the swing' of sauna-ing! You can stay in longer than other saunas as it's balmy rather than hot.

Good for   Warming and soothing aching muscles; making you sweat, so drawing out toxins.

See also   **Arctic shower**; **Aroma room**; **Heat treatment**; **Steam room**; **Wraps**

Scrub

Also known as a **body polish**, a scrub is a whole-body exfoliation treatment. Abrasive products – usually salts, sugars or ground rice or seeds – are massaged or brushed over and into your body, often mixed in warm oils which smooth and soften your skin at the same time. The scrub is usually showered off at stages throughout the treatment. If you're lucky, you'll have this treatment on a 'wet plinth' which is heated so that you don't get cold at all, and means you don't have to get up to be washed. A good body scrub or polish forms the basis of other body treatments: preparing your skin for an even tan or opening your pores ready for a wrap or mud treatment.

**New Park
Manor**, see
page 153

Different types of body scrub

Fruit (edible!) Some body scrubs mix crushed seeds with fruit oils, oatmeal and similar products to nourish and soothe the skin.

Herbal The exfoliating scrub is mixed with a herbal oil such as rosemary, lavender or aloe vera, depending on your skin type and whether the scrub is designed to wake you up or relax you.

Salt and oil Finely granulated salt is mixed with an essential, moisturising oil. The salt might be sea or mineral. (Also known as a **Salt glow**.)

Sugar is also used, mixed with oils or creams.

Good for   Smoothing and moisturising your skin; boosting the circulation of lymph and blood to the skin; improving the tone of the skin.

See also   **Exfoliation**; **Wraps**

Serail	See **Mud**
Shiatsu	See **Massage**
Shiroabhyanga	Another term for Indian head massage (see **Massage**)
Shirodhara	See **Massage**
Snehana	Another term for oleation (see **Massage**)
Spa ritual	A spa ritual describes a package of different body treatments that you get on the same day: use of the gym, a sauna and a light lunch, followed by a massage, a facial and, say, some **reflexology** or a **pedicure**.

Good for   A range of benefits depending on the treatments you choose, but whatever you have should take you out of the humdrum and allow you to experience something special.

See also   **Body treatment**; **Facial**; **Hydrotherapy massage**; **Scrub**; **Wraps**

Sports massage	See **Massage**
Steam room	A small room into which hot steam is piped. The effect of this warm, wet heat is to soothe and cleanse, warm and relax.

Good for   Relaxing; refreshing; drawing out toxins; soothing weary or aching muscles and joints; very sensual.

See also   **Floatation**; **Hammam**; **Heat treatment**; **Rasul**; **Sauna**; **Serail**; **Wraps**

t IS FOR...

Tai Chi

Similar to **Qi Gong**, this is a Chinese physical health practice of balancing postures and controlled breathing. Tai chi is a very graceful series of movements, and looks a little like slow-motion dancing.

Good for   Toning muscles; improving balance; relaxation.

See also   **Ai Chi**; **Pilates**; **Qi**; **Yoga**

Tanning

A tanning treatment will turn your skin golden brown in a fraction of the time that it would take you to do it naturally. It is also, broadly speaking, a much healthier way to do it than planting yourself in the sun for hours at a time. The most popular tanning treatments are the spray tans and the cream tans. Both look much more even when applied by a professional.

Good for   Making you look like you've been on holiday, or – perversely – as though you're healthy (despite the fact that we all know sunbathing ain't great for you…), relaxed and fabulous.

See also   **Hair removal**; **Scrub**

Tepidarium

A heat treatment – a warm(ish… as the 'tepid' part of the name suggests) seating area where you can relax between treatments.

Good for   They are a useful step up to, and step down from, more intense heat treatments.

See also   **Arctic shower**; **Aroma room**; **Heat treatment**; **Ice fountain**

Thai herbal heat treatment

See **Massage**

Thai massage

See **Massage**

Thalassotherapy

See **Mud** and **Wraps**

Thermo-auricular therapy

Also known as ear candling, this involves the insertion of a rolled cotton tube impregnated with beeswax, honey and herb extracts into your auditory canal while you lie on your side. The therapist lights the candle and allows it to burn down over the course of 10-15 minutes, during which it allegedly sucks impurities out of the ear canal. This treatment is said to be effective in reducing excess earwax, alleviating tinnitus (ringing in the ears) and relieving the build-up of catarrh during colds and flu. Many medical experts consider this procedure to be of little or no benefit, and potentially dangerous if carelessly applied.

You will also see this technique referred to as Hopi ear candling, from its supposed origins among the native Hopi people of North America, although spokespeople for the Hopi themselves have repeatedly said this practice is unknown in their customs.

Good for   In a word – nothing.

Thermotherapy   A blanket term to describe any spa treatment involving heat – of varying temperatures, and in various ways.

Good for   Soothing and relaxing you; drawing out impurities; easing muscular and joint pain.

See also   **Fangotherapy**; **Heat treatment**; **Laconium**; **Sauna**; **Steam room**; **Tepidarium**; **Wraps**

Traeger massage   See **Massage**

Trigger point therapy   This treatment puts pressure on certain trigger points, temporarily stopping blood flow to a particular part of the body, and then releasing it, flooding that body part with fresh blood.

Good for   Boosting your circulation and flooding oxygen to your limbs.

See also   **Thai massage**

Tropicarium   See **Indian blossom steam room**

Tui Na   See **Massage**

U IS FOR...

Ultra   This is a good prefix to look for when you're looking for an extra-special spa experience. 'Ultra pampering', 'ultra hydrating', 'ultra effective' – these are words to savour.

V IS FOR...

Vichy shower

(Also known as an **Affusion shower**.) This is a light, warm, mineral-rich shower that is sprayed or sprinkled over your body as you are lying down.

Good for   Relaxing; as part of a spa ritual.

See also   **Hydrotherapy**

W IS FOR...

Watsu

See **Massage**

Whirlpool

See **Baths**

Wraps

A wrap is a spa treatment designed to slim and tone the body, hydrate or firm the skin, relax and soothe the muscles, or draw out toxins and cleanse the skin. Whether you are looking to shape, bake or sweat, wraps come in varied and exciting packages, although some people get a bit apprehensive about the idea of being wrapped up. But think of a body wrap as a nourishing cocoon to warm, cleanse and moisturise.

Good for   Detoxifying, relaxing and revitalising; you may also notice some temporary inch loss and firmer skin.

See also   **Dead Sea mud**; **Heat treatment**

Y IS FOR...

Yoga

A physical practice involving postures and controlled breathing, to stretch and tone the body, and order and relax the mind.

Different types of yoga

Ananda yoga A gentle, meditative form of yoga, Ananda yoga is related to Hatha yoga and is designed to prepare you for meditation rather than give aerobic exercise.

Ashtanga (or **astanga vinyasana**) **yoga** Consists of faster, flowing sequences of dynamic postures that build physical strength and flexibility. Also known as 'hot yoga', astanga vinyasana yoga is often practised in warm rooms so that the muscles are relaxed and free. It is aerobic exercise and can be quite demanding.

Bath Spa Hotel, see page 37

Hatha yoga Focuses on physical forms, breathing and meditation. It is slower and more intense than other forms of yoga and concentrates on physical and mental balance and control.

Iyengar yoga Probably the most popular form of yoga in the UK. It is very much concerned with poise and balance.

Kundalini yoga The aim of Kundalini yoga is to energise you. The focus here is on postures, chanting and breathing exercises.

Power yoga A very aerobic version of Ashtanga yoga.

Good for   Improving balance, posture, muscular strength and tone; relaxing the mind.

See also   Pilates; Traegar massage; Thai massage

Z IS FOR...

Zen Shiatsu

See **Shiatsu**

Spas by region

From north to south, east to west, you're never too far from a 5-bubble spa…

London: 290-291

South East: 292-293

South West: 294

Midlands: 295

North: 296

Scotland: 297

Wales: 298

Northern Ireland: 298

Scotland

Northern Ireland

North

Midlands

Wales

South East

London

South West

London

South East

Channel Islands

Map	Spa	Town	County	Page
11	Chewton Glen	New Milton	Hampshire	71
12	The Club Hotel & Spa	St Helier	Jersey	74
13	Danesfield House	Marlow	Buckinghamshire	81
14	Donnington Valley Hotel and Spa	Newbury	Berkshire	87
15	Dove Spa Bromley	Bromley	Kent	90
16	Four Seasons	Hook	Hampshire	109
17	Fredrick's Hotel Spa	Maidenhead	Berkshire	111
18	Grand Jersey	St Helier	Jersey	117
19	Grayshott Spa	Hindhead	Surrey	118
20	Hartwell House	Aylesbury	Buckinghamshire	124
21	Horsted Spa at East Sussex National	Uckfield	East Sussex	126
22	Imagine Health and Spa	Kings Lynn	Norfolk	128
23	KuBu	Henley-on-Thames	Oxfordshire	131
24	Lansdowne Place Hotel	Hove	East Sussex	136
25	Luton Hoo	Luton	Bedfordshire	145
26	New Park Manor Hotel's Bath House Spa	Brockenhurst	Hampshire	153
27	Nirvana Spa	Wokingham	Berkshire	155
28	The Pavillion Spa (Cliveden House)	Taplow	Berkshire	162
29	Pennyhill Park Hotel and The Spa	Bagshot	Surrey	165
30	Royal Day Spa	Tunbridge Wells	Kent	181
31	Runnymede Hotel and Spa	Egham	Surrey	183
32	SenSpa at Carey's Manor	Brockenhurst	Hampshire	193
33	Sequoia Spa at The Grove	Watford	Hertfordshire	195
34	Sofitel London Heathrow	Hayes	Middlesex	205
35	Solent Hotel and Spa	Fareham	Hampshire	208
36	Spa Sirène at The Royal Yacht	St Helier	Jersey	215
37	Spa SPC at Stoke Park Club	Stoke Poges	Buckinghamshire	216
38	Sprowston Manor Marriott Hotel and Country Club	Norwich	Norfolk	217
39	The Treatment Rooms	Brighton	East Sussex	231
40	Utopia Spa at Rowhill Grange	Wilmington	Kent	232
41	The Vineyard at Stockcross	Newbury	Berkshire	237
42	Vitality Detox Retreat	West Wittering	West Sussex	239

South West

Midlands

Map	Spa	Town	County	Page
1	Amala Spa (Hyatt Regency Birmingham)	Birmingham	West Midlands	22
2	Center Parcs Sherwood	Newark	Nottinghamshire	57
3	Clumber Park Hotel and Spa (New Leaf Spa)	Sherwood Forest	Nottinghamshire	75
4	Eden Hall Day Spa	Newark	Nottinghamshire	97
5	Fawsley Hall (Grayshott Studio Spa and Gym)	Daventry	Northhamptonshire	101
6	Hoar Cross Hall	Yoxall	Staffordshire	125
7	Moddershall Oaks	Stone	Staffordshire	151
8	Petit Spa (Malmaison Hotel)	Birmingham	West Midlands	167
9	Ragdale Hall Health Hydro	Melton Mowbray	Leicestershire	171
10	Rookery Hall Hotel	Nantwich	Cheshire	177
11	Thoresby Hall Hotel and Spa	Newark	Nottinghamshire	227
12	Whittlebury Hall	Towcester	Northhamptonshire	241

North

Map	Spa	Town	County	Page
1	Alexandra House	Huddersfield	West Yorkshire	21
2	Armathwaite Hall Country House Hotel	Keswick	Cumbria	29
3	Brooklands Retreat and Health Spa	Garstang	Lancashire	49
4	Center Parcs Whinfell Forest	Penrith	Cumbria	58
5	The Devonshire Arms	Skipton	North Yorkshire	86
6	Eastthorpe Hall Health and Beauty Spa	Mirfield	West Yorkshire	95
7	Formby Hall Golf Resort and Spa	Formby	Merseyside	105
8	Harrogate Turkish Baths and Health Spa	Harrogate	North Yorkshire	123
9	Matfen Hall	Matfen	Newcastle upon Tyne	148
10	Oxley's at Underscar	Keswick	Cumbria	161
11	Portland Hall Spa	Southport	Lancashire	168
12	Serenity Spa at Seaham Hall	Seaham	County Durham	199
13	Thornton Hall Hotel and Spa	Thornton Hough	Merseyside	228
14	Titanic Spa	Linthwaite	West Yorkshire	229
15	Verbena Spa at the Feversham Arms	Helmsley	North Yorkshire	235
16	Waterfall Spa	Leeds	West Yorkshire	240

Scotland

Map	Spa	Town	County	Page
1	Balmoral Spa	Edinburgh	Edinburgh	35
2	Boath House Hotel	Nairn	Highland	44
3	Spa at the Carrick, Cameron House	Loch Lomond	Dunbartonshire	54
4	The Gleneagles Hotel	Auchterarder	Perthshire	115
5	Loch Lomond Golf Club	Luss	Dunbartonshire	141
6	Norton House Hotel and Spa	Edinburgh	Edinburgh	156
7	Old Course Hotel, Golf Resort and Spa	St Andrews	Fife	157
8	ONE Spa at the Sheraton Grand	Edinburgh	Edinburgh	159
9	The Scotsman	Edinburgh	Edinburgh	191
10	Serenity in the City	Edinburgh	Edinburgh	197
11	Stobo Castle Health Spa	Stobo	Peeblesshire	223
12	Zen Lifestyle Teviot Place	Edinburgh	Edinburgh	243

Wales

Map	Spa	Town	County	Page
1	Bodysgallen Hall and Spa	Llandudno	Conwy	46
2	The Forum Spa at The Celtic Manor Resort	Newport	Newport	107
3	Lake Vyrnwy Hotel and Spa	Llanwddyn	Powys	132
4	St Brides Spa Hotel	Saundersfoot	Pembrokeshire	219
5	St David's Hotel and Spa	Cardiff	Cardiff	221
6	Vale Hotel, Golf and Spa Resort	Hensol	Vale of Glamorgan	233

Northern Ireland

Map	Spa	Town	County	Page
1	Aura Day Spa	Belfast	County Antrim	30
2	Culloden Estate and Spa	Belfast	County Antrim	79
3	Galgorm Resort & Spa	Ballymena	County Antrim	113
4	Slieve Donard	Newcastle	County Down	203

Spa and treatment index

Photo credits

Original photography by James Pike, pp 3 and 13

Photographs reproduced with kind permission of: piv Loch Lomond Golf Club, Dunbartonshire, Scotland; p7 St David's Hotel and Spa, Cardiff, Wales; p8 Thermae Bath Spa, Bath; p11 The Vineyard at Stockcross, The Vineyard at Stockcross, Berkshire; p14 One Spa at The Sheraton Grand Hotel ; p17 Barnsley House, Gloucestershire; p19 The Gleneagles Hotel, Perthshire, Scotland; p20 Agua at Sanderson, London; p21 Alexandra House, West Yorkshire; p22 Amala Spa at Hyatt Regency Hotel, Birmingham; p23 Amida Spa Beckenham, Kent; p24 Aquarias Spa, Whatley Manor, Wiltshire; p26 Aquila Health Spa at the Spread Eagle Hotel, West Sussex; p28 Armathwaite Hall Country House & Spa, Cumbria; p31 Aura Day Spa, County Antrim, Northern Ireland; p32 Aveda Institute, London; p33 Ayush Wellness Spa at the Hotel de France, Jersey; p34 Bailiffscourt Hotel, West Sussex; p35 Balmoral Spa at the Balmoral Hotel, Edinburgh, Scotland; p36 Barnsley House, Gloucestershire; p37 Bath Spa Hotel, Bath; p38 The Bath Priory, Bath; p40 Bedruthan Steps Hotel and Spa, Cornwall; p41 The Berkeley Hotel, London; p42 Bishopstrow House Country Hotel and Halcyon Spa, Wiltshire; p43 Bliss, London; p44 Boath House Hotel, Highlands, Scotland; p45 Body Experience, Surrey; p46 Bodysgallen Hall and Spa, Conwy, Wales; p47 Bowood Hotel, Spa and Golf Resort, Wiltshire; p48 Brandshatch Place Hotel and Spa, Kent; p49 Brooklands Country Retreat and Health Spa, Lancashire; p50 Thalgo Group (UK); p51 Brown's Hotel, London; p52 Calcot Spa, Gloucestershire; p54 Cameron House, Dunbartonshire, Scotland; p55 Aqua Sana Spa at Center Parcs Elveden, Suffolk; p56 Aqua Sana Spa at Center Parcs Longleat, Wiltshire; p57 Aqua Sana Spa at Center Parcs Sherwood, Nottinghamshire; p58 Aqua Sana Spa at Center Parcs Whinfell Forest, Cumbria; p59 Champneys Town and City Spa – Brighton, East Sussex; p60 Champneys Town and City Spa – Chichester, West Sussex; p61 Champneys Henlow, Bedfordshire; p62 Champneys Tring, Hertfordshire; p64 Renaissance London Chancery Court Hotel, London; p66 Ila-Spa Ltd.; p67 Charlton House Hotel and Spa, Somerset; p68 Chelsea Club Escape Spa, London; p70 Chewton Glen, Hampshire; p72 The CityPoint Club, London; p74 The Club Hotel and Spa, Jersey; p75 Clumber Park Hotel and Spa, Nottinghamshire; p76 COMO Shambhala Urban Escape at Metropolitan Hotel, London; p77 Cowley Manor, Gloucestershire; p78 Culloden Estate and Spa, County Down, Northern Ireland; p80 Cupcake Spa, London; p81 Danesfield House Hotel and Spa, Buckinghamshire; p82 Dart Marina Hotel and Spa, Dartmouth; p84 Daylesford Hay Barn, Gloucestershire; p86 The Devonshire Arms Hotel and Spa, North Yorkshire; p87 Donnington Valley Hotel and Spa, Berkshire; p88 The Dorchester Spa, London; p90 Dove Spa Bromley, Kent; p91 Dove Spa City,

p212 Spa Intercontinental, London; p214 Spa NK Notting Hill, London; p215 Spa Sirène at The Royal Yacht Hotel, Jersey; p216 Spa SPC at Stoke Park Club, Buckinghamshire; p217 Sprowston Manor, Marriott Hotel and Country Club, Norfolk; p219 St Brides Spa Hotel, Pembrokeshire, Wales; p220 The St David's Hotel and Spa, Cardiff, Wales; p222 Stobo Castle Health Spa, Peeblesshire, Scotland; p224 Sura Detox, Devon; p226 Thermae Bath Spa, Somerset; p227 Thoresby Hall Hotel and Spa, Nottinghamshire; p228 Thornton Hall Hotel and Spa, Merseyside; p229 Titanic Spa, West Yorkshire; p230 The Treatment Rooms, East Sussex; p232 Rowhill Grange Hotel and Utopia Spa, Kent; 233 The Vale Hotel, Golf and Spa Resort, Vale of Glamorgan, Wales; p234 Verbena Spa at The Feversham Arms Hotel, North Yorkshire; p236 The Vineyard Spa, The Vineyard at Stockcross, Berkshire; p238 Vitality Detox Retreat, West Sussex; p240 Waterfall Spa, West Yorkshire; p241 Whittlebury Hall Hotel, Spa and Management Training Centre, Northamptonshire; p242 Zen Lifestyle Teviot Place, Edinburgh, Scotland; p243 The Gleneagles Hotel, Perthshire, Scotland; p244 Loch Lomond Golf Club, Scotland; p249 Hand Picked Hotels Ltd; p256 Bedruthan Steps Hotel and Spa, Cornwall; p260 Le Kalon Spa at The Bentley Hotel, London; p264 Scarlet Spa, Scarlet Hotel, Cornwall; p266 Brandshatch Place Hotel and Spa, Kent; p277 Bishopstrow House Country Hotel and Halcyon Spa, Wiltshire; p282 Bath House Spa, New Park Manor Hotel, Hampshire; p286 Bath Spa Hotel, Bath; p304 The Forum Spa at The Celtic Manor Resort, Newport, Wales

Every effort has been made to credit copyright holders correctly and the publishers will be happy to correct any omissions in future editions.